THE TREASURY OF DAVID

THE TREASURY OF DAVID

Charles Haddon Spurgeon

A General Books LLC Publication.

CONTENTS

SECTION 1

earth ; but when at the same time, his own daughter, in his own court gave princely education to Moses, their deliverer, did not God laugh ?

Short is the joy of the wicked. Is Dagon put up to his place again ? God's smile shall take nil' his head and his hands, and leave him neither wit to guide

nor power to subsist We may not judge of God's works until

the fifth act : the case, deplorable and desperate in outward appearance, may with one smile from heaven find a blessed issue. He permitted his temple to be sacked and rifled, the holy vessels to be profaned and caroused in ; but did not God's smile make Belshazzar to tremble at the handwriting on the wall ? Oh, what are his frowns, if his smiles be so terrible !|*Thomas Adams.*

Versed.|The expression, *"He that sitteth in the heavens,"* at once fixes our thoughts on a being infinitely exalted above man, who is of the earth, earthy. And when it is said, " He shall *laugh,* 1'1 this word is designed to convey to our minds the idea, that the greatest confederacies amongst kings and peoples, and their most extensive and vigorous preparations, to defeat His purposes or to injure ms servants, are in His sight altogether insignificant and worthless. He looks upon their poor and puny efforts, not only without uneasiness or fear, but He laughs at their folly ; He treats their impotency with derision. He knows how He can crush them like a moth when He pleases, or consume them in a moment with the breath of His mouth. How profitable is it for us to be reminded of truths such as these ! Ah ! it is indeed " *a tain thing"* for the potsherds of the earth to strive with the glorious Majesty of Heaven.|*David Pii.ca.irn.*

*Verse 4.|" The Lord,"*1 in Hebrew, Adonai, mystically signifieth my stays, or my sustainers|my pillars. Our English word " Lord " hath much the same force, being contracted of the old Saxon word " Llaford," or " Hlafford," which cometh from " Laef," to sustain, refresh, cherish.|*Henry Ainsworth.*

*Verse 4.|' He that sitteth in the heavens shall laugh at them: the Lord shall have them in derision.'*1" This, tautology or repetition of the same thing, which is frequent in the Scriptures, is a sign of the thing being established : according to the authority of the patriarch Joseph (Gen. xli. 82), where, having interpreted the dreams of Pharaoh, he said, " And for that the dream was doubled unto Pharaoh twice ; it is because the thing is established by God, and God will shortly bring it to pass." And therefore, here also, " *shall laugh at them,"* and " *shall have them in derision,"* is a repetition to show that there is not a doubt to be entertained that all these things will most surely come to pass. And the gracious Spirit does all this for our comfort and consolation, that we may not faint under temptation, but lift up our heads with the most certain hope; because "he that shall come will come, and will not tarry." Hebrews x. 37. |*Martin Luther.*

Verse 5.|" Vex them y" either by horror of conscience, or corporal plagues; one way or the other he will have his pennyworths of them, as he always has had of the persecutors of his people.|*John Trapp.*

Verses 5, 9.|It is easy for God to destroy his foes. . . . Behold Pharaoh, his wise men, his hosts, and his horses plouting and plunging, and sinking like lead in the Red sea. Here is the end of one of the greatest plots ever formed against God's chosen. Of thirty Roman emperors, governors of provinces, and others high in office, who distinguished themselves by their zeal and bitterness in persecuting the early Christians, one became speedily deranged after some atrocious cruelty, one was slain by his own son, one became blind, the eyes of one started out of his head, one was drowned, one was strangled, one died in a miserable captivity, one fell dead in a manner that will not bear recital, one died of so loathsome a disease that several of his physicians were put to death because they could not abide the stench that filled his room, two committed suicide, a third attempted it, but had to call for help to finish the work, five were assassinated by their own people or servants, five others died the most miserable and excruciating deaths, several of them having an untold complication of diseases,

and eight were killed in battle, or after being taken prisoners. Among these was Julian the apostate. In the days of his prosperity he is said to have pointed his dagger to heaven defying the Son of God, whom he commonly called the Galilean. But when he was wounded in battle, he saw that all was over with him, and he gathered up his clotted blood, and threw it into the air, exclaiming, " Thou hast conquered, O thou Galilean." Voltaire has told us of the agonies of Charles IX. of France, which drove the blood through the pores of the skin of that miserable monarch, after his cruelties and treachery to the Huguenots. *William S. Plumer, D.D., LL.D.,* 1867.

*Verse 6.l" Yet have I tet my King.'*1" Noticel1. The royal office and character of our glorious Redeemer : he is a King, " This name he hath on his vesture and on his thigh." Rev. xix. 10. 2. The authority by which he reigns ; he is " *my King,"* says God the Father, and I have set him up from everlasting : " The Father judgeth no man ; but hath committed all judgment unto the Son." The world disowns his authority, but I own it ; I have set him, I have "given him to be head over all things to the church." 8. His particular kingdom over which he rules ; it is over " *my holy 7iitt of Zion"*lan eminent type of the gospel church. The temple was built upon Mount Zion and therefore called a *holy hill.* Christ's throne is in his church, it is his head-quarters, and the place of his peculiar residence. Notice the firmness of the divine purpose with respect unto this matter. " *Tet have I set* " him " *King* ;" i.e., whatever be the plots of hell and earth to the contrary, ho reigns by his Father's ordination. *Stephen Charnock,* 1628l1680.

Verse 6.l" Yet hate I set my Kiko," etc.lJesus Christ is a threefold King. *First,* his enemies' King ; *secondly,* his saints' King ; *thirdly,* his Father's King.

First, Christ is his enemies' King, that is, he ia King over his enemies. Christ is a King above all kings. What are all the mighty men, the great, the honourable men of the earth to Jesus Christ ? They arc but like a little bubble in the water ; for if all the nations, in comparison to God, be but as the drop of the bucket, or the dust of the balance, as the prophet speaks in Isaiah xl. 15, how little then must be the kings of the earth ! Nay, beloved, Christ Jesus is not only higher than kings, but he is higher than the angels ; yea, he ia the head of angels ; and, therefore, all the angels in heaven are commanded to

worship him. Col. ii. 12 ; Heb. i. 6 He is King over all kingdoms,

over all nations, over all governments, over all powers, over all people.

Dan. vii. 14 The very heathen are given to Christ, and the uttermost

parts of the earth for his possession. Psalm ii. 8.

Secondly. Jesus Christ is his saints' King. He is King of the bad, and of the good ; but as for the wicked, he rules over them by his power and might ; but the saints, he rules in them by his Spirit and gracea. Oh 1 this is Christ's spiritual kingdom, and here he rules in the hearts of his people, here he rules over their consciences, over their wills, over their affections, over their judgments and understandings, and nobody hath anything to do here but Christ. Christ is not only the King of nations, but the King of saints ; the one he rules over, the other he rules in.

Thirdly. Jesus Christ is his Father's King too, and so his Father calls him : " *I have set my Kiny upon my holy hill of Ziun.'"* Well may he be our King, when he is God's King. But you may say, how is Christ the Father's King ? Because he rules for his Father. There is a twofold kingdom of God committed to Jesus Christ; *first,* a spiritual kingdom, by which he rules in the hearts of his people, and so is King of saints ; and, *secondly,* a providential kingdom, by which he rules the affairs of this world, nnd so he is King of nations. I *Condensed from William Dyer's Christ's Famous Titles,* 1665.

Verse 6.l" Zion.'" The *mime* " Zion" signifies a " distant view" *(speculum).* And the church is called " a distant view" *(specula),* not only because it views God and heavenly things by faith (that is, afar off), being wise unto the things that are above, not unto those that are on the earth ; but also, because thereare within her true viewers, or seers, and watchmen in the spirit, whose office is to take charge of the people under them, and to watch against the snares of enemies and sins ; and such are called in the Greek bishops *(exioKoxot),* that is, spyers or seers ; and you may for the same reason give them, from the Hebrew, the appellation of Zionians or Zioners.|*Martin Luther.*

Verse 7.|The dispute concerning the eternal filiation of our Lord betrays more of presumptuous curiosity than of reverent faith. It is an attempt to explain where it is far better to adore. We could give rival expositions of this verse, but we forbear. The controversy is one of the most unprofitable which ever engaged the pens of theologians. | *C. If. S.*

Verge 8.|" *Ask of me.* " The priesthood doth not appear to be settled upon Christ by any other expression than this, " Ask of me." The Psalm speaks of his investiture in his kingly office ; the apostle refers this to his priesthood, his commission for both took date at the same time ; both bestowed, both confirmed by the same authority. The office of asking is grounded upon the same authority as the honour of king. Ruling belonged to his royal office, asking to his priestly. After his resurrection, the Father gives him a power and command of asking.|*Stephen Charnock.*

Verse 8.|As the limner looks on the person whose picture he would take, and draws his lines to answer him with the nearest similitude that he can, so God looks on Christ as the archetype to which he will conform the saint, in suffering, in grace, in glory ; yet so that Christ hath the pre-eminence in all. Every saint must suffer, because Christ suffered : Christ must not have a delicate body under a crucified head ; yet never any suffered, or could, what he endured. Christ is holy, and therefore so shall every saint be, but in an inferior degree ; an image cut in clay cannot be so exact as that engraved on gold. Now, our conformity to Christ appears, that as the promises made to him were performed upon his prayers to his Father, his promises made to his saints are given to them in the same way of prayer : " *Ask of me,* " faith God to his Son, *"and I shall give thec."* And the apostle tells us, "Ye have not, because ye ask not." God hath promised support to Christ in all his conflicts. Isaiah xlii. 1. " Behold my servant, whom 1 uphold ;" yet he prayed " with strong cries and tears," when his feet stood within the shadow of death. A seed is promised to him, and victory over his enemies, yet for both these he prays. Christ towards us acts as a king, but towards his Father as a priest. All he speaks to God is by prayer and intercession. So the saints, the promise makes them kings over their lusts, conquerors over their enemies ; but it makes them priests towards God, by prayer humbly to sue out those great things given in the promise.| *William GurnaU, 1617|1679.*

Verse 8.|It will be observed in our Bible that two words of verse eight are in italics, intimating that they are not translations of the Hebrew, but additions made for the purpose of elucidating the meaning. Now if the " *thee"* and the "/or" are left out, the verse will read thus, " Ask of me, and I shall give the heathen, thine inheritance, and thy possession, the uttermost parts of the earth." And this reading is decidedly preferable to the other. It implies that by some previous arrangement on the part of God, he had already assigned an inheritance of the heathen, and the possession of the earth, to the person of whom he says, " Thou art my Son." And when God says, " I will give," etc., he reveals to his Anointed, not so much in what the inheritance consisted, and what was the extent of possession destined for him, as the promise of his readiness to bestow it. The heathen were already " the inheritance," and the ends of the earth " the possession," which God *bud purposed* to give to his Anointed. Now he says to him, " Ask of me," and he *promises* to fulfil his purpose. This is the idea involved in the words of the text, and the importance of it will become more apparent, when we consider its application to the *s)riritual* David, to the true Son of God, " whom he hath appointed the heir of all things."

Verte 9.|The " *rod* " has a variety of meanings in Scripture. It might be of different materials, as it was employed for different purposes. At an early period, a -wooden rod came into use as one of tbe insignia of royalty, under the name of sceptre. By degrees the sceptre grew in importance, and was regarded as characteristic of an empire, or of the reign of some particular king. A golden sceptre denoted wealth and pomp. The right, or straight sceptre, of which we read in Psalm xlv. 6, is expressive of the justice and uprightness, the truth and equity, which shall distinguish Messiah's reign, after his kingdom on earth has been established. But when it is said in Rev. xix. 15, that he, " whose name is called the Word of God," will smite the nations, and " rule them with a rod of iron," if the rod signifies "his sceptre," then the " inen" of which it is made must be designed to express the severity of the judgments which this omnipotent " King of kings" will inflict on all who resist his authority. But to me it appears doubtful whether the " rod of iron" symbolises the royal sceptre of the Son of God at his second advent. It is mentioned in connection with "a sharp sword," which leads me to prefer the opinion that it also ought to be regarded as a weapon of war ; at all events, the " rod of iron" mentioned in the Psalm we are endeavouring to explain, is evidently not the emblem of sovereign power, although represented as in the hands of a king, but an instrument of correction and punishment.. In this sense

the word " rod " is often used When the correcting rod, which

usually was a wand or cane, is represented as in this second Psalm, to be of " iron," it only indicates how weighty, now severe, how effectual the threatened chastisement will belit will not merely bruise, but it will break. " *Thou nhalt break them with a rod of iron.*11

Now it is just such a complete breaking as would not readily be effected excepting by *an iron rod,* that is more fully expressed in the following clause of the verse, "Thou shall dash them in pieces like a potter's vessel." The completeness of the destruction, however, depends on two things. Even an iron rod, if gently used, or used against a hard and firm substance, might cause little injury ; but, in the case before us, it is supposed to be applied with great force, " Thou shalt *dash* them ;" and it is applied to what will prove as brittle and frangible as " *a potter's vessel* "|" Thou shalt dash them *in piece.*" .... Here, as in other respects, we must feel that the predictions and promises of this Psalm were but very partially fulfilled in the history of" the literal David. Their real accomplishment, their awful completion, abides the day when the spiritual David shall come in glory and in majesty as Zion's King, with a rod of iron to diish in pieces the great antichristian confederacy of kings and peoples, and to take possession of his long-promised and dearly-purchased inheritance. And the signs of the times seem to indicate that the coming of the Lord draws nigh.|*David Pitcairn.*

Verse 1Q.|" *Be mse now, therefore, 0 ye kings,"* etc As Jesus is King of kings and Judge of judges, so the gospel is the teacher of the greatest and wisest. If any are so great as to spurn its admonitions, God will make little of them ; and if they are so wise as to despise its teachings, their fancied wisdom, shall make fools of them. The gospel takes a high tone before the rulers of the earth, and they who preach it should, like Knox and Melvill, magnify their office by bold rebukes and manly utterances even in the royal presence. A clerical sycophant is only fit to be a scullion in the devil's kitchen.| *C. H. S.*

Verse 11.| *"Serve the Lord with fear."* This fear of God qualifies our joy. If you abstract fear from joy, joy will become light and wanton ; and if you abstract joy from fear, fear then will become slavish.| *William Bate, D.D.,* 1625|1699.

Verse 11.|" *Serte the Lord with fear, and rejoice with trembling."* There are two kinds of serving and rejoicing in God. First, a serving in security, and a. rejoicing in the Lord without fear ; these are peculiar to hypocrites, who aresecure, who please themselves, and who appear to themselves to be not unuseful servants, and to have great merit on their side, concerning whom it is said (Psalm x. 5), " Thy judgments are far aboje out of his sight;" and also afterwards (Psalm xxxvi. 1), " There is no fear of God before his eyes." These do righteousness without judgment at all times ; and permit not Christ to be the Judge to be feared by all, in whose sight no man living is justified. Secondly, a serving with fear and a rejoicing with trembling ; these are peculiar to the righteous who do righteousness at all times, and always rightly attemper both ; never being without judgments, on the one hand, by which they are terrified and brought to despair of themselves and of all their own works ; nor without that righteousness, on the other, on which they rest, and in which they rejoice in the mercy of God. It is the work of the whole lives of these characters to accuse themselves ia all things, and in all things to justify and praise God. And thus they fulfil that word of Proverbs, " Blessed is the man that feareth alway" (xxvifi. 14); and also that of Philip, iv. 4, "Rejoice in the Lord alway." Thus, between the upper and nether mill-stone (Deut. xxiv. 6), they are broken in pieces and humbled, and the husks being thus bruised off, they come forth the all-pure wheat of Christ.|*Martin Luther.*

Verse 11.|The fear of God promotes spiritual joy ; it is the morning star which ushers in the sunlight of comfort. " Walking in the fear of God, and in. the comfort of the Holy Ghost." God mingles joy with fear, that fear may not be slavish.|*Thomat Watson,* 1660.

Verse 12.|" Jfiss," a sign of love among equals: Gen. xxxiii. 4; 1 Sam. xx. 41 : Rom. xvi. 1C ; 1 Cor. xvi. 20. Of subjection in inferiors : 1 Sam. x. 1. Of religious adoration in worshippers : 1 Kings xix. 18 ; Job xxxi: 27. |*John Richardson, Bishop of Ardagh,* 1655.

Verse 12.|" *Kiss the Son, lest ha le angry."'* From the Person, *the Son,* we shall pass to the act *(Osculamini, kiss the Son)* ; in which we shall see, that since this is an act which licentious men have depraved (carnal men do it, and treacherous men do it|*Judas* betrayed his Master by a kiss), and yet God commands this, and expresses love in this ; everything that hath, or may be abused, must not therefore be abandoned ; the turning of a thing out of the way, is not a taking of that thing away, but good things deflected to ill uses by some, may be by others reduced to their first goodness. Then let us consider and magnify the goodness of God, that hath brought us into this distance, that we may *kiss the Son,* that the expressing of this love lies in our hands, and that, whereas the love of the church, in the Old Testament, even in the Canticle, went no farther but to the *Oseulatur me (0 that he would kiss me with the kisses of his mouth !* Cant. i. 1), now, in the Christian church, and in the visitation of a Christian soul, he hath invited us, enabled us to kiss him, for he is presently amongst us. This leads us to give an earnest persuasion and exhortation *to kiss the Son,* with all those affections, which we shall there find to be expressed in the Scriptures, in that testimony of true love, *a holy kiss.* But then, lest that persuasion by love should not be effectual and powerful enough to us, we shall descend from that duty, to the danger, from love, to fear, " *lest he le angry;"* and therein see first, that God, who is love, can be angry ; and then, that this God who is angry here, is the Son of God, he that hath done so much for us, and therefore in justice may be angry ; he that is our Judge, and therefore in reason we are to fear his anger : and then, in a third branch, we shall see how easily this anger departs|a kiss removes it.

Verse 12.|" *Kits the Son."* That is, embrace him, depend upon him all these ways : as thy kinsman, as thy sovereign ; at thy going, at thy coming ; at thy reconciliation, in the truth of religion in thyself, in a peaceable unity with the church, in a reverent estimation of those men, and those means, whom he sends. Kiss him, and be not ashamed of kissing him ; it is that which the spouse desired, " *I would kiss thee, and not le despised.'*1" Cant. vii. 1. If thou be despised for loving Christ in his gospel, remember that when David was thoughtbase, for dancing before the ark, his way was to be more base. If them be thought frivolous for thrusting in at service, in the forenoon, be more frivolous, and corae again in the afternoon : " *Tanto major requies, quantv ab amore Jetu nulla requies* ;" "The more thou troublest thyself, or art troubled by others for Christ, the more peace thou hast in Christ." .... " *Lett he be angry."* Anger, as it is a passion that troubles, and disorders, and discomposes a man, *Bo* it is not in God ; but anger, as it is a sensible discerning of foes from friends, and of things that conduce, or disconduce to his glory, so it is in God. In a word, Hilary hath expressed it well: " *Pcena patientis, ira decernentu ;"* "Man's suffering is God's anger." When God inflicts such punishments as a king justly incensed would do, then God is thus angry. Now here, our case 13 heavier ; it is not this great, and almighty, and majestical God, that may be angry -that is like enough ; but even the *Son,* whom wo must *kiss,* may be *angry ;* it is not a person whom we consider merely as God, but as man ; nay not as man neither, but *a worm, and no man,* and he may be angry, and angry to

our run *"Kits the Son,"* and he will not *be angry;* if he be, kiss the

rod, i.od be will be angry no longer|love him lest he be : fear him when he is angry : the preservative is easy, and so is the restorative too : the balsamum of this kiss is all, to suck spiritual milk out of the left breast, as well as out of the right, to find mercy in his judgments, reparation in his ruins, feasts in his lents, joy A his anger.|*from Hermans of John Donne, D.D., Dean of tit. Paul's.* 1621|1631.

Verse 12.|" *Kis the Son."* To make peace with the Father, kiss the Son. " Let him k.s me," was the church's prayer. Cant. i. 2. Let us kiss him|that be our endea-our. Indeed, the Son must first kiss us by his mercy, before we can kiss him oy our piety. Lord, grant in these mutual kisses and interchangeable embraces now, that we may come to the plenary wedding supper hereafter ; when the choir of heaven, even the voices of angels, shall sing epithalaimums, nuptial songs, at the bridal of the spouse of the Lamb. | *Thoma Adams.*

Verse 12.|" *If his wrath be kindled but a little ;"* the Hebrew is, if his nose or nostril be kindled but a little ; the nostril, being an organ of thr; body in which wrath shows itself, is put for wrath itself. Paleness and snuffling of the nose are symptoms of anger. In our proverbials, to take a thing in snuff, is to take it in anger.|*Joseph Caryl.*

Verse 12.|" *His wrath."* Unspeakable must the wrath of God be when it is kindled fully, since perdition may come upon the *kindling of it but a little.*| *John NewUm.*

HINTS TO THE VILLAGE PREACHER.

Whole Ptalm.|Shows us the nature of sin, and the terrible results of it if it could reign.

Verse 1.|*Nothing is more irrational than irreligion.* A weighty theme.

The reasons why sinners rebel against God, stated, refuted, lamented, and repented of.

The crowning display of human sin in man's hatred of the Mediator.

Verses 1 *and* 2.|Opposition to the gospel, unreasonable and ineffectual.|*Two termons by John Newton.*

Verses 1 *and* 2.|These verses show that all trust in man in the service of God is vain. Inasmuch as men oppose Christ, it is not good to hang our trust upon *the multitude* for their number, *the earnest* for their zeal, *the mighty* for their countenance, or *the wise* for their counsel, since all these are far oftener against Christ than for him.

Gregory.

Verse 2.|" Spurgeon's Sermons," No. 495, " The Greatest Trial on Record."

Verse 3.|The true reason of the opposition of sinners to Christ's truth, viz. : their hatred of the lestruints of godliness.

Verge 4.|God's derision of the rebellious, both now and hereafter.

Verse 5.|*The voice of wrath.* One of a series of sermons upon the voices of xhe divine attributes.

Verse 6.|*Chrufi sovereignty. 1.* The opposition to it: *"yet."* 2. The certainty of its existence : " *Yet fiave I set."*| 3. The power which maintains it : "Aarelsei." 4. The place of its manifestation : " *my holy hillofZion.'"* 5. Th blessings Sowing from it.

Verse 7.|The divine decree concerning Christ, in connection with the decrees of election and providence. The Sonship of Jesus.

This verse teachcth us faithfully to declare, and humbly to claim, the gifts and calling that God hath bestowed upon us.|*Thomas Wilcocks.*

Verge 8.|Christ's inheritance.| *William Jay.*

Prayer indispensable.|*Jesus must aik.*

Verse 9.|*The ruin of the wicked.* Certain, irresistible, terrible, complete, irretriev- able, " like a potter's vessel."

The destruction of system of error and oppression to be expected. The gospel an iron rod quite able to break mere pots of man's making.

Verse 10.|True wisdom, fit for kings and judges, lies in obeying Christ.

The gospel, a school for those who would learn how to rule and judge well. They may consider its principles, its exemplar, its spirit, etc.

Verse .–Minyled experience. See the case of the women returning from the sepulchre. Matt, xxviii. 8. This may be rendered a very comforting subject, if the Holy Spirit direct the mind of the preacher.

True religion, a compound of many virtues and emotious.

Verse 12.|An earnest invitation. 1. *The command.* 2. *The argument.* 3. *The benediction* upon the obedient.|" Spurgeon's Sermons," No. 260.

*Lout clause.|Nature, object, and blessedness of saving faith.

WORK UPON THE SECOND PSALM.

Zian's King : the Second Psalm expounded in the Light of History and Prophecy. By the Kev. David Pitcairn. 1851.

PSALM III.

Titlk.|"A Psalm of David, when lie fled from Absalom bis Son." *Ton win* remember *the sad story of David's flight from his own palace, when, in the dead of the night, he forded the brook Kedron, and went with a few faithful followers to hide himself for awhile from the fury of his rebellious son. Remember that David in this was a type of the Lord Jesus Christ. He, too, fled ; he, too, passed over the brook Kedron when his own petqile were in rebellion against him, and with a feeble band of followers he went to the garden of Geth- semane. Jle, too, drank of ike brook by the way, and therefore doth he lift up the head. By very many expositors this is entitled* The Mokninq Hymn. *May we ever wake with holy confidence in our hearts, and a song upon our lips]*

Division.|*This Psalm may be divided into four parts of two verses each. Indeed, many of the Psalms cannot be well understood unless we attentively regard the parts into which they should be divided. They are not* continuous *descriptions of one scene, but a set of pictures of many kindred subjects. As in our modern sermons, we divide our discourse into different heads, so is it in these Psalms. There is always unity, but it is the unity of a bundle of arrows, and not of a single solitary shaft. Let us now look at the Psalm before us. In tlie first two verses you have David making a complaint to (Jod concerning his enemies; he then declares his confidence in the Lord (3, 4), sings of his safety in sleep (5, C), and strengthens himself for future connict (7, 8).*

EXPOSITION.

LORD, how are they increased that trouble me ! many *are* they that rise up against me.

2 Many *there be* which say of my soul, *There is* no help for him in God. Selah.

The poor broken-hearted father complains of the multitude of his enemies : and if you turn to 2 Samuel xv. 12, you will find it written that " the conspiracy was strong ; for the people increased continually with Absalom," while the troops of David constantly diminished ! " *Lord, how are they increased that trouble me!"* Here is a note of exclamation to express the wonder of woe which amazed and perplexed the fugitive father. Alas ! I see no limit to my misery, for my troubles are enlarged ! There was enough at first to sink me very low ; but lo ! my enemies multiply. When Absalom, my darling, is in rebellion against me, it is enough to break my heart; but lo! Ahithophel hath forsaken me, my faithful counsellors have turned their backs on me ; lo 1 my generals and soldiers have deserted my standard. " How are they increased that trouble me 1" Troubles always come in flocks. Sorrow hath a numerous family.

"Many are they that rise up against me." Their hosts are far superior to mine ! Their numbers are too great for my reckoning !

Let us here recall to our memory the innumerable hosts which beset our Divine Redeemer. The legions of our sins, the armies of fiends, the crowd of bodily pains, the host of spiritual sorrows, and all the allies of death and hell, set themselves in battle against the Son of Man. O how precious to know and believe that he has routed their hosts, and trodden them down in his anger ! They who would have troubled us he has removed into captivity, and those who would have risen up against us he has laid low. The dragon lost his sting when he dashed it into the soul of Jesus.

David complains before his loving God of the worst weapon of his enemies' attacks, and the bitterest drop of his distresses. "Oh!" saith David, *"many there lie that say of my soul, There is no help for him in God."* Some of his distrustful friends said this sorrowfully, but his enemies exultingly boasted of it, and longed to see their words proved by his total destruction. This was the un- kindest cut of all, when they declared that his God had forsaken him. Yet David knew in his own conscience that he had given them some ground for this exclamation, for he had committed sin against God in the very light of day. Then they flung his crime with Bathsheba into his face, and they said, " Go up, thou bloody man ; God hath forsaken thee and left thee." Shimei cursed him, and swore at him to his very face, for he was bold because of his backers, since multitudes of the men of Belial thought of David in like fashion. Doubtless, Duvid felt this infernal suggestion to be staggering to his faith. If all the trials which come from heaven, all the temptations which ascend from hell, and all the crosses which arise from earth, could be mixed and pressed together, they would not make a trial so terrible as that which is contained in this verse. It is the most bitter of all afflictions to be lead to fear that there is no help for us in God. And yet remember our most blessed Saviour had to endure this in the deepest degree when he cried, " My God, my God, why hast thou forsaken me ?" He knew full we'll what it was to walk in darkness and to see no light. This was the curse of the curse. This was the wormwood mingled with the gall. To be deserted of his Father was worse than to be the despised of men. Surely we should love him who suffered this bitterest of temptations and trials for our sake. It will be a delightful and instructive exercise for the loving heart to mark the Lord in his agonies as here pourtrayed, for there is here, and in very many other Psalms, far more of David's Lord than of David himself.

" &fa/." This is a musical pause ; the precise meaning of which is not known. Some think it simply a rest, *a* pause in the music ; others say it means, " Lift up the strain|sing more loudly|pitch the tune upon a higher key|there is nobler matter to come, therefore retune your harps." Harp-strings soon get out of order and need to be screwed up again to their proper tightness, and certainly our heart-strings are evermore getting out of tune. Let " Selah" teach us to pray

" O mav ray heart In tune he found
Like David's harp of solemn sound."

At least, we may learn that wherever we see " Selah," we should look upon it as a note of observation. Let us read the passage which precedes and succeeds it with greater earnestness, for surely there is always something excellent where we are required to rest and pause and meditate, or when we are required to lift up our hearts in grateful song. " Selah."

3 But thou, O Lord, *art* a shield for me ; my glory, and the lifter up of mine head.

4 I cried unto the Lord with my voice, and he heard me out of his holy hill. Selah.

Here David avows his confidence in God. " *Tluru, O Lord, art a shield for me.*" The word in the original signifies more than a shield ; it means a buckler round about, a protection which shall surround a man entirely, a shield above, beneath, around, without and within. Oh ! what a shield is God for his people I He wards off the fiery darts of Satan from beneath, and the storms of trials from above, while, at the same instant, he speaks peace to the tempest within the breast. Thou art "my *glory.*'1' David knew that though he was driven ,from his capital in contempt and scorn, he should yet return in triumph, and by faith he looks upon God as honouring and glorifying him. O for grace to see our future glory amid present shame ! Indeed, there is a present glory in our afflictions, if we could but discern it ; for it is no mean thing to have fellowship with Christ in his sufferings. David was honoured when he made the ascent of Olivet, weeping, with his head covered ; for he was in all this made like unto his Lord. May we learn, in this respect, to glory in tribulations also ! " *And the lifter up of mine head*'1'1lthou shalt yet exalt me. Though I hang my head insorrow, I shall very soon lift it up in joy and thanksgiving. What a divine trio of mercies is contained in this verse !ldefence for the defenceless, glory for the despised, and joy for the comfortless. Verily wo may well say, " there is like the God of Jeshurun."

" *I cried unto the Ijord with my voice.*" "Why doth he say, " with my voice ?" Surely, silent prayers are heard. Yes, but good men often find that, even in secret, they pray better aloud than they do when they utter no vocal sound. Perhaps, moreover, David would think thus :l" My cruel enemies clamour against me ; *they* lift up their voices, and, behold, / lift up mine, and my cry outsoars them all. They clamour, but the cry of my voice in great distress pierces the very skies, and is louder and stronger than all their tumult ; for there is one in the sanctuary who hearkens to me from the seventh heaven, and he hath ' *heard me out of his holy hill.*'1 " Answers to prayers are sweet cordials for the soul. "We need not fear a frowning world while we rejoice in a prayer-hearing God.

Here stands another *Selah.* Rest awhile, O tried believer, and change the strain to a softer air.

5 I laid me down and slept; I awaked ; for the Lord sustained me.

6 I will not be afraid of ten thousands of people, that have set *themselves* against me round about.

David's faith enabled him to *lie down;* anxiety would certainly have kept him on tiptoe, watching for an enemy. Yea, he Whs able to sleep, *to steep* in the midst of trouble, surrounded by foes. " So he giveth his beloved sleep." There is a sleep of presumption ; God deliver us from it ! There is a sleep of holy confidence ; God help us so to close our eyes I But David says' he *tupaktd* also. Some sleep the sleep of death ; but he, though exposed to many enemies, reclined his head on the bosom of his God, slept happily beneath the wing of Providence in sweet security, and then awoke in safety. " *For the ford sustained me.*" The sweet influence of the Pleiades of promise shone upon the sleeper, and he awoke conscious that the Lord had preserved him. An excellent divine has well remarked|" This quietude of a man's heart by faith in God, is a higher sort of work than the natural resolution of manly courage, for it is the gracious operation of God's Holy Spirit upholding a man above nature, and therefore the Lord must have all the glory of it."

Buckling on his harness for the day's battle, our hero sings, " *I will not lie afraid of ten thousands of people, that hate set themselves ayainst me round about.*" Observe that he does not attempt to under-estimate the number or wisdom of his enemies. He reckons them at tens of thousands, and he views them as cunning huntsmen chasing him with cruel skill. Yet he trembles not, but looking his foeman in the face he is ready for the battle. There may be no wny of escape ; they may hem me in as the deer are surrounded by a circle of huntets ; they may surround me on every side, but in the name of God I will dash through them ; or, if I remain in the midst of them, yet shall they not hurt me ; I shall be free in my very prison.

But David is too wise to venture to the battle without prayer ; he therefore betakes himself to his knees, and cries aloud to Jehovah.

7 Arise, O Lord ; save me, O my God : for thou hast smitten all mine enemies *upon* the cheek bone ; thou hast broken the teeth, of the ungodly.

His only hope is in his God, but that is so strong a confidence, that he feels the Lord hath but to *arise* and he is saved. It is enough for the Lord to stand up, and all is well. He compares his enemies to wild beasts, and he declares that God hath broken their jaws, so that they could not injure him ; " *Thou hast broken the teeth of the ungodly.*" Or else he alludes to the peculiar temptationsto -which he was then exposed. They had spoken ngainst him ; God, therefore, has smitten them upon the cheek bone. They seemed as if they would devour him with their mouths ; God hath broken their teeth, and let them say what they will, their toothless jaws shall not be able to devour him. Rejoice, O believer, thou hast'to do with a dragon whose head is broken, and with enemies whose teeth are dashed from their jaws !

8 Salvation *belongcth* unto the Lord : thy blessing *is* upon thy people. Selah.

This verse contains the sum and substance of Calvinistic doctrine. Search Scripture through, and you must, if you read it with a candid mind, be persuaded that the doctrine of salvation by grace alone is the great doctrine of the word of God : " *Saltation belongeth unto the Lord.*" This is a point concerning which -we are daily fighting. Our opponents say, " Salvation belongeth to the free will of man ; if not to man's merit, yet at least to man's will ;" but we hold and teach that salvation from first to last, in every iota of it, belongs to the Most High God. It is God that chooses his people. *He* calls them by his grace ; *he* quickens them by his Spirit, and keeps them by his power. It is not of man, neither by man ; " not of him that willeth, nor of him that runneth, but of God that showeth mercy." Hay we all learn this truth experimentally, for our proud flesh and blood will never permit us to learn it in any other way. In the last sentence the peculiarity and speciality of salvation are plainly stated : " *'//'/./ Vetting is upon thy people.* Neither upon Epypt, nor upon Tyre, nor upon Nineveh ; thy blessing is upon thy chosen, thy blood-bought, thine everlastingly- beloved people. " *Selah:*" lift up your hearts, and pause, and meditate upon this doctrine. " Thy blessing is upon thy people." Divine, discriminating, distinguishing, eternal, infinite, immutable love, is a subject for constant adoration. Pause, my soul, at this *Selah,* and consider thine own interest in the salvation of God ; and if by humble faith thou art enabled to see Jesus as thine by his own free gift of himself to thee, if this greatest of all blessings be upon thee, rise up and sing|

" Rise, my soul! ndore and wonder!
Ask, ' O why such love to me ?'
Grace hath put me in the number
Of the Saviour's family :

Hallelujah!
Thanks, eternal thanks, to thee!"

EXPLANATORY NOTES AND QUAINT SAYINGS.

Title.|With regard to the authority of the Titles, it becomes us to speak with diffidence, considering the very opposite opinions which have been offered upon this subject by scholars of equal excellence. In the present day, it is too much the custom to slight or omit them altogether, as though added, nobody knows when or by whom, and as, in many instances, inconsistent with the subject-matter of the Psalm itself : while Augustine, Theodoret, and various other early writers of the Christian church, regard them as a part of the inspired text; and the Jews still continue to make them a part of their chant, and their rabbins to comment upon them.

It is certainly unknown who invented or placed them where they are ; but it *is* unquestionable that they have been so placed from time immemorial ; they occur in the Septuagint, which contains also in a few instances titles to Psalms that are without any in the Hebrew ; and they have been copied after the Septua- gint by Jerome. So far as the present writer has been able to penetrate the obscurity that occasionally hangs over them, they re a direct and most valuable key to the general history or subject of the Psalms to which they are prefixed ; and, excepting where they have been evidently misunderstood or misinterpreted, he has never met with a single instance in which the drift of the title and its respective Psalm do not exactly coincide. Many of them were, doubtless, composed by Ezra at the time of editing his own collection, at which period some critics suppose the whole to have been written ; but the rest appear rather to be coeval, or nearly so, with the respective Psalms themselves, and to have been written about the period of their production.|*John Mason Good, M.D., F.H.S.,* 1854.

See title. Here we have the first use of the word *Psalm.* In Hebrew, *Mizmor,* which hath the signification of pruning, or cutting off superfluous twigs, and is applied to songs made of short sentences, where many superfluous words are put away.|*Uenry Ainnworth.*

Upon this note an old writer remarks, " Let us learn from this, that in times of sore trouble men will not fetch a compass and use fine words in prayer, but will offer a prayer which is pruned of all luxuriance of wordy speeches."

Whole Psalm.|Thus you may plainly see how God hath wrought in his church in old time, and therefore should not discourage yourselves for any sudden change ; but with David, acknowledge your sins to God, declare unto him how many there be that vex you and rise up against you, naming you Huguenots, Lutherans, Heretics, Puritans, and the children of Belial, as they named David. Let the wicked idolaters brag that they will prevail against you and overcome you, and that God hath given you over, and will be no more your God. Let them put their trust in Absalom, with his large golden locks ; and in the wisdom of Ahithophel, the wise counsellor ; yet say you, with David, " *Thou, 0 Lord, art my defender, and the lifter up of my head.*" " Persuade yourselves, with David, that the Lord is your defender, who hath compassed you round about, and is, as it were, a " *shield"* that doth cover you on every side. It is he only that may and will compass you about with glory and honour. It is he that will thrust down those proud hypocrites from their seat, and exalt the lowly and meek. It is he which will *"smite"*1 your "enemies on *the check lone,"*1 and burst all their teeth in sunder. He will hang up Absalom by his own long hairs ; and Ahithophel through desperation shall hang himself. The bunds shall be broken, and you deb'vered ; for this belongeth unto the Lord, to save his from their enemies, and to bless his people, that they may safely proceed in their pilgrimage to heaven without fear.|*Thomas Tymme's "Silver Watch Bell,"* 1634.

Verge 1.|Absalom's faction, like a snowball, strangely gathered in its motion. David speaks of it as one amazed ; and well he might, that a people he had so many ways obliged, should almost generally revolt from him, and rebel against him, and choose for their head such a silly, giddy young fellow as Absalom was. How slippery and deceitful are the many ! And how little fidelity and constancy is to be found among men ! Duvid had had the hearts of his subjects as much as ever any king had, and yet now of a sudden he had lost them ! As people must not trust too much to princes (Psalm cxlvi. 3), so princes must not build too much upon their interest in the people. Christ the Son of David had many enemies, when a great multitude came to seize him, when the crowd cried, " Crucify him, crucify him," how were they then increased that troubled him ! Even good people must not think it strange if the stream be against them, and the powers that threaten them grow more and more formidable.|*Matthew Henry.*

Verse 2.|When the believer questions the power of God, or his interest in it, his joy gusheth out as blood out of a broken vein. This verse is a sore stab indeed.| *William Qumall.*

Verse 2.|A. child of God startles at the very thought of despairing of help in God ; you cannot vex him with anything so much as if you offer to persuade him, " *There* is no *help for him in God."* David comes to God, and tells him what his enemies said of him, as Hezekiah spread Rabshakeh's blasphemous letter before the Lord ; they say, " *There is no help for me in thee ;"* but, Lord, if it be so, I am undone. They say to my soul, " *There is no salvation"* (for so the word is) *"for him in Ood ;"* but, Lord, do thou say unto my soul, " *I am thy salvation"* (Psalm xxxv. 3), and that shall satisfy me, and in due time silence them.|*Matthew Henry.*

Verses 2, 4, 8.|" *Selah."* rnp. Much has been written on this word, and still its meaning does not appear to be wholly determined. It is rendered in the Targum or Chaldee paraphrase, I' 1??.??, *lealmin, for ever,* or *to eternity.* In the Latin Vulgate, it is omitted, as if it were no part of the text. In the Septuagint it is rendered Aiua?,//0, supposed to refer to some variation or modulation of the voice in singing. Schleusner, *Lex.* The word occurs seventy- three times in the Psalms, and three times in the book of Habukkuk (iii. 3, 9, 13). It is never translated in our version, but in all these places the original word *Stlalt* is retained. It occurs only in poetry, and is supposed to have had some reference to the singing or cantillation of the poetry, and to be probably a musical term. In general, also, it indicates a pause in the sense, as well as in the musical performance. Gesenius *(Lex.)* supposes that the most probable meaning of this musical term or note is *silence* or *pause,* and that its use was, in chanting the words of the Psalm, to direct the singer *to be silent, to pause a little,* while the instruments played an interlude or harmony. Perhaps this is all that can now be known of the meaning of the word, and this is enough to satisfy every reasonable enquiry. It is probable, if this was the use of the term, that it would commonly correspond with the sense of the passage, and be inserted where the sense made a pause suitable ; and this will doubtless be found usually to be the fact. But any one acquainted at all with the character of musical notation, will perceive at once that we are not to suppose that this would be invariably or necessarily the fact, for the musical pauses by no means always correspond with pauses in the sense. This word, therefore, can furnish very little assistance in determining the meaning of the passages where it is found. Ewald supposes, differing from this view, that it rather indicates that in the places where it occurs the voice is to be raised, and that it is synonymous with *up, higher, loud,* or *distinct,* from 0, *sal,* SSo, *salal, to ascend.* Those who are disposed to enquire further respecting its meaning, and the uses of musical pauses in general, may be referred to Ugolin, " Thesau. Antiq. Sacr.," torn. xxii. |*Albert Barnes,* 1868.

Verses 2, 4, 8.|*Selah,* iT75, is found seventy-three times in the Psalms, generally at the end of a sentence or paragraph ; but in Psalm Iv. 19 and Ivii. 3, it stands in the middle of the verse. While most authors have agreed in considering this word as somehow relating to the *music,* their conjectures about its precise meaning have varied greatly. But at present these two opinions chiefly obtain. Some, including Herder, be Wette, Ewald *(Poet. Bucher,* i. 179), and Delitzscli, derive it from i"1/?! or ' -? '" *raise,* and understand an *elevation* of the voice or music ; others, after Gesenius, in *Thesaurus,* derive it from 7170, *to be still* or *silent,* and understand a pause in the singing. So Rosen- muller, Hengstenberg, and Tholuck. Probably *seldh* was used to direct the singer to be silent, or to pause a little, while the instruments played an interlude (so Sept., ... or symphony. In Psalm ix. 16, it occurs in the expression *hiygaion selah,* which Gesenius, with much probability, renders *instrumental music, pause; i.e.,* let the instruments strike up a symphony, and let the singer pause. By Tholuck and Hengstenberg, however, the two wordsare rendered *meditation, pause ; i.e.,* let the singer meditate while the music rtope. *Benjamin Datie, Ph. D., LL.D., article Psalm, in KMo' Cyclopadia of Biblical Literature.*

Vene 3.|" *Lifter vp of my head."* God will have the body partaVe with the soul|as in matters of grief, so in matters of joy ; the lanthorn shines in the light of the candle within.|*Kichard Sibbs,* 1639.

There U a lifting up of the head by elevation to office, as with Pharaoh's butler ; this we trace to the divine appointment. There is a lifting up in honour after shame, in health after sickness, in gladness after sorrow, in restoration after a fall, in victory after a temporary defeat.; in all these respects the Lord is the lifter up of our head.|*C. II. 8.*

Verse 4.|When prayer leads the van, in due time deliverance brings up the rear. | *Thomas Walton.*

Verted.|" lie heard me." I have often heard persons say in prayer, "Thou art a prayer-hearing and a prayer-answering God," but the expression contains a superfluity, since for God to hear is, according to Scripture, the same thing as to answer.|C. H. S.

Verse 5.|" *I laid me down and slept; 1 awaked ; for the Lord sustained me."* The title of the Psalm tells us when David hud this sweet night's rest ; not when he lay on his bed of down in his stately palace at Jerusalem, but when he fled for his life from his unnatural son Absalom, and possibly was forced to lie in the open field under the canopy of heaven. Truly it must be a soft pillow indeed that could make him forget his danger, who then had such a disloyal army at his back hunting of him ; yea, so transcendent is the influence of this peace, thiit it can make the creature lie down as cheerfully to sleep in the grave, as on the softest bed. You will say that child is willing that calls to be put to bed ; some of the saints have desired God to lay them at rest in their beds of dust, and that not in a pet and discontent with their present trouble, as Job did, but from a sweet sense of this peace in their bosoms. " Now let thy servant depart in peace, for mine eyes have seen thy salvation," was the swan-like song of old Simeon. He speaks like a merchant that had got all his goods on ship-board, and now desires the master of the ship to hoist sail, and be gone homewards. Indeed, what should a Christian, that is but a foreigner here, desire to stay any longer for in the world, bur. to get his full lading in for heaven ? And when hath he that, if not when he is assured of his peace with God ? This peace of the gospel, and sense of the love of God in the soul, doth so admirably conduce'to the enabling of a person in all difficulties, and temptations, and troubles, that ordinarily, before he calls his saints to any hard service, or hot work, he gives them a draught of this cordial wine next their hearts, to cheer them up and embolden them in the conflict.| *William Ournall.*

Verne 5.|Gurnall, who wrote when there were houses on old London Bridge, has quaintly said, " Do you not think that they sleep as soundly who dwell on London Bridge as they who live at Whitehall or Cheapside f for they know that the waves which rush under them cannot hurt them. Even Fo may the saints rest quietly over the floods of trouble or death, and fear no ill."

Vena 5.|Xerxes, the Persian, when he destroyed all the temples in Greece, caused the temple of Diana to be preserved for its beautiful structure : that soul which hath the beauty of holiness shining in it, shall be preserved for the glory of the structure ; God will not suffer his own temple to be destroyed. Would you be secured in evil times ? Get grace and fortify this garrison ; a good conscience is a Christian's fort-royal. David's enemies lay round about him ; yet, saith he, "*/ laid me down anl slept."* A. good conscience can sleep in the mouth of a cannon ; grace is a Christian's coat of mail, which fears not the arrow or bullet. True grace may be shot at, but can never be shot through ; grace puts the soul into Christ, and there it is safe, as the bee in the hive, asthe dove in the ark. " There is no condemnation to them which arc in Christ Jesus." Rom. viii. 1.|*Thomas Ynison.*

Vfrte 5.|" *The Lord sustained me."* It would not be unprofitable to consider the sustaining power manifested in us while we lie asleep. In the flowing of the blood, heaving of the lung, etc., in the body, and tho continuance of mental faculties while the image of death is upon us.|C. *1L &.*

Terse 0.|" *1 icill not he afraid of ten thousands rf peojile, that hate set them- tflrc against me round about.*" The psalmist will trust, *deipite appearances.* He will not be afiaid though ten thousands of people have set themselves against him round about. Let us here limit our thoughts to this one idea, " despite appears noes." What could look worse to human sight than this nrray of ten thousands of people ? Ruin seemed lo stare him in the face ; wherever he looked an enemy was to be seen. What was one against ten thousand I It often happens that God's people come into circumstances like this ; they say, " All these things are against me ;" they seem scarce able to count their troubles ; they cannot see !X loophole through which to escape ; tilings look very black indeed : it is great faith and trust which says under these circumstances, " I will not be afraid."

These were the circumstances under which Luther was placed, as he journeyed towards Worms. His friend Spalatin heard it said, by the enemies of the Reformation, that the safe conduct of a heretic ought not to be respected, and became alarmed for the reformer. "At the moment when the latter was apprcaching the city, n messenger appeared before him with this advice from the chaplain, ' Do not enter Worms !' And this from his best fiiend, the elector's confidant, from Spalatin himself ! . . . But Luther, undismayed, turned his eyes upon the messenger, and replied, ' Go and tell your master, that even should theie be as many devils in Worms as tiles upon the housetops, still I would enter it.' The messenger returned to Worms, with this astounding answer : ' I was then undaunted,' said Luther, a few days before his death, ' I feared nothing.' "

At such seasons as these, the reasonable men of the world, those who walk by sight and not by faith, will think it reasonable enough that the Christian should be afraid; they themselves would be very low if they were in such a predicament. Wenk believers are now ready to make excuses for us, and we are only too rendy to make them for ourselves ; instead of rising above the week- ness of the flesh, we take refuge under it, and use it as an excuse. But let us think prayerfully for a little while, and we shall see that it should not be thus witli us. To trust only when appearances are favourable, is to sail only with the wind and tide, to believe only when we can see. Oh ! let us follow the example of the psalmist, and seek that unreservedness of faith which will enable us to trust God, come what will, and to say as he said, " *I will not be afraid of ten thousands of people, that hate set themselces against me roundabout.*"|*Philip Bennett Power's ' I trills*1 *of the Psalms,* 1862.

Verne G.|" *1 will r,ot lie afraid,*"1 etc. It makes no matter what our enemies be, though for number, legions ; for power, principalities ; for subtlety, serpents; for cruelty, dragons ; for vantage of place, a prince of the air ; for maliciousness, spiritual wickedness ; stronger is he that is in us, than they who are against us ; nothing is able to separate us from the love of God. In Christ Jesus our Lord, we shall be more than conquerors.| *William Cowper,* 1G12.

Verse 1.|" *Arise, O Lord,*" Jehovah ! This is a common scriptural mode of calling upon God to manifest his presence and his power, either in wrath or favour. By a natural anthropomorphism, it describes the intervals of such manifestation as periods of inaction or of slumber, out of which he is besought tc rouse himself. " *Sate me,"* even me, of whom they say there is no help for him in God. " *Sane me, 0 my Go/1,"* mine by covenant and mutual engagement, to whom I therefore have a right to look for deliverance and protection. This confidence is warranted, moreover, by experience. *"For ttwu hast,"* in former

2

SECTION 2

---

exigencies, " *smitten all mine enemies,"* without exception " *(on the) cheek* " or jaw, an act at once violent and insulting.|*J. A. Alexander, D.D.*

Verse 7.|" *Upon tfie cheek bone.* "|The language seems to be taken from a comparison of his enemies with wild beasts. The cheek bone denotes the bone in which the teeth are placed, and to break that is to disarm the animal. *Albert Barnes, in loc.*

Verse 7.|When God takes vengeance upon the ungodly, he will smite in such a manner as to make them feel his almightiuess in every stroke. All his power ahull be exercised in punishing and none in pitying. O that every obstinate sinner would think of this, and consider his unmeasurable boldness in thinking himself able to grapple with Omnipotence !|*titqihen Charnock.*

Verse 8.|" *Salvation belongeth unto the Lord:"* parallel passage in Jonah ii. 9, " *Saltation is of the Lord."* The mariners might have written upon their ship, instead of Castor and Pollux, or the like device, *Salvation is tlie Lord's;* the Ninevites might have written upon their gates, *Salvation is the Lord's;* and whole mankind, whose cause is pitted and pleaded by God against the hardness of Jonah's heart, in the last, might have written on the palms of their hands, *Salvation is tfte Lord's.* It is the argument of both the Testaments, the staff and supportation of heaven and earth. They would both sink, and all their joints be severed, if the salvation of the Lord were not. The birds in the air sing no other notes, the beasts in the field give no other voice, than *Stilus Jehotce,* Salvation is the Lord's. The walls and fortresses to our country's gates, to our cities and towns, bars to our houses, a surer cover to our heads thau a helmet of steel, a better receipt to our bodies than the confection of apothecaries, a better receipt to our souls than the pardons of Rome, is *Salus Jehovoj,* the salvation of the Lord. *The salvation of the Lord* blesseth, prcserveth, upholdeth all that we have ; our basket and our store, the oil in our cruses, our presses, the sheep in our folds, our stalls, the children in the womb, at our tables, the corn in our fields, our stores, our garners ; it is not the virtue of the stars, nor nature of all things themselves, that giveth being and continuance to any of these blessings. And, " What shall I more say 2" as the apostle asked (Ileb. xi.) when he had spoken much, and there was much more behind, but time failed him. Rather, what should I not say ? for the world is my theatre at this time, and I neither think nor can feign to myself anything that hath not dependence upon this acclamation, *Salvation is the Lord's.* Plutarch writeth, that the Amphictious in Greece, a famous council assembled of twelve sundry people, wrote upon the temple of Apollo Pythius, instead of the Iliads of Homer, or songs of Pindarus (large and tiring discourses), short sentences and memoratives, as, *Know thyself, Use moderation, Beware of suretyship,* and the like ; and doubtless though every creature in the world, whereof we have use, be a treatise and narration unto us of the goodness of God, and we might weary our flesh, and spend our days in writing books of that inexplicable subject, yet this short apothegm of Jonah comprehendeth all the rest, and standeth at the end of the song, as the altars and stones that the patriarch set up at the parting of the ways, to give knowledge to the after-world by what means lie was delivered. I would it were daily preached in our temples, sung in our streets, written upon our door-posts, painted upon our walls, or rather cut with an adamant claw upon the tables of our hearts, that we might never forget salvation to be the Lord's. "We have need of such remembrances to keep us in practice of revolving the mercies of God. For nothing decayeth sooner than love ; *nihil facilius quam amt/r putrescit.* And of all the powers of the soul, memory is most delicate, tender, and brittle, and first waxcth old, *memoria delicata, tenera, fra- gili, in gwim primum senectus incurrit ;* and of all the apprehensions of memory, first benefit, *primum senescit beneficium.\John King's Commentary on Jonah,* 1594.

*Verse 8.\" Thy blessing is upon thy people.'*1" The saints are not only blessed when they are comprehensors, but while they are viators. They are blessedbefore they are crowned. This seems a paradox to flesh and blood : what, reproached and maligned, yet blessed ! A man that looks upun the children of God with a carnal eye, and sees how they are afflicted, and like the ship in the gospel, which was covered with waves (Matt. viii. 24), would think they were far from blessedness. Paul brings a catalogue of his sufferings (2 Cor. xi. 24|26), " Thrice was I beaten with rods, once was I stoned, thrice I suffered shipwreck," etc. And those Christians of the first magnitude, of whom the world was not worthy, " Had trials of cruel mockings and scourgings, they were sawn asunder, they were slain with the sword." Hcb. xi. 36, 37. What ! and were all these during the time of their sufferings blessed ? A carnal man would think, if this be to be blessed, God deliver him from it. But, however sense would give their vote, our Saviour Christ pronounceth the godly man blessed ; though a mourner, though a martyr, yet blessed. Job on the dunghill was blessed Job. The saints are blessed when they are cursed. Shimei did curse David (2 Samuel xvi. 5), " He came forth and cursed him ;" yet when he was cursed David he was blessed David. The saints though they are bruised, yet they are blessed. Not only they shall be blessed, but they are so. Psalm cxix. 1. "Blessed are the undefiled." Psalm iii. 8. " *Thy blessing is upon thy people."|Thomas Watson.*

At a curious instance of Luther's dogmatical interpretations, vie give very considerable extracts from his rendering of this Psalm without in any degree endorsing them.|C. H. S.

*Whole Psalm.|*That the meaning of this Psalm is not historical, is manifest from many particulars, which militate against its being so understood, And first of all, there is this which the blessed Augustine has remarked ; that the words, " I laid me down to sleep and took my rest," seem to be the words of Christ rising from the dead. And then that there is at the end the blessing of God pronounced upon the people, which manifestly belongs to the whole church. Hence, the blessed Augustine interprets the Psalm in a threefold way : first, concerning Christ the head ; secondly, concerning the whole of Christ, that is, Christ and his church, the head and the body ; and thirdly, figuratively, concerning any private Christian. Let each have his own interpretation. I, in the meantime, will interpret it concerning Christ; being moved Bo to do by the game argument that moved Augustine|that the fifth verse does not seem appropriately to apply to any other but Christ. First, because, " Lying down" and " sleeping," signify in this place altogether a natural death, not a natural sleep. Which may be collected from this|because it then follows, " and rose again." "Whereas if David had spoken concerning the sleep of the body, he would have said, " and awoke ;" though this does not make so forcibly for the interpretation of which we are speaking, if the Hebrew word be closely examined. But again, what new thing would he advance by declaring that he laid him down and slept ? Why did lie not say also that he walked, ate, drank, laboured, or was in necessity, or mention particularly some other work of the body ? And moreover, it seems an absurdity under so great a tribulation, to boast of nothing else but the sleep of the body ; for that tribulation would rather force him to a privation from sleep, and to he in peril and distress ; especially since those two expressions, " I laid me down," and " I slept," signify the quiet repose of one lying down in his place, which is not the state of one who falls asleep from exhaustive through sorrow. But this consideration makes the more forcibly for us|that he therefore glories in his rising up again because it was the Lord that sustained him, who raispd him up while sleeping, and did not leave him in sleep. How can such a glorying agree, and whut new kind of religion can make it agree, with any particular sleep of fho body ? viorin that case, would it not apply to the daily sleep also T) and especially, when this sustaining of God indicates at the same time an utterly forsaken state in the person sleeping, which is not the case in corporal sleep ; for there the person sleeping may be protected even by men being his guards ; but this sustaining being altogether of God, implies, uot a sleep, but a heavy conflict. And lastly, the word Hekizothi itself favours such an interpretation ; which, being here put absolutely and transitively, signifies, " I caused to arise or awake." As if he had said, "I caused myself to awake. I roused myself." Which certaiuly more aptly agrees with the resurrection of Christ than with the sleep of the body ; both because those who are asleep are accustomed to be roused and awaked, and because it is no wonderful matter, nor a matter worthy of so important a declaration, for any one to awake of himself, seeing that it is what takes place every day. But this matter being introduced by the Spirit as a something new and singular, is certaiuly different from all that which attends common sleeping and waking.

Verse 2.|" There it no help for him in hit Ood." In the Hebrew the expression is simply, " in God," without the pronoun " Aw," which seems to me to give clearness and force to the expression. As if he had said. They say of me that I am not only deserted and oppressed by all creatures, but that even God, who is present with all things, and preserves all things, and protects all things, forsakes me as the only thing out of the whole universe that he does not preserve. Which kind of temptation Job seems also to have tasted wlieie he says, " Why hast thou set me as a mark against thee ?" vii. 20. For there is no temptation, no, not of the whole world together, nor of all hell combined in one, equal unto that wherein God stands contrary to a man, which temptation Jeremiah prays against (xvii. 17), " Be not a terror unto me ; thou art my hope in the day of evil ;" and concerning which also the sixth Psalm following saith, " O Lord, rebuke me not in thine anger ;" and we find the same petitions throughout the psaltery. This temptation is wholly unsupportable, and is truly hell itself ; as it is said in the same sixth Psalm, " for in death there is no remembrance of thee," etc. In a word, if you have never experienced it, you can never form any idea of it whatever.

Verse 3.|" Far thou, 0 Lord, art my helper, my glory, and the lifter up of my he id." David here contrasts three things with three; helper, with many troubling ; glory, with many rising up ; and the lifter up of the head, with the blaspheming and insulting. Therefore, the person here represented is indeed alone in the estimation of man, and even according to his own feelings also ; but in the sight of God, and in a spiritual view, he is by no means alone ; but protected with the greatest abundance of help ; as Christ saith (John xvi. 32), " Behold, the hour cometh when ye shall leave me alone ; and yet I am not

alone, because the Father is with me." The words contained in

this verse are not the words of nature, but of grace ; not of free-will, but of the spirit of strong faith ; which, even though seeing God, as in the darkness of the storm of death and hell, a deserting God, acknowledges him a sustaining God ; when seeing him as a persecuting God, acknowledges him a helping God ; when seeing him as a condemner, acknowledges him a Saviour. Thus this faith does not judge of things according as they seom to be, or are felt, like a horse or mule which have no understanding ; but it understands things which are not seen, for " hope that is seen is not hope : for what a man seeth, why doth he yet Jiopefor?" Romans viii. 24.

Verse 4.|" I cried unto the Lord with my voice, and he heard me out of hit holy hill." In the Hebrew, the verb is in the future; and is, as Hieronymus translates it, " I will cry," and, " he shall hear ;" and this pleases me better than the perfect tense ; for they are the words of one triumphing in, and praising and glorifying God, and giving thanks unto him who sustained, preserved, and lifted him up, according as he had hoped in the preceding verse. For it is usual with those that triumph and rejoice, to speak of those things which they have done and suffered, and to sing a song of praise unto their helper anadeliverer; as in Psalm lxvi. 16, " Come, then, all ye that fear God, and I will declare what he hath done for my soul. I cried unto him with my mouth, and he was extolled with my tongue." And also Psalm Ixxxi. 1," Sing aloud unto God our strength." And so again, Exodus xv. 1, " Let us sing unto the Lord, for he hath triumphed gloriously." And so here, being filled with an overflowing sense of gratitude and joy, he sings of his being dead, of his having slept and rose up again, of his enemies being smitten, and of the teeth of the ungodly being broken. This it is which causes the change ; for he who hitherto had been addressing God in the second person, changes on a sudden his address to others concerning God, in the third person, saying, " *and he heard me,*"' not "and thon heardest me ;" and also, " *I cried unto the Lord,*" not " I cried unto thee," for he wants to make all know what benefits God has heaped upon him ; which is peculiar to a grateful mind.

Verse 5.|" *Ilaid me down and slept; I awaked; for the Lord suttained me."*

Christ, by the words of this verse, signifies his death and .burial For

it is not to be supposed that he would have spoken so importantly concerning mere natural rest and sleep ; especially since that which precedes, and that which follows, compel us to understand him as speaking of a deep conflict and a glorious victory over his enemies. By all which things he stirs us up and animates us to faith in God, and commends unto us the power and grace of God ; that he is able to raise us up from the dead ; an example of which he sets before

us, and proclaims it unto us as wrought in himself

And this is shown also farther in his using gentle words, and such as tend wonderfully to lessen the terror of death. " *I laid me down* (saith he), *and tltpt."* He does not say, I died and was buried ; for death and the tomb had lost both their name and their power. And now death is not death, but a sleep; and the tomb not a tomb, but a bed and resting place ; which was the reason why the words of this prophecy were put somewhat obscurely and doubtfully, that it might by that means render death most lovely in our eyes (or rather most contemptible), as being that state from which, aafrom the sweet rest of sleep, an undoubted arising and awaking are promised. For who is not most sure of an awaking and arising, who lies down to rest in a sweet sleep (where death does not prevent) ? This person, however, does not say that he died, but that he laid him down to sleep, and that therefore he awaked. And moreover, as sleep is useful and necessary for a better renewal of the powers of the body (as Atnbrosius says in his hym'n), and as sleep relieves the weary limbs, so is death also equally useful, and ordained for the arriving at a better life. And this is what David says in the following Psalm, " 1 will lay me down in peace, and take my rest, for thou, Lord, in u singular manner hast formed me in hope." Therefore, in considering death, we are not so much to consider death itself, as that most certain life and resurrection which are sure to those who are in Christ; that those words (John viii. 51) might be fulfilled, " If a man keep my saying, he shall never see death." But how is it that he shall never see it ? Shall he not feel it ? Shall he not die ? No ! he shall only see sleep, for, having the eyes of his faith fixed upon the resurrection, he so glides through death, that he does not even see death ; for death, as I have said, is to him no death at all. And hence, there is that also of John xi. 25, " He that believeth in me, though he were dead, yet shall he live."

Verse 7.l" For thou hast smitten all mine enemies upon the cheek lone; thou hast trolcen the teeth of the ungodly." Hieronymus uses this metaphor of " *cheek tone,"* and " *teeth,"* to represent cutting words, detractions, calumnies, and other injuries of the same kind, by which the innocent are oppressed : according to that of Proverbs xxx. 14, " There is a generation whose teeth are as swords, and their jw-teeth as knives, to devour the poor from off the earth, and the needy from among men." It was by these that Christ was devoured, when, before Pilate, he was condemned to the cross by the voices and accusations of his enemies. And hence it is that the apostle saith (Gal. v. 15), " But if ye bite and devour one another, take heed that ye be not consumed one of another."

Verse 8.l" Salvation is of the Lord, and thy Messing is upon thy -people." A most beautiful conclusion this, and, as it were, the sum of all the feelings spoken of. The sense is, it is the Lord alone that saves and blesses : and even though the whole mass of all evils should be gathered together in one against a man, still, it is the Lord who saves : salvation and blessing are in his hands. What then shall I fear ? What shall I not promise myself ? When I know that no one can be destroyed, no one reviled, without the permission of God, even though all should rise up to curse and to destroy ; and that no one of them can be blessed and saved without the permission of God, how much soever they may bless and strive to save themselves. And as Gregory Nazianzen says, " Where God gives, envy can avail nothing ; and where God does not give, labour can avail nothing.1' And in the same way also Paul saith (Rom. viii. 31), " If God be for us, who can be against us ?" And so, on the contrary, if God be against them, who can be for them? And why? Because " *salvation it of the Lord,'*l" and not of them, nor of us, for " vain isthe help of man."|*Martin Luther.*

HINTS TO THE VILLAGE PREACHER.

Verse 1. | *The saint telling his griefs to his God.* (1) His right to do so.

(2) The proper manner of telling them. (3) The fair results of such holy com-muuications with the Lord.

When may we expect increased troubles ? Why are they sent ? What is our wisdom in reference to them ?

Verse 2.|The lie against the saint and the libel upon his God.

Verse 3.|The threefold blessing which God affords to his suffering ones| Defence, Honour, Joy. Show how all these may be enjoyed by faith, even in our worst estate.

Verse 4.|(1) In dangers we should pray. (2) God will graciously hear.

(3) We should record his answers of grace. (4) We may strengthen ourselves lor the future by remembering the deliverances of the past.

Verge 5.|(1) Describe sweet sleeping. (2) Describe happy waking. (8) Show how both are to be enjoyed, " *for the Lord sustained me."*

Verse 6.|Faith surrounded by enemies and yet triumphant.

Verse 7.|(1) Describe the Lord's past dealing with his enemies ; " thou hast." (2) Show that the Lord should be our constant resort, " O Lord," " O my God." (8) Enlarge upon the fact that the Lord is to be stirred up : " Arise." (4) Urge believers to use the Lord's past victories as an argument with which to prevail with him.

Verge 7 *(last clause).*|Our enemies vanquished foes, toothless lions.

Verse 8 *(firtt clause).*|Salvation of God from first to last. (See the exposition.)

Verse 8 *(last clause).*|They were blessed *in* Christ, *through* Christ, and shall be blessed *with* Christ. The blessing rests upon their persons, comforts, trials, labours, families, etc. It flows from grace, is enjoyed by faith, and is insured by oath, etc.|*James Smith's Portions,* 1802|1802.

PSALM IV.

Tttlje.|*This Psalm is apparently intended to accompany the third, and make a* pairtoUA *ii. If the last may be entitled* The Mobnino I';-, u „m , *this from its matter is equally deserving of the title of* The Evening Hymn. *May the choice* words *of the Slh verse be our swett sang of rest as* ice *retire to our repose I*

" Thus with in v thoughts composed to peace,

I'll give miue eyes to sleep;

Thy liand In safety keeps my days,

And will my slumbers keep."

The Inspired title runs thus: " To the chief Musician on Neginoth, a Psalm of David." *The chief musician was the master or director of the sacred music of the sanctuary. Concerning this person carefully read* 1 Vhron. vi. 31, 32 ; xv. 16|22 ; xxv. 1, 7. *In these passages will be found much Hint is interesting to the lover of sacred song, and very much that will throw a light upon the mode of praising Qod in the temple. Some of the litlet of the Psalms are, we doubt not, derived from the names of certain renowned singers, who composed the music to which they were set.*

On Neginoth, *that is, on stringed instruments, or* hand *instruments, which were played on with the hand alone, as harps and cymbals. The joy of the Jewish church was so great that they needed music to set forth the delightful feelings of their souls. Our holy mirth is none th less overflowing because we prefer to express it in a more spiritual manner, as becometh a more spiritual dispensation. In allusion to these instruments to be played on with the hand, Kazianzen says, " Lord, I am an instrument for thee to touch." Let us lay ourselves open to the Spirit's touch, so shall toe make melody. May we be full of faith and love, and we shall be living instruments of music.*

Hawker says: " *The Septuagint read the word which we have rendered in our translation chief musician* Lamenetz, in.it" nl *of* Lamenetzoth, *the meaning of which is* nnto the end. *from whence the Greek and Latin fathers imagined, that all psalms which bear this inscription refer to the Messiah,* the great end. *If so, this Psalm is addressed to Christ; and well it may, for it is att of Christ, and spoken by Christ, and hath respect only to his people as being one with Christ. The Lord the Spirit give the reader to see this, and he will find it most blessed,*

Division.|*Inthe first verse David*pleads with *Qod for help. In the second*he expos-*tulates with his enemies, and continues to address them to the end of verse 5. Then from verse 6 to the close he delightfully contrasts his own satisfaction and safety with the disquietude of the ungodly in their best estate. The Psalm was most probably written upon the same occasion as the preceding, and is another choice flower from the garden of affliction. Happy is it for us that David was tried, or probably we should never have heard these sweet sonnets of faith.*

EXPOSITION.

HEAR me when I call, O God of my righteousness : thou hast enlarged me *when I was* in distress; have mercy upon me, and hear my prayer.

This is another instance of David's common habit of pleading past mercies as a ground for present favour. Here he reviews his Ebenezers and takes comfort from them. It is not to be imagined that he who has helped us in six troubles will leave us in the seventh. God docs nothing by halves, and he will never cease to help us until we cease to need. The manna shall fall every morning until we cross the Jordan.

Observe, that David speaks first to God and then to men. Surely we should ill speak the more boldly to men if we had more constant converse with God. He who dares to face his Maker will not tremble before the sons of men.

The name by which the Lord is here addressed, " *God, of my righteousneui,'*1" deserves notice, since it is not used in any other part of Scripture. It means,Thou art the author, the witness, the maintainer, the judge, and the rewardcr of my righteousness ; to thee I appeal from the calumnies and harsh judgments ot men. Herein is wisdom, let us imitate it and always take our suit, not to the putty courts of human opiuion, but into the superior court, the King's Bench of heaven.

' *Thou, halt enlarged me when 1 was in distress."* A figure taken from an army enclosed in a defile, and hardly pressed by the surrounding enemy. God hath dashed down the rocks and given me room ; he hath broken the barriers and set me in a large place. Or, we may understand it thus:l' God hath enlarged my heart with joy and comfort, when I was like a man imprisoned by grief and sorrow." God is a never-failing comforter.

"*Htioe mercy upon, me."* Though thou mayest justly permit my enemies to destroy me, on account of my many and great sins, yet I flee to thy mercy, and I beseech thee *hear my prayer,* and bring thy servant out of his troubles. The best of men need mrcy as truly as the worst of men. All the deliverances of, saints, as well as the pardons of sinners, are the free gifts of heavenly grace.

2 O ye sons of men, how long *will ye turn* my glory into shame ? *how long* will ye love vanity, *and* seek after leasing ? Selah.

In this second division of the Psalm, we are led from the closet of prayer into the field of conflict. Remark the undaunted courage of the man of God. He allows that his enemies are great men (for such is the import of the Hebrew words translatedl*ton. of men),* but still he believes them to be foolish men, aril therefore chides them, as though they were but children. He tells them that they *lone witty, and seek after leasing,* that is, lying, empty fancies, vain conceits, wicked fabrications. He asks them *haw tony* they mean to make his honour a jest, and his fame a mockery ? A little of such mirth is too much, why need they continue to indulge in it ? Had they not been long enough upon the watch for his halting ? Had not repeated disappointments convinced them that the Lord's anointed was not to be overcome by all their calumnies ? Did they in in to jest their souls into hell, and go on with their laughter until swift vengeance should turn their merriment into howling ? In the contemplation of thoir perverse continuance in their vain and lying pursuits, the Psalmist solemnly pine ani inserts a *Selah.* Surely we too may stop awhile, and meditate upon the deep-seated folly of the wicked, their continuance in evil, and their sure destruction ; and we may learn to admire that grace which has made us to differ, uni taught us to *loot* truth, and *seek* after righteousness.

3 But know that the LORD hath set apart him that is godly for himself; the Lord will hear when I call unto him.

" *B-it kn/u.*" Fools will not learn, and therefore they must again and again be told tha sams thing, especially when it is such a bitter truth which is to be taught them, viz. :lthe fact that the godly aro the chosen of God, and are, by distinguishing grace, set apart and separated from among men. Election is a doctrine which unrenewed men cannot endure, but nevertheless, it is a glorious ani well-attested truth, and one which should comfort the tempted believer. Election is ths guarantee of complete salvation, and an argument for success at the throne of grace. He who chose us for himself will surely hear our prayers. The Lord's elect shall not be condemned, nor shall their cry be unheard. David was king by divine decree, and we are the Lord's people in the same manner ; let us tell our enemies to their faces, that they fight against God and destiny, when they strive to overthrow our souls. O beloved, when you are on your knees, the fact of your being *set apart* as God's own peculiar treasure, should give you courage and inspire you with fervency and faith. " Shall not God avenge his own elect, which cry day and night unto him ?" Since he chose to love us he cannot but choose to hear us.

4 Stand in awe, and sin not : commune with your own heart upon your bed, and be still. Selah.

" *Tremble and tin not.*" How many reverse this counsel and sin but tremble not. O that men would take the advice of this verse and *commune with their oirn hearts.* Surely u want of thought must be one reason why men are so mad as to despite Christ und hate their own mercies. O that for once their passions would be quiet and let them *be still,* that so in solemn silence they might review the past, and meditate upon their inevitable doom. Surely a thinking man might have enough sense to discover the vanity of sin and the worthless- ness of the world. Stay, rash sinner, stay, ere thou take the last leap. Go to *thy bed* and think upon thy ways. Ask counsel of thy pillow, and let the quietude of night instruct thee ! Throw not away thy soul for nought! Let reason speak ! Let the clamorous world be still awhile, and let thy poor soul plead with thee to bethink thyself before thou seal its fate, and ruin it for ever ! *tidah.* O sinner 1 pause while I question thee awhile in the words of a sacred poet,l

" Sinner, is thy heart ut rest ?
Is thy bosom void of fear ?
Art thou not by guilt oppress'd ?
Speuka not conscience in thine ear T

Can this world afford thee bliss ?
Can it chase away thy gloom ?
Fluttering, false, nnd vain it is ;

Tremble at the worldling's doom I
Think, O sinner, on thy end,

See the judgment-day appear,
Thither must thy spirit wend,

There thy righteous sentence bear.
Wretched, ruin'd. helpless soul.
To a Saviour's blood apply j
Htf nlone can make thee whole,

Fly to Jesus, sinner, fly !"
5 Offer the sacrifices of righteousness, and put your trust in the Lord.

Provided that the rebels had obeyed the voice of the Inst verse, they would now be crying,l" What shall we do to be saved ?" And in the present veise, they are pointed to the *sacrifice,* and exhorted to *trust in the Lurd.* When the Jew offered sacrifice righteously, that is, in a spiritual manner, he thereby set forth the Redeemer, the great sin-atoning Lamb ; there is, therefore, the full gospel in this exhortation of the Psalmist. O sinners, flee ye to the sacrifice of Calvary, and there put your whole confidence and *trust,* for he who died for men i the Lord Jehovah.

6 *T/tere be* many that say, Who will shew us *any* good ? LORD, lift thou up the light of thy countenance upon us.

We have now entered upon the third division of the Psalm, in which the f.iith of the afflicted one finds utterance in sweet expressions of contentment and Jk-hcc.

There were many, even among David's own followers, who wanted to *gee* r:ither than to believe. Alas! this is the tendency of us all ! Even the regenerate sometimes groan after the sense and sight of prosperity, and are sad when darkness covers all good from view. As for worldlings, this is their unceasing cry. " *Who will shew us any goodf"* Never satisfied, their gaping mouths arc turned in every direction, their empty hearts are ready to drink in any fine delusion which impostors may invent; and when these fail, they soon yield to despair, and declare that there is no good thing in either heaven or earth. The true believer is a man of a very different mould. His face is not downward like the beasts', but upward like the angels'. He dtinks not fromthe muddy pools of Mammon, but from the fountain of life above. The light of God's countenance is enough for him. This is his riches, his honour, his limith, his ambition, his ease. Give him this, and he will ask no more. This is joy unspeakable, and full of glory. Oh, for more of the indwelling of the Holy Spirit, that our fellowship with the Father and with his Son Jesus Christ may be constant and abiding I

7 Thou hast put gladness in my heart, more than in the time *that* their corn and their wine increased.

"It is better," said one, "to feel God's favour one hour in our repenting souls, than to sit whole ages under the warmest sunshine that this world affordetb." Christ in the heart is better than corn in the barn, or wine in the vat. Corn and wine are but fruits of the world, but the light of God's countenance is the ripe fruit of heaven. " Thou art with me," is a far more blessed cry than " Harvest home." Let my granary be empty, I am yet full of blessings if Jesus Christ smiles upon me ; but if I have all the world, I am poor without Him.

We should not fail to remark that this verse is the *saying* of the righteous man, in opposition to the saying of the many. How quickly doth the tongue betray the character 1 " *Speak,* that I may see thee !" said Socrates to a fair boy. The metal of a bell is best known by its sound. Birds reveal their nature by their song. Owls cannot sing the carol of the lark, nor can the nightingale hoot like the owl. Let us, then, weigh and watch our words, lest our speech should prove us to be foreigners, and aliens from the commonwealth of Israel.

8 I will both lay me down in peace, and sleep : for thou, Lord, only makest me dwell in safety.

Sweet Evening Hymn I I shall not sit up to watch through fear, but I will *lie down;* and then I will not lie awake listening to every rustling sound, but I will lie down *in peace and sleep,* for I have nought to fear. He that hath the wings of God above him needs no other curtain. Better than bolts or bars is the protection of the Lord. Armed men kept the bed of Solomon, but we do not believe that he slept more soundly than his father, whose bed was the hard ground, and who was haunted by blood-thirsty foes. Note the word " *only,"* which means that God alone was his keeper, and that though alone, without man's help, he was even then in good keeping, for he was " alone with God." A quiet conscience is a good bedfellow. How many of our sleepless hours might be traced to our untrusting and disordered minds. They slumber sweetly whom faith rocks to sleep. No pillow so soft as a promise ; no coverlet so warm as an assured interest in Christ.

O Lord, give us this calm repose on thee, that like David we may lie down in peace, and sleep each night while we live ; and joyfully may we lie down in the appointed season, to sleep in death, to rest in God !

Dr. Hawker's reflection upon this Psalm is worthy to be prayed over and fed upon with sacred delight. We cannot help transcribing it.

" Reader ! let us never lose sight of the Lord Jesus while reading this psalm. He is the Lord our righteousness ; and therefore, in all our approaches to the mercy seat, let us go there in a language corresponding to this which calls Jesus the Lord our righteousness. While men of the world, from the world are seeking their chief good, let us desire his favour which infinitely transcends corn and wine, and all the good things which perish in the using. Yes, Lord, *tly favour w 'better than life itself.* Thou causest them that love thee to inherit substance, and fillest all their treasure.

" Oh 1 thou gracious God and Father, hast thou in such a wonderful manner set apart one in our nature for thyself ? Hast thou indeed chosen one out of the neople ? Hast thou beheld him in the purity of his nature,las one in every point Godly ? Hast thou given him as the covenant of the people ?And hast thou declared thyself well pleased in him ? Oh ! then, well may my sonl be well pleased in him also. Now do I know that my God and Father will hear me when I call upon him in Jesus' name, and when I look up to him for acceptance for Jesus' *sake* ! Yes, my heart is fixed, O Lord, my heart is fixed ; Jesus is my hope and righteousness ; the Lord will hoar me when I call. And henceforth will I both lay me down in peace and sleep securely in Jesus, accepted in the Beloved ; for *thu i the rest wherewith the Lord causeth the weary to rest, and this i the refreshing."*

EXPLANATORY NOTES AND QUAINT SAYINGS.

Verne 1.*|"Hear me when I call,"* etc. Faith is a good orator and a noble disputer in a strait; it can reason from God's readiness to hear : " *Hear me when I call, 0 God."* And from the everlasting righteousness given to the man in the justification of his person : " *0 God of my righteousness."* And from God's constant justice in defending the righteousness of his servant's cause : " *O God of my righteousness.*'1" And from both present distresses and those that are by-past, wherein he hath been, and from by-gone mercies received : " *Thou hast enlarged me when I was in distress.*'11 And from God's grace, which is able to answer all objections from the man's unworthiness or ill- deserving : " *Hate mercy vpon me, and hear my prayer.*'1'1|*David Dickson,* 1653.

Verse I.|"Hear me." The great Author of nature nnd of all things does nothing in vain. He instituted not this law, and, if I may so express it, art of praying, as a vain and insufficient thing, but endows it with wonderful efficacy for producing the greatest and happiest consequences. He would have it to be the key by which all the treasures of heaven should be opened. He has constructed it as a powerful machine, by which we may, with easy and pleasant labour, remove from us the most dire and unhappy machinations of our enemy, and may with equal ease draw to ourselves what is most propitious and advantageous. Heaven and earth, and all the elements, obey and minister to the hands which are often lifted up to heaven in earnest prayer. Yea, all works, and, which is yet more and greater, all the words of God obey it. "Well known in the sacred Scriptures are the examples of Moses and Joshua, and that which James (v. 17) particularly mentions of Elijah, whom he expressly calls S//otnira6 s, *a man subject to like infirmities* with ourselves, that he might illustrate the admirable force of prayer, by the common and human weakness of the person by whom it was offered. And that Christian legion under Antoninus is well known and justly celebrated, which, for the singular ardour and efficacy of its prayers, obtained the name of *Kepavvo@67io$, the thundering legion.|Robert Leighton, D.D., Archbishop of Glasgow,* 1611|1684.

Verse 2.|" O ye tons of men, how long will ye turn my glory into shame f June long will ye lore vanity, and seek after leasing f Selah." Prayer soars above the violence and impiety of men, and with a swift wing commits itself to heaven, with happy omen, if I may allude to what the learned tell us of the augury of the ancients, which I shall not minutely discuss. Fervent prayers stretch forth a strong, wide-extended wing, nnd while the birds of night hover beneath, they mount aloft, and point out, as it were, the proper seats to which we should aspire. For certainly there is nothing that cuts the air so swiftly, nothing that takes so sublime, so happy, and so auspicious a flight as prayer, which bears the soul on its pinions, and leaves far behind all the dangers, and even the delights of this low world of ours. Behold this holy man, who just before was crying to God in the midst of distress, and with urgent importunityentreating that he might be heard, now, as if he were already possessed of all he had asked, taking upon him boldly to rebuke his enemies, how highly soever they were exalted, and how potent soever they might be even in the royal palace *Robert teigkton, D.D.*

Verte 2.|" 0 ye ions of men, how long will ye turn my glory into shame ?" etc. We might imagine every syllable of this precious Paul in used by our Master some evening, when about to leave the temple for the day, uud retiring to his wonted rest at

Bethany (v. 8), after another fruitless expostulation with the men of Israel. And we may read it still as the very utterance of his heart, longing over man, and delighting in God. But, further, not only is this the uttei- ance of the Head, it is also the language of one of his members in full sympathy with him in holy feeling. This is a Psalm with which the righteous may maku their dwellings resound, morning and evening, as they cast u sad look over a world that rejects God's grace. They may sing it while they cling more and more every day to Jehovah, as their all-sufficient heritage, now and in the age to come. They may sing it, too, in the happy confidence of faith and hope, when the evening of the world's day is coming, and may then fall asleep in the cet- taiuty of what shall greet their eyes on the resurrection moiningl " Sleeping embosomed In his grace, Till muruiug-shodows flee."

Andrew A. Bonar, 1850.

Verte 2.l*"Late Vanity."* They that lovo sin, love *vanity;* they chase a, bubble, they lean upon a iced, their hope is as a spider's web.

" *Leasing."* This is an old Saxon word signifying falsehood.

Verse 2.l*" How long will ye lane vanity, and seek after leafing?"* "Vanity of vanities, and all is vanity." This our first parents found, and therefore named their second son Abel, or vanity. Solomon, that had tried these things, and could best tell the vanity of them, he preacheth this sermon over again and again, " Vanity of vanities, and all is vanity." It is sad to think how many thousands there be that can say with the preacher, " Vanity of vanities, all is vanity ;" nay, swear it, and yet follow after these things as if there were no other glory, nor felicity, but what is to be found in these things they call vanity. Such men will sell Christ, heaven, and their souls, for a trifle, that call these things vanity, but do not cordially believe them to be vanity, but set their hearts upon them as if they were their crown, the top of all their royalty and glory. Oh ! let your souls dwell upon the vanity of all things here below, till your hearts be so thoroughly convinced and persuaded of the vanity of them, as to trample upon them, and make them a footstool for Christ to get up, and ride in a holy triumph in your hearts.

Gilemex, king of Vandals, led in triumph by Belisarius, cried out, " Vanity of vanities, all is vanity." The fancy of Lucian, who placeth Charon on the top of a high hill, viewing all the affairs of men living, and looking on their greatest cities as little birds' nests, is very pleasant. Oh, the imperfection, the ingratitude, the levity, the inconstancy, the perfidiousness of those creatures we most servilely affect 1 Ah, did we but weigh man's pain with his payment, his crosses with his mercies, his miseries with his pleasures, we should then see that there is nothing got by the bargain, and conclude, " Vanity of vanities, all is vanity." Chrysostom said once, " That if he were the fittest in the world to preach a sermon to the whole world, gathered together in one congregation, and had some high mountain for his pulpit, from whence he might have a prospect of all the world in his view, and were furnished with a voice of brass, a voice as loud as the trumpets of the archangel, that all the world might hear him, he would choose to preach upon no other text than that in the Psalms, O mortal men, ' *How long will ye love vanity, and follow after leaning* ?' "|*Thomas Brooks,* IKIdl1080.

Verse 2.l*"Love vanity."* Men's affections are according to their principles; and every one loves that most *witliout him* which is most suitable to somewhat *within him: liking* ia founded in *likenens,* and has therefore that word put upon it. It is so in whatsoever we can imagine ; whether in temporals or spirituals,

as to the things of this life, or of a better. Men's love is according to some working and impression upon their own spirits. And so it is here in the point of vanity ; those which are vain persons, they delight in vaiH things ; as children, they love such matters as are most agreeable to their childish dispositions, and as do suit them in that particular. Out of the heart comes all kind of evil.| *Thomas Uorton,* 1675.

Verse 3.|" The Lord hath set apart him that is godly for himself." When God chooseth a man, he chooseth him for himself ; for himself to converse with, to communicate himself unto him as a friend, a companion, and his delight. Now, it is holiness that makes us fit to live with the holy God for ever, since without it we cannot see him (Heb. xii. 14), which is God's main aim, and more than our being his children ; as one must be supposed a man, one of mankind, having a soul reasonable, ere we can suppose him capable of adoption, or to be another man's heir. As therefore it was the main first design in God's eye, before the consideration of our happiness, let it be so in ours.| *Thomas Goodwin,* 1600| 1679.

*Verse 3.|*What rare persons the godly are : " The righteous is more excellent than his neighbour." Prov. xii. 26. As the flower of the sun, as the wine of Lebanon, as the sparkling upon Aaron's breastplate, such is the orient splendour of a person embellished with godliness. . . .' . The godly are precious, therefore they are set apart for God, " *Know that the Lord hath set apart him that is godly for himself."* We set apart things that are precious ; the godly are set apart as God's peculiar treasure (Psalm cxxxv. 4) ; as his garden of delight (Cant. iv. 12) ; as his royal diadem (Isaiah xliii. 3) ; the godly are the excellent of the earth (Psalm xvi. 3) ; comparable to fine gold (Lam. iv. 2) ; double refined. Zech. xiii. fl. They are the glory of the creation. Isaiah xlvi. 13. Origen compares the saints to sapphires and crystals : God calls them jewels. Mai. iii. 17. *Thoma-i Watson.*

Verse 3.|" The Lord will hear when, I call unto him." | Let us remember that the experience of one of the saints concerning the verity of God's promises, and of the certainty of the written privileges of the Lord's people, is a sufficient proof of the right which all his children have to the same mercies, and a ground of hope that they also shall partake of them in their times of need. *Daaid Dickson,* 1653.

Verse 4.|" Stand in awe and sin not." Jehovah is a name of great power and efficacy, a name that hath in it five vowels, without which no language can be expressed ; a name that hath in it also three syllables, to signify the Trinity of persons, the eternity of God, One in Three and Three in One ; a name of such dread and reverence amongst the Jews, that they tremble to name it, and therefore they use the name *Adonai (Lord)* in all their devotions. And thus ought every one to " *stand in awe, and sin not,"* by taking the name of God in vain ; but to sing praise, and honour, to remember, to declare, to exalt, to praise and bless it; for holy and reverend, only worthy and excellent is his name.|*JRaymentf* 1630.

Versed.|" Commune with your own heart." The language is similar to that which we use when we say, "Consult your better judgment," or "Take counsel of your own good sense."|*Albert Barnes, in loc.*

Verse 4.|If thou wouldst exercise thyself to godliness in solitude, accustom thyself to soliloquies, I mean to conference with thyself. He needs never be idle that hath so much business to do with his own soul. It was a famous answer which Antisthenes gave when he was asked what fruit he reaped by all his studies. By them, saith he, I have learned both to live and talk with myself. Soliloquies are the best disputes ; every good man is best company for himself of all the creatures. Holy David enjoineth this to others, " *Commune with your own hearts vpon your bed, and be ttill.*" " *Commune with your own hearts;*" when ye have none to speak with, talk to yourselves. Ask yourselves for what end ye weremade, what lives ye have led, what times ye have lost, what love ye have abused, what wrath ye have deserved. Call yourselves to a reckoning, how ye have improved your talents, how true or fafse ye have been to your trust, what provision ye have laid in for an hour of death, what preparation ye have made for a great day of account. " *Upon your beds.*" Secrecy is the best opportunity for this duty. The silent night is a good time for this speech. When we have no outward objects to disturb us, and to call our eyes, as the fools' eyes are always, to the ends of the earth ; then our eyes, as the eyes of the wise, may be in our heads ; and then our minds, like the windows in Solomon's temple, may be broad inwards. The most successful searches have been made in the night season ; the soul is then wholly shut up in the earthly house of the body, and hath no visits from strangers to disquiet its thoughts. Physicians have judged dreams a probable sign whereby they might find out the distempers of the body. Surely, then, the bed is no bad place to examine and search into the state of the soul. *"And be still.*" Self-communion will much help to curb your headstrong, ungodly passions. Serious consideration, like the casting up of earth amongst bees, will allay inordinate affections when they are full of fury, and make such a hideous noise. Though sensual appetites and unruly desires are, as the people of Ephesus, in an uproar, pleading for their former privilege, and expecting their wonted provision, as in the days of their predominancy, if conscience use its authority, commanding them in God's name, whose officer it is, to keep the king's peace, and argue it with them, as the town-clerk of Ephesus, " We are in danger to le called in question for this day's uproar, there being no cause whereby we may

five an account of this day's concourse ;" all is frequently by this means ushed, and the tumult appeased without any further mischief.|*George Swin- nock,* 1627|1678.

Verse 4.|" *Commune with your own heart upon your bed, and be still.*" When we are most retired from the world, then we are most fit to have, and usually have, most communion with God. If a man would but abridge himself of sleep, and wake with holy thoughts, when deep sleep falleth upon sorrowful labouring men, he might be entertained with visions from God, though not such visions as Eliphaz and others of the saints have had. yet visions he might have. Every time God communicates himself to the soul, there is a vision of love, or mercy, or power, somewhat of God in his nature, or in his will, is showed unto us. David shows us divine work when we go to rest. The bed is not all for sleep : " *Commune with your own heart vpon your bed, and be still.*" Be still or quiet, and then commune with your hearts ; and if *you* will commune with your hearts. God will come and commune with your hearts too, his Spirit will give you a loving visit and visions of his love.|*Joseph Caryl. Verse* 4.|" *Stand in awe.*"

With sacred *aim* pronounce his name,
Whom words nor thoughts can reach.

John Needham, 1768.

Verse 6.|Where Christ reveals himself there is satisfaction in the slenderest portion, and without Christ there is emptiness in the greatest fulness.|*Alexander Q-rosse, on enjoying Christ,* 1632.

Verse 6.|" *Many,"* said David, " *asJc who wU shew vt any goodf"* meaning riches, and honour, and pleasure, which are not good. But when he came to godliness itself, he leaves out " *many,"*1 and prayeth in his own person, " *Lord, lift ihou up the light of thy countenance upon us ;"* aa if none would join with him. *Henry Smith.*

Verse 6.|" *Who mill shew us any good"* This is not a fair translation. The word *any* is not in the text, nor anything equivalent to it ; and not a few have quoted *it,* and preached upon the text, placing the principal emphasis upon this illegitimate. The place is sufficiently emphatic. There are *multitudes who nay, Who wiU shete us good f* Man wants *good;* he hates *evil* as evil, because he has *pain, suffering,* and *death* through it; and he wishes to find that *supreme good* which -will content his heart, and save him from evil. But men mistake this good. They look for a good that is to gratify their *passions;* they have no notion of any happiness that does not come to them through the *medium of their tenses.* Therefore they reject *spiritual good,* and they reject the supreme God, by whom alone all the powers of the soul of man can be gratified.|*Adam Clarice.*

Verne 6.|" *Lift thou up,"* etc. ,This was the blessing of the high priest and is the heritage of all the saints. It includes reconciliation, assurance, communion, benediction, in a word, the fulness of God. Oh, to be filled therewith I *C. H. 8.*

Verges 6, 7.|Lest riches should be accounted evil in themselves, God sometimes gives them to the righteous ; and lest they should be considered as the *chief good,* he frequently bestows them on the wicked. But they are more generally the portion of his enemies than his friends Alas ! what is it to receive and not to be received ? to have none other dews of blessing than such as shall be followed by showers of brimstone ? We may compass ourselves'with sparks of security, and afterwards be secured in eternal misery. This world is a floating island, and so sure as we cast anchor *upon* it, we shall be carried away *Try* it. God, and all that he has made, is not more than God without anything that he has made. He can never want treasure who has such a golden mine. *He* is enough without the creature, but the *creature* is not anything without him. It is, therefore, better to enjoy him without anything else, than to enjoy everything else without him. It is better to be a wooden vessel filled with wine, than a golden one filled with water.| *William Seeker's Nonsuch Professor,* 1060.

Verse 7.|"What madness and folly is it that the favourites of heaven should envy the men of the world, who at best do but feed upon the scraps that come from God's table ! Temporals are the bones ; spirituals are the marrow. Is it below a man to envy the dogs, because of the bones ? And is it not much more below a Christian to envy others for temporals, when himself enjoys spirituals ? *Thomas Brooks.*

Verse 7.|" *Thou hast put gladress in my heart.'*1" The comforts which God reserves for his mourners are filling comforts (Rom. xv. 13) ; " The God of hope fill you with joy" (John xvi. 24) ; "Ask that your joy may be full." When God pours in the joys of heaven they fill the heart, and make it run over (2 Cor. ii. 4) ; "I am exceeding joyful;" the Greek is, I overflow with joy, as a cup that is filled with wine till it runs over. Outward comforts can no more fill the heart than a triangle can fill a circle. Spiritual joys are satisfying (Psalm lxiii. 5) ; " My heart shall be satisfied as with marrow and fatness ; and my mouth shall praise thee with joyful lips ;" " *Thou hast put gladness in my heart.*" Worldly joys do put gladness into the face, but the spirit of God puts gladness into the heart ; divine joys are heart joys (Zech. x. 7 ; John xvi. 22) ; " Your heart shall rejoice" (Luke i. 47) ; " My spirit rejoiced in God." And to show how filling these comforts are, which are of a heavenly extraction, the psalmist says they create greater joy than when *"corn and wine increase."* Wine and oil may delight but not satisfy ; they have their vacuity and indigence. We may say, as Zech. x. 2, " They comfort in vain ;" outward comforts do sooner cloy than cheer, and sooner weary than fill. Xerxes offered great rewards to him that could find out a new pleasure ; but the comforts of the Spirit are satisfactory, they recruit the heart (Psalm xciv. 19), " Thy comforts delight my soul." There is as much difference between heavenly comforts and earthly, as between a banquet that is eaten, and one that is painted on the wall.|*Thomas Watson.*

Verse 8.|It is said of the husbandman, that having cast his seed into the ground, he sleeps and riseth day and night, and the seed springs and grows he knoweth not how. Mark iv. 26, 27. So a good man having by faith and prayer cast his care upon God, he resteth night and day, and is very easy, leaving it to his God to perform all things for him according to his holy will.| *Matthew Henry.*

Verse 8.|When you have walked with God from morning until night, it remaineth that you *conclude* the day well, when you would give yourself to rest at night. Wherefore, first, look back and take a strict view of your whole carriage that *(lay past.* Reform what you find amiss ; and rejoice, or be grieved, as you find you have done well or ill, as you have advanced or declined in grace that day. Secondly, since you cannot sleep in safety if God, who is your *ker)er* (Psalm cxxi. 4, 5), do not *wake and watch for you* (Psalm cxxvii. 1) : and. though you have *Ood* to watch when you sleep, you cannot be safe, if he that wateheth be your *enemy.* Wherefore it is very convenient that at night you renew and confirm your pence with God by faith and prayer, commending and committing yourself to God's tuition by prayer (Psalm iii. 4, 5 ; Psalm xcii. 2), with thanksgiving before you go to bed. Then shall you *lie down in. safety.* Psalm iv. 8. All this being done, yet while you are *putting off* your apparel, when you are *lying down,* and when you are *in bed,* before you sleep, it is good that *you commune with* your *own heart.* Psalm iv. 4. If possibly you can fait asleep with *some htavenly meditation,* then will your sleep be *more sv-eet* (Prov. iii. 21. 24, 2-3) ; and *mare secure* (Prov. vi. 21, 22) ; your *dreams* fewer, or more *comfortable;* your head will be fuller of good thoughts (Prov. vi. 22), and your heart will be in a *better frame* when you *awake,* whether in the night or in the morning. | *Condensed from Henry Scudders Daily Walk,* 1688.

Verse 8.|" *I will both,* " etc. We have now to retire for a moment from the strife of tongues and the open hostility of foes, into the stillness and privacy of the chamber of sleep. Here, also, we find the " I will " of trust. " *I trill both lay me down in. peace, and sleep ; for thou, Lord, only makest me dwell in safety."* God is here revealed to us as exercising *personal care in the still chamber.* And there is something here which should be inexpressibly sweet to the believer, for this shows the minuteness of God's care, the individuality of his love ; how it condescends and stoops, and acts, not only in great, but also in little spheres ; not only where glory might be procured from great results, but where nought is to be had save the gratitude and love of a poor feeble creature, whose life has been protected and preserved, in a period of helplessness and sleep. How blessed would it be if we made a larger recognition of God in the still chamber ; if we thought of him as being there in all hours of illness, of weariness, and pain ; if we believed that his interest and care are as much concentrated upon the feeble believer there as upon his people when in the wider battle field of the strife of tongues. There is something inexpressibly touching in this " lying down" of the Psalmist. In thus lying down ho voluntarily gave up any guardianship of himself ; he resigned himself into the hands of another ; he did so completely, for in the absence of all care he slept; there was here a perfect trust. Many a believer lies down, but it is not to sleep. Perhaps he feels safe enough so far as his body is concerned, but cares and anxieties invade the privacy of bis chamber ; they come to try his faith and trust; they threaten, they frighten, and alas ! prove too strong for trust. Many a poor believer might say, " I will lay me down, but not to sleep." The author met with a touching instance of this, in the case of an aged minister whom he visited in severe illness. This worthy man's circumstances were narrow, and his family trials were great; he said, " The doctor wants me to sleep, but how can I sleep with care sitting on my pillow ?" It is the experience of some of the Lord's people, that although equal to an emergency or a continued pressure, a re-action sets in afterwards ; and when they come to be alone their spirits sink, and they do not realise that strength from God, or feel that confidence in him which they felt while the pressure was

exerting its force There is a trial in stillness ; and oftentimes the

still chamber makes a larger demand upon loving trust than the battle field. O that we could trust God more and more with personal things ! O that he were the God of our chamber, as well as of our temples and houses ! O that we could bring him more and more into the minutiae of daily life 1 If we did thus, we should experience a measure of rest to which we arc, perhaps, strangers now ; we should have less dread of the sick chamber ; we should havethat unharasscd mind which conduces most to repose, in body and soul ; we should be able to say, " I will lie down and sleep, *and leave to-morrow with God /"* Ridley's brother offered to remain with him during the night preceding his martyrdom, but the bishop declined, saying, that " he meant to go to bed, and sleep as quietly :is ever he did in his life."|*Philip Bennett Power's ' / Wills ' of the Psalms.*

Verge 8.|Due observation of Providence will both beget and secure inward tranquil-lity in your minds amidst the vicissitudes and revolutions of things in this unstable vain world. *"/ will both lay me down in peace, ai.d sleep; for the Lard only mateth me dwell in safety."* He resolves that sinful fears of events shall not rob him of his inward quiet, nor torture his thoughts with anxious presages ; he will commit nil his concerns into that faithful fatherly hand that had hitherto wrought all things for him ; and he means not to lose the comfort of one night's rest, nor bring the evil of to-morrow upon the day ; but knowing in whose hand he was, wisely enjoys the sweet felicity of a resigned will. Now this tranquillity of our minds is as much begotten and prcfervi-d by due consideration of providence as by anything whatsoever.|*John Flavel, 1627|1691.*

Verge 8.|Happy is the Christian, who having nightly with this verse, committed himself to his bed as to his grave, shall at last, with the snmc words, resign himself to his grave as to his bed, from which he expects in due time to arise, and sing a morning hymn, with the children of the resurrection.|*Qeorge Home, D.D., 1776.*

Verte 9.|*"Sleep."*

" How blessed wns that *tlerp*
The sinless Saviour knew!
In vain the storm-winds blew,
Till lie awoke to others' woes,
And hushed the billows to repose.

How beautiful Is *ifoep*|
The .,'/.' that Christians know!
Yc mourners ! cease your woe,
While soft upon his Saviour's breaot,
The righteous sinks to endless rest."

Mrs. M'Cartree.
HINTS TO THE VILLAGE PREACHER.
Verse 1.|Is full of matter for a sermon upon, *past mercies a plea for present help.* The first sentence shows that believers desire, expect, and believe in a God that heareth prayer. The title|*Ood of my righteousness,* may furnish a text (see exposition), and the last sentence may suggest a sermon upou "The best of saints must slill appeal to God's mercy and sovereign grace."

Verne 2.|*Depravity of mim* as evinced (1) by continuance in despising Christ, (2) loving vanity jn his heart, and (3) seeking lies in his daily life.

Verte 2.|The length of the sinner's sin. "How long?" May be bounded by repentance, shall be by death, and yet shall continue in eternity.

Verse 3.|*Elent.ion.*|Its aspects towards God, our enemies, and ourselves.

Verte 3.|" *The Lord will hear when I call unto him.* " Answers to prayer certain to special persons. Mark out those who can claim the favour.

Verse 3. | *The gracious Separatist.* Who is he? Who separated him? With what end ? How to make men know it ?

Verse 4.|The sinnpr directed to review himself, that he may be convinced of sin.|*Andrew Fuller, 1754|1815.*

Verted.|"fife *still.* " Advice|good, practical, but hard to follow. Times when season-able. Graces needed to enable one to be still. Results of quietness. Persons who most need the advice. Instances of its practice. Here is much material for a sermon.

Verte 6.|The nature of those sacrifices of righteousness which the Lord's people are expected to offer.| *William ford Vance, J827.*

Verse 6.|The cry of the world and the church contrasted. *Voxpoptdi* not always *Vox Dei.*

Verse 6.|The cravings of the soul all satisfied in God.

Verses 6, 7.|An assurance of the Saviour's love, the source of unrivalled joy.

Verse. 7.|The believer's joys. (1) Their source, " *Thou;'* 1" (2) their season |even now|" *Thou hast;"* (3) their position, "in *my heart;"* (4) their excellence, " *more than in the time that their corn and their wine increased.'"*

Another excellent theme suggests itself|" The superiority of the joys of grace to the joys of earth ;" or, " Two sorts of prosperity|which is to be the more desired ?"

Verse 8.|The peace and safety of the good man.|*Joseph Lathrop, D.D.,* 1805.

Verse 8.|A bedchamber for believers, a vesper song to sing in it, and a guard to keep the door.

Verse 8. |The Christian's good-night.

Verses 2 to 8.|The means which a believer should use to win the ungodly tc Christ. (1.) Expostulation, verse 2. (2.) Instruction, verse 3. (8.) Exhortation, verses 4, 5. (4.) Testimony to the blessedness of true religion, as in verses 8, 7. (5.) Exemplification of that testimony by the peace of faith, verse 8.

WORKS UPON THE FOURTH PSALM.

Choice and Practical Expositions on four select Psalms: namely, the Fourth Psalm, in eight Sermons, etc. By Thomas Horton, D.D. 1675.

Meditations, Critical and Practical, on Psalm IV., in Archbishop Leighton's Works.

PSALM V.

Titt.e.|"To the Chief Musician upon Nehiloth, a Psalm of David." *The Hebrew word Xetiilolh is taken from another word, signifying "to perforate" "to bore through," whence it comes to mean a pipe or a flute; so lliat this song was probably intended to be sung with an accompaniment of wind instruments, suck as the horn, the trumpet, flute, or tornet. Hotctver, it is proper to remark that we are not sure of the interpretation of these ancient titles, for the Septuagini translates it, " For him who shall obtain inheritance," and Alien Ezra thinks it denotes some old and well fcnoion melody to which this Psalm was to be played. The best scholars confess that great darkness hangs over the precise interpretation of the title; nor is this much to be regretted, for it furnishes an internal evidence of the great antiquity of the Book. Throughout the first, second, third, and fourth I'salms, you wiU haw noticedthat the subject is a contrast between the position. Vie character, and the prospects of the righteous and of the wicked. In this Psalm you will note the same. The Psalmist carries out a contra.it between himself made righteous by God's grace, and the wicked who opposed Urn. To the devout mind there is here presented a precious view of the Lord Jesus, of whom ii is said that in the days of his flesh, he offered up prayers and supplication with strong crying and tears.*

Division.|*The Psalm should be divided into two parts, from the first to the seventh verse, and thenfrom the eigltth to the twelfth. In the first part of the Psalm David most vehemently beseeches the lard to hearken to his prayer, and in the second part he retraces the same ground.*

EXPOSITION. *f* IVE ear to my words, O Lord, consider my meditation.

There are two sorts of prayers|those expressed in words, and the unuttered longings which abide as silent meditations. Words are not the essence but the garments of prayer. Moses at the Red Sea cried to God, though he said nothing. Yet the use of language may prevent distraction of mind, may assist the powers of the soul, and may excite devotion. David, we observe, uses both modes of prayer, and craves for the one a hearing, and for the other a *consideration.* What in expressive word ! " *Consider my meditation.*'1" If I have asked that which ! - right, give it to me ; if I have omitted to ask that which I most needed, fill up the vacancy in my prayer. "Consider my meditation." Let thy holy eoul *consider* it as presented through my all-glorious Mediator : then regard thou it in thy wisdom, weigh it in the scales, judge thou of my sincerity, and of the true state of my necessities, and answer me in due time for thy mercy's wke ! There may be prevailing intercession where there are no words ; and alas ! there may be words where there is no true supplication. Let us cultivate the *tpirit* of prayer which is even better than the *habit* of prayer. There may be seeming prayer where there is little devotion. We should begin to pray before we kneel down, and we should not cease when we rise up.

2 Hearken unto the voice of my cry, my King, and my God : for unto thee will I pray.

" *The voice of my* ory." In another Psalm we find the expression, "The voice of my weeping." Weeping has a voicela melting, plaintive tone, aii car-piercing shrillness, which reaches the very heart of God ; and *crying* hath a voicela soul-moving eloquence ; coming from *our* heart it reaches *Qed't* heart. Ah ! my brothers and sisters, sometimes we cannot put our prayers into words : they are nothing but a *cry:* but the Lord can comprehend the meaning, for he hoars a voice in our cry. To a loving father his children's cries are, music, and they have a magic influence which his heart cannot resist. " *MyKing, and my Qod."* Observe carefully these little pronouns, *"my* King, and *my* God." They are the pith and marrow of the plea. Here is a grand argument why God should answer prayerlbecause he is *our* King and *our* God. We are not aliens to him : he is the King of our country. Kings are expected to hear the appeals of their own people. We are not strangers to him ; we are his worshippers, and he is our God : ours by covenant, by promise, by oath, by blood.

"For unto thee will I pray.'1'1 Here David expresses his declaration that he will seek to God, and to God alone. God is to be the only object of worship : the only resource of our soul in times of need. Leave broken cisterns to the godless, and let the godly drink from the Divine fountain alone. " Uiito thee *will* /pray." He makes a resolution, that as long as he lived he would pray. He would never cease to supplicate, even though the answer should not come.

3 My voice shalt thou hear in the morning, O LORD ; in the morning will I direct *my prayer* unto thee, and will look up.

Observe, this is not so much a prayer as a resolution, " ' *My toice shalt thou hear ;* ' I will not be dumb, I will not be silent, I will not withhold my speech, I *will* cry to thee. for the fire that dwells within compels me to pray." We can sooner die than live without prayer. None of God's children are possessed with a dumb devil.

" *In the morning.*'1" This is the fittest time for intercourpe with God. An hour in the morning is worth two in the evening. While the dew is on the grass, let grace drop upon the soul. Let us give to God the mornings of our days and the morning of our lives. Prayer should be the key of the day and the lock of the night. Devotion should be both the morning star and tho evening star.

If we merely read our English version, and want an explanation of these two sentences, we find it in the figure of an archer, " *I will direct my prayer unto thee,"* I will put my prayer upon the bow, I will direct it towards heaven, and then when I have shot up my arrow, *I will look up* to see where it has gone. But the Hebrew has a still fuller meaning than this!" I will *direct* my prayer." It is the word that is used for the laying in order of the wood and the pieces of the victim upon the altar, and it is used also for the putting of the shewbread upon the table. It means just this : " I will arrange my prayer before thee ;" I will lay it out upon the altar in the morning, just as the priest lays out the morning sacrifice. I will *arrange* my prayer ; or, as old Master Trapp has it, " I will marshal up my prayers," I will put them in order, cull up all my powers, and bid them stand in their proper places, that I may pray with all my might, and pray acceptably.

" *And will look up,"* or, as the Hebrew might better be translated, " ' I will look out,' I will look out for the answer : after I have prayed, I will expect that the blessing shall come." It is a word that is used in another place where we read of those who watched for the morning. So will I watch for thine answer, O my Lord ! I will spread out my prayer like the victim on the altar, and I will look up, and expect to receive the answer by fire from heaven to consume the sacrifice.

Two questions are suggested by the last part of this verse. Do we not miss very much of tho sweetness and efficacy of prayer by a want of careful meditation before it, and of hopeful expectation after it ? We too often rush into the presence of God without forethought or humility. We are like men who present themselves before a king without a petition, and what wonder is it that we often miss the end of prayer ? We should be careful to keep the stream of meditation always running ; for this is the water to drive the mill of prayer. It is idle to pull up the flood-gates of a dry brook, and then hope to see the whetl revolve. Prayer without fervency is like hunting with a dead dog, and prayer without preparation is hawking' with a blind falcon. Prayer is the work of theHoly Spirit, but he works by means. God made man, but he used the dust of the earth as a material : the Holy Ghost is the author of prayer, but he employs the thoughts of a fervent soul as the gold with which to fashion the vessel. Let not our prayers and praises be the flashes of a hot and hasty brain, but the steady burning of a well-kindled fire.

But, furthermore, do we not forget to watch the result of our supplications ? We are like the ostrich, which lays her eggs and looks not for her young. We sow the seed, and are too idle to seek a harvest. How can we expect the Lord to open the windows of his grace, and pour us out a blessing, if we will not open the windows of expectation and look up for the promised favour ? Let holy preparation link hands with patient expectation, and we shall have far larger answers to our prayers.

4 For thou *art* not a God that hath pleasure in wickedness : neither shall evil dwell with thee.

5 The foolish shall not stand in thy sight : thou hatest all workers of iniquity.

6 Thou shalt destroy them that speak leasing : the Lord will abhor the bloody and deceitful man.

And now the Psalmist having thus expressed his resolution to pray, you hear him putting up his prayer. He is pleading against his cruel and wicked enemies. He uses

SECTION 2 **41**

a most mighty argument. He begs of God to put them away from him, because they were displeasing to God himself. " *For thou art not a Qod that hath pleasure in wickedness: neither shall evil dwell with thee."* "When I pray against my tempters," says David, " I pray against the very things which thou thyself abhorrest." *Thou* hatest evil: Lord, I beseech thee, deliver *me* from it!

Let us learn here the solemn truth of the hatred which a righteous God must bear towards sin. *lie ha no pleasure in wickedness,* however wittily, grandly, and proudly it may array itself. Its glitter has no charm for him. Men may bow before successful villainy, and forget the wickedness of the battle in the gaudinesa of the triumph, but the Lord of Holiness is not such-an-one as we are. *"Neither shall evil dteell with thee.""* He will not afford it the meanest shelter. Neither on earth nor in heaven shall evil share the mansion of God. Oh, how foolish are we if we attempt to entertain two guests so hostile to one another as Christ Jesus and the devil! Rest assured, Christ will not live in the parlour of our hearts if we entertain the devil in the cellar of our thoughts. " *The foolish shall not stand in thy sight.*'1'1 Sinners are fools written large. A little sin is a great folly, and the greatest of all folly is great sin. Such sinful fools as these must be banished from the court of heaven. Earthly kings were wont to have fools in their trains, but the only wise God will have no fools in his palace above. " *Thou hatest all workers of iniquity."* It is not a little dislike, but a thorough hatred which God bears to workers of iniquity. To be hated of God is-an awful thing. O let us be very faithful in warning the wicked around us, for it will be a terrible thing for them to fall into the hands of an angry God ! Observe, that evil speakers must be punished as well as evil workers, for " *thou shalt destroy them that speak leasing.*'1" All liars shall have their portion in the lake which burneth with fire and brimstone. A man may lie without danger of the law of man, hut he will not escape the law of God. Liars have short wings, their flight shall soon be over, and they shall fall into the fiery floods of destruction. " *The Lord will abhor the bloody and deceitful man,*'1'1 Bloody men hall be made drunk with their own blood, and they who began by deceiving others shall end with'being deceived themselves. Our old proverb saith, " Bloody and deceitful men dig their own graves." The voice of the people is in this instance the voice of God. How forcible is the word *abhor !* Does it not show M how powerful and deep-seated is the hatred of the Lord against the workers of iniquity ?

7 But as for me, I will come *into* thy house in the multitude of thy mercy : *and* in thy fear will I worship toward thy holy temple.

"With this verse the first part of the Psalm ends. The Psalmist has bent his knee in prayer ; he has described before God, as an argument for his deliverance, the character and the fate of the wicked : and now he contrasts this with the condition of the righteous. " *But as for me, I will come into thy house."* I will not stand at a distance, I will come into thy sanctuary, just as a child comes into his father's house. But I will not come there by my own merits ; no, I have a multitude of sins, and therefore I will come *in the multitude of thy mercy.* I will approach thee with confidence because of thy immeasurable grace. God's judgments are all numbered, but his mercies are innumerable ; he gives his wrath by weight, but without weight his mercy. " *And in thy fear will I worship toward thy holy temple,"*ltowards the temple of thy holiness. The temple was not built on earth at that time ; it was but a tabernacle ; but David was wont to turn his eyes spiritually to that temple of God's holiness where between the wings of the Cherubim Jehovah dwells in light ineffable. Daniel opened his window towards Jerusalem, but we open our hearts towards heaven.

8 Lead me, O Lord, in thy righteousness because of mine enemies ; make thy way straight before my face.

Now we come to the second part, in which the Psalmist repeats his arguments, and goes over the same ground again.

" *Lead me, 0 Lord,"* as a little child is led by its father, as a blind man is guided by his friend. It is safe and pleasant walking when God leads the way. " *In thy righteousness,""* not in *my* righteousness, for that is imperfect, but in *thine,* for thou art righteousness itself. " *Make thy way,"* not *my* way, " *straight tefare my face."* Brethren, when we have learned to give up our own way, and long to walk in God's way, it is a happy sign of grace ; and it is no small mercy to see the way of God with clear vision straight before our face. Errors about duty may lead us into a sea of sins, before we know where we are.

9 For *there is* no faithfulness in their mouth ; their inward part *is* very wickedness ; their throat *is* an open sepulchre ; they flatter with their tongue.

This description of depraved man has been copied by the Apostle Paul, and, together with some other quotations, he has placed it in the second chapter of Romans, as being an accurate description of the whole human race, not of David's enemies only, but of all men by nature. Note that remarkable figure, " *Their throat is an open sepulchre,"* a *tepukhre* full of loathsomeness, of miasma, of pestilence and death. But, worse than that, it is an *open* sepulchre, with all its evil gases issuing forth, to spread death and destruction all around. So, with the throat of the wicked, it would be a great mercy if it could always be closed. If we could seal in continual silence the mouth of the wicked it would be like a sepulchre shut up, and would not produce much mischief. But " their throat is an *open* sepulchre," consequently all the wickedness of their heart exhales, and comes forth. How dangerous is an open sepulchre ; men in their journeys might easily stumble therein, and find themselves among the dead. Ah ! take heed of the wicked man, for there is nothing that he will not say to ruin you ; he will long to destroy your character, and bury you in the hideous sepulchre of his own wicked throat. One sweet thought here, however. At the resurrection there will 1)6 a resurrection not only of bodies, but characters. This should be a great comfort to a man who has been abused and slandered. " Then shall the righteous, shine forth as the sun." The world may think you vile, and bury your character ; but if you have been upright, in the day when the graves shall give up their dead, this open sepulchre of the sinner's throat shall be compelled to give up your heavenly character, and you shall come forth and be honoured in the sight ofmen. " *They fatter with their tongue.*'1" Or, as we might read it, " They have an oily tongue, a smooth tongue." A smooth tongue is a great evil ; many have been bewitched by it. There be many human ant-eaters that with their long tongues covered with oily words entice and entrap the unwary and make their gain thereby. When the wolf licks the lamb, he is preparing to wet his teeth in its blood.

10 Destroy thou them, O God ; let them fall by their own counsels ; cast them out in the multitude of their transgressions ; for they have rebelled against thee.

x " *Against thee:* 11 not against *me.* If they were my enemies I would forgive them, but I cannot forgive *thine.* We are to forgive *our* enemies, but God's enemies it is not in our power to forgive. These expressions have often been noticed by men of over refinement as being harsh, and grating on the ear. " Oh !" say they, "they are vindictive and revengeful." Let us remember that they might be translated as prophecies, not as wishes ; but we do not care to avail ourselves of this method of escape. We have never heard of a reader of the Bible who, after perusing these passages, was made revengeful by reading them, and it is but fair to test the nature of a writing by its effects. When we hear a judge condemning a murderer, however severe his sentence, we do not feel that we should be justified in condemning others for any private injury done to us. The Psalmist here speaks as a judge, *ex officia;* he speaks as God's mouth, and in condemning the wicked he gives us no excuse whatever for uttering anything in the way of malediction upon those who hare caused us personal offence. The most shameful way of cursing another is by pretending to bless him. We were all somewhat amused by noticing the toothless malice of that wretched old priest of Rome when he foolishly cursed the Emperor of France with his blessing. He was blessing him in form and cursing him in reality. Now, in direct contrast we put this healthy commination of David, which is intended to be a blessing by warning the sinner of the impending curse. O impenitent man, be it known unto thee that all thy godly friends will give their solemn assent to the awful sentence of the Lord, which he shall pronounce upon thee in the day of doom ! Our verdict shall applaud the condemning curse which the Judge of all the earth shall thunder against the godless.

In the following verse we once more find the contrast which has marked the preceding Psalms.

11 But let all those that put their trust in thee rejoice : let them ever shout for joy, because thou defendest them : let them also that love thy name be joyful in thee.

Joy is the privilege of the believer. When sinners are destroyed our rejoicing shall be full. They laugh first and weep ever after ; we weep now, but shall rejoice eternally. When they howl we shall *shout,* and as they must groan for ever, so shall we *ever shout* for joy. This holy bliss of ours has a firm foundation, for, O Lord, we are *joyful in thee.* The eternal God is the well-spring of our bliss. We love God, and therefore we delight in him. Our heart is at ease in our God. We fare sumptuously every day because we feed on him. We have music in the house, music in the heart, and music in heaven, for the Lord Jehovah is our strength and our song ; he also is become our salvation.

12 For thou, LORD, wilt bless the righteous ; with favour wilt thou compass him as *with* a shield.

Jehovah has ordained his people the heirs of blessedness, and nothing shall rob them of their inheritance. With all the fulness of his power he will bless them, and all his attributes shall unite to satiate them with divine contentment. Nor is this merely for the present, but the blessing reaches into the long and unknown future. *"l%ou, Lord, wilt tkss the righteous."* This is a promise of infinite length, of unbounded breadth, and of unutterable prcciousness.

As for the defence which the believer needs in this land of battles, it is here promised to him in the fullest measure. There were vast shields used by the ancients as extensive as a man's whole person, which would surround him eatirely. So says David, " *With favour wilt thou comjiass him n with a shield.'"* According to Ainsworth there is here also the idea of being crowned, so that we wear u royal helmet, which is at once our glory and defence. O Lord, ever give to ua this gracious coronation 1

EXPLANATORY NOTES AND QUAINT SAYINGS.

*Verie 1.|" Give ear to my word, 0 Lord, consider my meditation.'*1" It is certain that the greater part of men, as they babble out vain, languid, and inefficacious prayers, most unworthy the ear of the blessed God, so they seem in some degree to set a just estimate upon them, neither hoping for any success from them, nor indeed seeming to be at all solicitous about it, but committing them to the wind as vain words, which in truth they are. But far be it from a wise and pious man, that he should so foolishly and coldly trifle in so serious an aff.iir ; his pniyer has u certain tendency and scope, at which he aims with assiduous and repeated desires, and doth not only pray that he may pray, but that he may obtain an answer ; and as he firmly believes that it may be obtained, so he firmly, and constantly, and eagerly urges his petition, that he may not flatter himself with an empty hope.|*Robert Leighton, D.D.*

Verses 1, 2.|Observe the order and force of the words, " *my* cry," " *the voice of my prayer;"* and also, " *give ear,'*1'1 "consider," "hearken." These expressions all evince the urgency and energy of David's feelings and petitions. First, we have, " *give ear ;"* that is, hear me. But it is of little service for the words to he heard, unless the " cry," or the roaring, or the meditation, be *considered.* As if he had said, in a common way of expression, I speak with deep anxiety and concern, but with a failing utterance ; and I cannot express myself, nor make myself understood as I wish. Do thou, therefore, understand from my feelings more than I am able to express in words. And, therefore, I add my " *cry ;"* that what I cannot express in words for thce to hear, I may by my " cry" signify to thine understanding. And when thou hast understood me, then, O Lord, *"Hearken unto the voice of my prayer,"* and despise not what thou hast thus heard and understood. We are not, however, to understand that hearing, understanding, and hearkening, are all different acts in God, in the same way as they are in us ; but that our feelings towards God are to be thus varied and increased ; that is, that we are first to desire to be heard, and then, that our prayers which are heard may be understood ; and then, that being understood, they may be hearkened unto, that is, not disregarded.|*Martin Luther.*

Verse 1.|" Meditation" fits the soul for supplication ; meditation fills the soul with good liquor, and then prayer broaches it, and sets it a-running. David first mused, and then spake with his tongue, " Lord, make me to know mine end." Psalm xxxix. 3, 4. Nay, to assure us that meditation was the mother which bred and brought forth prayer, he calls the child by its parent's name, " *O-ive ear to my words, 0 Lord, consider my meditation.'"* Meditation is like the charging of a piece, and prayer the discharging of it. " Isaac went into the field to meditate." Genesis xxiv. 63. The Septuagint, the Geneva translation, and Tremellius, in his marginal notes on it, read it to " pray ;" and the Hebrew word 1171 used there signifieth both to *pray* and *meditate;* whereby we may learn they are very near akin ; like twins, they be in the same womb, in the sameword. Meditation is the best beginning of prayer, and prayer is the best conclusion of meditation. When the Christian, like Dun id, hath first opened the windows of his soul by contemplation, then he may kneel down to prayer.| *George Swinnock.*

Verse 3.|" My voice shalt thou hear in the morning, 0 Lord."

When first thy eyes unveil, give tliy soul leave
To do the like; our bodies but forerun
The spirit's duty true hearts spread and heave

Unto their God, as flowers do to the sun;
Give him thy first thought, then, so shalt thou keep
Him company all day, and iu him sleep.

Tet never sleep the sun up; prayer should
Dawn with the day, there are set awful hours
'Twixt heaven and us ; the manna was not good

After sun-rising, for day sullies flowers.
Kisu to prevent the sun; sleep riolh sins glut,
And heaven's gate opens wheu the world's Is shut

Walk with thy fellow-creatures; note the hush
And whisperings amongbt them. Not a spring
Or leaf but hnth his *moniing* hymn ; each bush

And oak doth know I AM|canst thou not sing?
O leave thy cares and follies ! Go this way,
And thou art sure to prosper all the day.

Henry Vavghan, 1621|1695.

Verse 3.|" Ify voice shalt thou hear in the morning." " In the morning shall my *prayer present thee,"* said Heman. That is the fittest time for devotion, you being then fresh in your spirits, and freest from distractions. Which opportunity for holy duties may fitly be called *the wings of the morning.|Edward Jleyner,* 1658.

*Verse 3.|" In the morning.'*1" "In the days of our fathers," says Bishop Burnet, " when a person came early to the door of his neighbour, and desired to speak with the master of the house, it was as common a thing for the servants to tell him with freedom|' My master is at prayer,' as it now is to say, ' My master is not up.' "

Verse 8.|" In the morning 1 mil direct my prayer unto thee, and will look up," or, | *will marshal my prayer,* I will bring up petition after petition, pleading after pleading, even till I become like Jacob, a prince with God, till I have won the field and got the day. Thus the word is applied by a metaphor both to disputations with men and supplications to God. Further, we may take the meaning plainly without any strain of rhetoric, *Set thy words in oi'der before me.* Method is good in everything, either an express or covert method. Sometimes it is the best of art to cover it; in speaking there is a special use of method, for though, as one said very well (speaking of those who are more cuiious about method than serious about matter), " *Method neter converted any man;"* yet method and the ordering of words is very useful. Our speeches should not be heaps of words, but words bound up ; not a throng of words, but words set in array, or, as it were, in rank and file.| *Joseph Caryl.*

Verse 3.|" I will direct my prayer unto thee and will look up." In the words you may observe two things : first, David's posture in prayer ; secondly, liif practice after prayer. First, his posture in prayer, " *I will direct my prayer vntothee."* Secondly, his practice after prayer, " *And Iirill look up."* The prophet in these words, makes use of two military words. First, he would not only pray, but marshal up his prayers, he would put them in battle array ; so much the Hebrew word)UJ imports. Secondly, when he had done this, then he would be as a spy upon his watch-tower, to see whether he prevailed, whether he got the day or no ; and so much the Hebrew word HDV imports. When David had set his prayers, his petitions, in rank and file, in good array, then he was resolved he would look abroad, he would look about him to see at what door God wouldsend in an answer of prayer. He is either a fool or a madman, he is either very weak or very wicked, that prays and prays, but never looks after his prayers ; that shoots msny an arrow towards heaven, but never minds where his arrows alight.|*Thomas Brooks.*

Verse 3.|David wo'uld direct hit prayer to God and look up; not down to the world, down to corruption, but up to God what he would speak. Psalm Ixxxv. 8. " I will hear what God the Lord will speak," Let the resolution of the prophet be thine, " I will look unto the Lord ; I will wait for the God of my salvation : my God will hear me." Micah vii. 7.| *William GreenhUl,* 1650.

Verse 3.|" I will direct my prayer to thee, and will look up," that is, I will trade, I will send out my spiritual commodities, and expect a gainful return : I will make my prayers, and not give them for lost, but look up for an answer. God will bring man home by a way contrary to that by which he wandered from him. Man fell from God by distrust, by having God in suspicion ; God will bring him back by trust, by having good thoughts of him. Oh, how richly laden might the vessel which thou sendest out come home, wouldst thou but long aud look for its return !|*George Swinnock.*

*Verse 3.|*Faith hath a supporting act after prayer ; it supports the soul to expect a gracious answer : " *I will direct my prayer unto thee, and will look up,"* or I will look ; for what, but for a return ? An unbelieving heart shoots at random, and never minds where his arrow lights, or what comes of his praying ; but faith fills the soul with expectation. As a merchant, when he casts up his estate, he counts what he hath sent beyond sea, as well as what he hath in hand ; so doth faith reckon upon what he hath sent to heaven in prayer and not received, as well as those mercies which he hath received, and are in hand at present. Now this expectation which faith raiseth in the soul after prayer, appears in the power that it hath to quiet and compose the soul in the interim between the sending forth, as I may say, the ship of prayer, and its return home with its rich lading it goes for, and it is more or less, according as faith's strength is. Sometimes faith comes from prayer in triumph, and cries, *Victoria.* It gives such a being and existence to the mercy prayed for in the Christian's soul before any likelihood of it appears to sense and reason, that the Christian can silence all his troubled thoughts with the expectation of its coining. Yea, it will make the Christian disburse his praises for the mercy long before it is received For want of looking up many a prayer is lost. If you

do not believe, why do you pray ? And if you believe, why do you not expect ? By praying you seem to depend on God ; by not expecting, you again renounce your confidence. What is this, but to take his name in vain ? O Christian, stand to your prayer in a holy expectation of what you have begged upon the

credit of the promise Mordecai, no doubt, had put up many prayers for

Esther, and therefore he waits at the king's gate, looking what answer God would in his providence give thereunto. Do thou likewise.| *William Gvrnall.*

Verse 4.|" *Thou art not a God that hath pleasure in wickedness.*1' As a man that cutteth with a dull knife is the cause of cutting, but not of the ill-cutting and hacking of the knife|the knife is the cause of that; or if a man strike upon an instrument that is out of tune, he is the cause of the sound, but not of the jarring sound|that is the fault of the untuned strings ; or, as a man riding upon a lame horse, stirs him|the man is the cause of the motion, but the horse himself of the halting motion : thus God is the author of every action, but not of the evil of that action|that is from man. He that makes instruments and tools of iron or other metal, he maketh not the rust and canker which corrupteth them, thnt is from another cause ; nor doth that heavenly workman, GoJ Almighty, bring in sin and Iniquity ; nor can he be justly blamed if his creatures do soil and besmear themselves with the foulness of sin, for he mude them good.|*Spencer's Things New and Old.*

Verses 4|6. |Here the Lord's alienation from the wicked is set forth gradually, and seems to rise by six steps. First, *he hath no pleasure in them;*secondly, *they shall not dwell with him;* thirdly, he casteth them forth, *they shall not stand in hit sight;* fourthly, his heart turns from them, *thou hatest all the workers of iniquity;* fifthly, his hand is turned upon them, *thou ihalt destroy them that speak leasing;* sixthly, his spirit riseth against them, and is alienated from them, *the Lrrd will abhor the Uoody man.* This estrangement is indeed a *strange* (yet a certain) *punishment to* "*the workers of iniquity.*" These words, " *the workers of iniquity,'*1" may be considered two ways. First, as intending (not all degrees ot sinners, or sinners of every degree, but) the highest degree of sinners, great, and gross sinners, resolved and wilful sinners. Such as sin industriously, and, as it were, artificially, with skill and care to get themselves a name, as if they had an ambition to be accounted *workmen* that need not be ashamed in doing that whereof all ought to be ashamed ; these, in strictness of Scripture sense, are " *worl-crs of iniquity."*" Hence note, *notorious sinners make tin their butiness, or their trade.* Though every sin be *a work of iniquity,* yet only some sinners are " *workers of iniquity* /" and they who are called so, make it their calling to sin. We read of some *who love and make a lie.* Rev. xxii. 15. A lie may be told by those who neither love nor make it ; but there are lie-makers, and they, sure enough, are lovers of a lie. Such craftsmen in sinning are also described in Psalm lviii. 2|" Yea, in heart ye work wickedness ; ye weigh the violence of your hands in the earth." The psalmist doth not say, they had wickedness in their heart, but they did work it there ; *the heart is a shop within, an underground shop;* there they did closely contrive, forge, and hummer out their wicked purposes, and fit them into actions.|*Joseph Caryl.*

Verse 5.|What an astonishing thing is sin, which maketh the God of love and Father of mercies an enemy to his creatures, and which could only be purged by the blood of the Son of God ! Though all must believe this who believe the Bible, yet the exceeding sinfulness of sin is but weakly apprehended bv those who have the deepest sense of it, and will never be fully known in this w'orld.|*Thomas Adam's Private Thoughts,* 1701|1784.

Verse 5 (last clause).|*" Thou hatest all workers of iniquity. "* For what God thinks of sin, see Deut. vii. 22 ; Prov. vi. 16 ; Rev. ii. 6, 15 ; where he ex- presseth his detestation and hatred of it, from which hatred proceeds all those direful plagues and judgments thundered from the fiery mouth of his most holy law against it; nay, not only the work, but *workef* also of iniquity becomes the object of his hatred.| *William Ournall.*

Verse 5 (last clause).|*" Thou hatest all workers of iniquity.'*1" If God's hatred be against the workers of iniquity, how great is it against iniquity itself 1 If a man hate a poisonous creature, he hates poison much more. The strength of God's hatred is against sin, and so should we hate sin, and hate it with strength ; it is an abomination unto God, let it be so unto us. Prov. vi. 16|19, " These six things doth the Lord hate ; yea, seven are an abomination unto him ; a proud look, a lying tongue, and hands that shed innocent blood, an heart that deviseth wicked imaginations, feet that be swift in running to mischief, a false witness that speaketh lies, and he that soweth discord among brethren."|*William (freenhiil.*

Verm 5 (last clause).|*those* whom the Lord hates must perish. But he hates impen- itent sinners, " *Thou hatest all workers of iniquity.'*1' 1 -Now, who are so pro- jierly workers of iniquity as those who are so eager at it that they will not leave this work, though they be in danger to perish for it ? Christ puts it out of doubt. The workers of iniquity must perish. Luke xiii. 27. Those whom the Lord will tear in his wrath must perish with a witness ; but those whom he Imtes, he tears, &c. Job xvi. 8. What more due to such impenitent sinners than hatred ! What more proper than wrath, since they treasure up wrath ? Rom. ii. Will he entertain those in the bosom of love whom his soul hates ? No ; destruction is their portion. Prov. xxi. 15. If all the curses of the law, all the threatenings of the gospel, all judgments in earth or in hell, will be the ruin of him, he must perish. If the Lord's arm be strong enough to wound him dead, be must die. Psalm Ixviii. 21 Avoid all that Christ hates. If youlove, approve, entertain that which is hateful to Christ, how can he love you ? What is that which Christ hates ? The psalmist (Psalm xlv. 7) tells us,

making it one of Christ's attributes, to hate wickedness As Christ hates

iniquity, so the *"workers of iniquity.'*1" You must not love them, so as to be intimate with them, delight in the company of evil doers, openly profane, scoruers of godliness, obstructors of the power of it. 2 Cor. vi. 14|18. If you love so near relations to wicked men, Christ will have no relation to you. If you would have communion with Christ in sweet acts of love, you must have no fellowship with the unfruitful works of darkness, nor those that act them.|*David Clark&m, B.D.,* 1021|1686.

Verse 6.|*" Thou shalt destroy them that speak leasing, "* whether in jest or earnest. Those that lie in jest will (without repentance) go to hell in earnest. *John Trapp.*

Verse 6.|*" Thou shall destroy them that speak leasing,'*1" etc. In the same field wherein Absalom raised battle against his father, stood the oak that was his gibbet. The mule whereon he rode was his hangman, for the mule carried him to the tree, and the hair wherein he gloried served for a rope to hang. Little know the wicked how everything which now they have shall be a snare to trap them when God begins to punish them.| *William Gtncper,* 1612.

Verse 7.|"In thy fear will I iconhip.'" As natural fear makes the spirits retire from the outward parts of the body to the heart, so a holy fear of miscarrying in so solemn a duty would be a means to call thy thoughts from all exterior carnal objects, and fix them upon the duty in hand. As the sculpture is on the seal, so will the print on the wax be ; if the fear of God be deeply engraven on thy heart, there is no doubt but it will make a suitable impression on the duty thou performest.| *William Gurnall.*

*VerteT.|*David saith, " *In thy fear will I worship toward thy holy temple."* The temple did shadow forth the body of our Lord Christ, the Mediator, in. whom only our prayers and services are accepted with the Father which Solomon respected in looking towards the temple.|*Thomas Manton, D.D.,* 1620|1677.

Verse 7.|" Butasfor me," etc. A blessed verse this ! a blessed saying 1 The words and the sense itself, carry with them a powerful contrast. For there are two things with which this life is exercised, Hope and Fear, which are, as it were, those two springs of Judges i. 15, the one from above, the other from beneath. *Fear* comes from beholding the threats and fearful judgments of God ; as being a God in whose sight no one is clean, every one is a sinner, every one is damnable. But *hope* comes from beholding the promises, and the all-sweet mercies of God ; as it is written (Psalm xxv. 0), " Remember, O Lord, thy loving kindnesses, and thy tender mercies which have been ever of old." Between these two, as between the upper and nether millstone, we must always be ground and kept, that we never turn either to the right hand or to the left. For this turning is the state peculiar to hypocrites, who are exercised with the two contrary things, security and presumption.|*Martin Luther.*

*Verse 9.|*If the whole soul bo infected with such a desperate disease, what a great and difficult work is it to regenerate, to restore men again to spiritual life ftnd vigour, when every part of them is seized by such a mortal distemper ! How great a cure doth the Spirit of God effect in restoring a soul by sanctifying it! To heal but the lungs or the liver, if corrupted, is counted a great cure, though performed but upon one part of thee ; but all thy inward parts are very rottenness. *"For there is no faithfulness in their mouth; their inward part it very wickedness ; their throat is an open sepulchre; they flatter with their tongue."* How great a cure is it then to heal thee 1 Such as is only in the skill and power of God to do.| *Thomas Goodwin.*

Verse 9.|" Their throat is an open sepulchre.' 1" This figure graphically portraysthe filthy conversation of the wicked. Nothing can be more abominable to the senses than an open sepulchre, when a dead body beginning to putrefy steams forth its tainted exhalations. What proceeds out of their mouth is infected and putrid ; and as the exhalation from a sepulchre proves the corruption within, so it is with the corrupt conversation of sinners.|*Mobert Haldane'a " Expositions of the Epiu'le to the Jiornans,"* 1835.

Verse 9.|" Their throat is an open sepulchre.' 1" This doth admonish us, (1) that tbe speeches of natural unregenerate men are unsavory, rotten, and hurtful to others ; for, as a sepulchre dotli send out noisome savours and filthy smells, o evil men do utter rotten and filthy words. (2) As a sepulchre doth consume and devour bodies cast into it, so wicked men do with their cruel words destroy others ; they are like a gulf to destroy others. (3) As a sepulchre, having devoured many corpses, is still ready to consume more, being never satisfied, so wicked men, having overthrown many with their words, do proceed in their outrage, seeking whom they may devour. | *Thomas Wilson,* 1658.

Vers$9.|" Their inward part, " etc. Their hearts are storehouses for the deviL|*John Trapp.*

Verge 10.|All those portions where we find apparently prayers that breathe revenge, are never to be thought of as anything else than the *breathed assent of righteous souh* to the justice of their God, who taketh vengeance on sin. When taken as the words of Christ himself, they are no other than an echo of the Intercessor's acquiescence at last in the sentence on the barren fig-tree. It is as if he cried aloud, " Hew it down now, I will intercede no longer, the doom is righteous, *destroy them, O God ; cast them out in* (or, for) *the multitude of their transgressions, for they have rebelled against thee."* And in the same moment he may be supposed to invite his saints to sympathise in his decision ; just as in Rev. iviii. 20, " Rejoice over her. thou heaven, and ye holy apostles and prophets." In like manner, when one of Christ's members, in entire sympathy with his Head, views the barren fig-tree from the same point of observation, and sees the glory of God concerned in inflicting the blow, he too can cry, " Let the axe smite !" Had Abraham stood beside the angel who destroyed Sodom, and seen how Jehovah's name required the ruin of these impenitent rebels, he would have cried out, " Let the shower descend ; let the fire and brimstone come down !" not in any spirit of revenge ; not from want of tender love to souls, but from intense earnestness of concern for the glory of his God. We consider this explanation to be the real key that opens all the difficult passages in this book, where curses seem to be called for on the head of the ungodly. They are no more than a carrying out of Deut. xxvii. 15|26, "Let all the people say, Amen," and an entering into the Lord's holy abhorrence of sin, and delight in acts of justice expressed in the "Amen, hallelujah," of Rev. xix. 8.|*Andrew A. Bonar,* 1859.

Verse 10.|(*Or imprecatory passages generally.*) Lord, when in my daily service I read David's Psalms, give me to alter the accent of my soul according to their several subjects. In such Psalms wherein he confesseth his sins, or requfsteth thy pardon, or praiseth for former, or prayeth for future favours, in all these give me to raise my soul to as high a pitch as may be. But when I come to such Psalms wherein he curseth his enemies, O there let me bring my out down to a lower note. For those words were made only to fit David's mouth. I have the like breath, but not the same spirit to pronounce them. Nor let me flatter myself, that it is lawful for me, with David, to curse thine enemies, lest my deceitful heart entitle mine enemies to be thine, and so what was religion in David, prove malice in me, whilst I act revenge under the pretence of piety.|*Thomas Fuller, D.D.,* 1608|1661.

Verse 12.|When the strong man armed comes against us, when he darts his fiery darts, what can hurt us, if God compass us about with *his lomngkindness as icith a shield f* He can disarm the tempter and restrain his malice, and tread him under our feet. If God be not with us, if he do not give us sufficientgrace, so subtle, so powerful, so politic an enemy, will be too hard for us. How surely are we foiled, and get the worse, when we pretend to grapple with him in our own strength ! How many falls, and how many bruises by those falls have we got, by relying too much on our own skill ? How often have we had the help of God when we have humbly asked it 1 And how sure we we to get ttiu victory, *if Christ pray for u t/utt we do not fail!* Luke xxii. 31. Where can we go for shelter but unto God our Maker 1 When this lion of the forest does begin to roar, how will he terrify aud vex us, till he that permits him for awhile to trouble us, be pleased to chain him up again !|*Timothy Rogers,* 1691.

Verse 12.|" *A with a shield."* Luther, when making his -way into the prcsenqe of Cardinal Cajetan, who had summoned him to answer for his heretical opinions at Augsburg, was asked by one of the Cardinal's minions, where he should find a shelter, if his patron, the Elector of Saxony, should desert him f " Under the shield of heaven !" was the reply. The silenced minion turned round, and went his way.

Verse 12.|" *With favour will thou compass Mm as with a shield."* The shield is not for the defence of any particular part of the body, as almost all the other pieces are : helmet, fitted for the head ; plate, designed for the breast; and so others, they have their several parts, which they are fastened to ; but the shield ia a piece that is intended for the defence of the whole body. It was used therefoi e to be made very large ; for its broadness, called a gate or door, because so long and large, as in a manner to cover the whole body. And if the shield were not large enough at once to cover every part, yet being a movable piece of armour, the skilful soldier might turn it this way or that way, to catch the blow or arrow from lighting on any part they were directed to. And this iudeed doth excellently well set forth the universal use that faith is of to the Christian. It defends the whole man : every part of the Christian by it is preserved. . . . The shield doth not only defend the whole body, but it is a defence to the soldier's armour also ; it keeps the arrow from the helmet as well as head, from the breast and breastplate also. Thus faith, it is armour upon armour, a grace that preserves all the other graces.|*William Gumatt.*

HINTS TO THE VILLAGE PREACHER.

Versesl, 2.|Prayer in its threefold form. " *Words, meditation, a-y."* Showing how utterance is of no avail without heart, but that fervent longings and silent desires are accepted, even when unexpressed.

Verse 3.|The excellence of morning devotion.

Verse 3 *(last two dames).*|1. Prayer directed. 2. Answers expected.

Verse 4.|God's hatred of sin an example to his people.

Verse 5.|" *The foolish."* Show why sinners are justly called fools.

Verne 7.|" *Multitude of thy mercy.'*1" Dwell upon the varied grace and goodness of God. : Verse 7.|The devout resolution.

Verse 7.|I. Observe the *singularity* of the resolution. H. Mark the *object* of the resolution. It regards the service of God in the sanctuary. " I will come into thine *house. ...* in thy fear will I *worship* towards thy *holy temple.'*1'1 III. The *manner* in which he would accomplish the resolution. (1) Impressed with a sense of the divine goodness : " I will come into thy house in *the multitude of thy mercy."* (2) Filled with holy veneration : " And *in thy fear* will I worship.'1 *William Jay,* 1842.

Yerte 8.|God's guidance needed always, and especially -when enemies are watching us.

Verse 10.|Viewed as a threatening. The sentence, " Cast them out in the multitude of their transgressions," is specially fitted to be the groundwork of a very solemn discourse.

FSrMll.II. The character of the righteous : *faith and lore.* II. The privileges of the righteous. (1) *Joy*|great, pure, satisfying, triumphant, *(shout)* constant *(eter).* (2) *Defence*|by power, providence, angels, grace, etc.

Verge 11.|Joy in the Lord both a duty and a privilege.

Verse 12 *(first clause).*|*The divine blessing upon the righteous.* It is ancient, effectual, constant, extensive, irreversible, surpassing, eternal, infinite.

Verse 12 *(second clause).*|A sense of divine favour a defence to the soul.

PSALM VI.

Title.|*Tliis Psalm is commonly known as the first of* Tite Peniteotiaj, Psai.ms," *and certainly its language well becomes the lip of a penitent, for U expresses at once the sorroir., (verses* 3, 8, 7), *the humiliation (verms 2 ami 4), and the haired of sin (verse* 8), *which are the unfailing marks of the contrite spirit when it turns to God. 0 Holy Spirit, begft in , the true repentance which needelh not to be repented of. The title of this Psalm is, " To i h chief Musician on Negiuoth upon Sheminith.f A Psalm of David," that is, to the chief musician with stringed instruments, upon the eirjhth, proliably the octave. Home think' it refers to the bass or tenor key, which would certainly be wtll adapted to this mournful ode. Hut we are not able to understand these old musical terms, and ei-en theterm " &lah," still remains untranslated. Thit, however, should be no difficulty in our way. We prubuliiy lose but very little by our ignorance, and it may serve to confirm our faith. It is o proof nf the h'ujh antiquity of these Psalms that they contain words, the meaning of which is lost even to the best scholar of the, Hebrew language. Surely these are but incidental (accidental I migM almost say, if I did not believe them to be. designed by (*|*od proofs of their being, ic.'wrf they profess to be, the ancient writings of King David of olden times.*

Division.| *You, will observe that the Psalm is readily divided into two parts. First, there is the Psalmist's plea in his great distress, reaching from the first to the end of the seventh verse. Then you have, from the eighth to the end, quite a different theme. Tfie Psalmist Ims changed his note. lie leaves the minor key, and betakes himself to sublimer strains. He tunes his note to the high key of confidence, and declares that God hath heard his prayer, ami hath delivered him out of all his troubles.*

EXPOSITION.

OLORD, rebuke me not in thine anger, neither chasten me in thy hot displeasure.

2 Have mercy upon me, O LORD ; for I *am* weak : O LORD, heal me ; for my bones are vexed.

3 My soul is also sore vexed : but thou, O Lord, how long?

4 Return, O Lord, deliver my soul : oh save me for thy mercies' sake.

5 For in death *there is* no remembrance of thee : in the grave who shall give thec thanks ?

6 I am weary with my groaning ; all the night make I my bed to swim ; I water my couch with my tears.

7 Mine eye is consumed because of grief; it waxeth old because of all mine enemies.

Having read through the first division, in order to see it ss a whole, we will now look at it verse by verse. " *O Lord, rebut me not in thine anger.*'1" The Psalmist is very conscious that he deserves to be rebuked, and he feels, moreover, that the rebuke in some form or other must come upon him, if not for condemnation, yet for conviction and sanctifitation. " Corn is cleaned with wind,' and the soul with chastenings." It were folly to pray against the golden hand which enriches us by its blows. He does not ask that the rebuke may be totally withheld, for he might thus lose a blessing in disguise ; but, " Lord, rebuke me not *in thine anger.*" If thou remindest me of my sin, it is good ; but. oh, remind me not of it as one incensed against me, lest thy servant's heart should sink in

The other six are, xxxii., rxivUL, 11., oil., cxxz., cxlili. t 1 Chron. xv. 2L

despair. Thus saith Jeremiah, " O Lord, correct me, but with judgment; not in thine anger, lest thou bring me to nothing." I know that I must be chastened, and though I shrink from the rod yet do I feel that it will be for my benefit ; but, oh, my God, " *chasten me not in thy hot displeasure,*" lest the rod become a sword, and lest in smiting, thou shouldest also kill. So may we pray that the chastisements of our gracious God, if they may not be entirely removed, may at least be sweetened by the consciousness that they are " not in anger, but in his dear covenant love."

2, 3. " *Hum mercy upon me, O Lord; for I am weak.*'1" Though I deserve destruction, yet let thy mercy pity my frailty. This is the right way to plead with God if we would prevail. Urge not your goodness or your greatness, but plead your sin and your littleness. Cry, " *I am weak,*" therefore, O Lord, give me strength and crush me not. Send not forth the fury of thy tempest agiunsc so weak a vessel. Temper the wind to the shorn lamb. Be tender and pitiful to a poor withering flower, and break it not from its stem. Surely this is the plea that a sick man would urge to move the pity of his fellow if he were striving with him, "Deal gently with me, 'for I am weak.' " A sense of sin had so spoiled the Psalmist's pride, so taken away his vaunted strength, that he found himself weak to obey the law, weak through the sorrow that was in him, too weak, perhaps, to lay hold on the promise. " *lam weak.*" The original may be read, " I am oue who droops," or withered like a blighted plant. Ah ! beloved, we know what this means, for we, too, have seen our glory stained, and our beauty like a faded flower.

" *O Lord, heal me; for my lones are vexed..*" Here he prays for *healing,* not merely the mitigation of the ills he endured, but their entire removal, and the curing of the wounds which had arisen therefrom. His bones were *"shaken,"* as the Hebrew has it. His terror had become so great that his very bones shook ; not only did his flesh quiver, but the bones, the solid pillars of the house of manhood, were made to tremble. "My bones are shaken." Ah, when the soul has a sense of sin, it is enough to make the bones shake ; it is enough to make a man's hair stand up on end to see the flames of hell beneath him, an angry God above him, and danger and doubt surrounding him. Well might he say, "My bones are shaken." Lest, however, we should imagine that it was merely bodily sicknesslalthough bodily sickness might be the outward signlthe Psalmist goes on to say, " *My soul is also sore vexed.*" Soul-trouble is the very soul of trouble. It matters not that the bones shake if the soul be firm, but when the soul itself is ulso sore vexed this is agony indeed. " *But thou, 0 Lord, how long?*" This sentence ends abruptly, for words failed, and grief drowned the little comfort which dawned upon him. The Psalmist had still, however, some hope ; but that hope was only in his God. He therefore cries, " 0 Lord, how long ?" The coming of Christ into the soul in his priestly robes of grace is the grand hope of the penitent soul; and, indeed, in some form or other, Christ's appearance is, and ever has been, the hope of the saints.

Calvin's favourite exclamation was," Domine usquequo"|*"OLord, how long f"* Nor could his sharpest pains, during a life of anguish, force from him any other word. Surely this is the cry of the saints under the altar, " O Lord, how long ?" And this should be the cry of the saints waiting for the millennial glories, " Why are his chariots so long in coming ; Lord, how long ?" Those of us who have passed through conviction of sin knew what it was to count our minutes hours, and our hours years, while mercy delayed its coming. We watched for the dawn of grace, as they that watch for the morning. Earnestly did our anxious spirits ask, " O Lord, how long ?"

4. *"Return, 0 Lord ; deliver my soul."* As God's absence was the main cause of his misery, so his return would be enough to deliver him from his trouble. " *Oh tare me for thy mercies*1 sake." He knows where to look, and what arm to lay hold upon. He does not lay hold on God's left hand of justice, but on his right hand of mercy. He knew his iniquity too well to think of merit, or appeal to anything but the grace of God.

" *For thy mercies' sale."* What a plea that is! How prevalent it is with God ! If we turn to justice, what plea can we urge ? but *if* we turn to mercy we may still cry, notwithstanding the greatness of our guilt, " Save me for thy mercies' sake."

Observe how frequently David here pleads the name of Jehovah, which is always intended where the word Lord is given in capitals. Five times in four verses we here meet with it. Is not this a proof that the glorious nnmu is full of consolation to the tempted saint? Eternity, Infinity, Immutability, Self- existence, are all in the name Jehovah, and all are full of comfort.

5. And now David was in great fear of death|death temporal, and perhaps death eternal. Read the passage as you will, the following verse is full of power. " *For in death there is no remembrance of thee; in the graze who shall gite thee thanks?"* Churchyards are silent places; the vaults of the sepulchre echo not with songs. Damp earth covers dumb mouths. " O Lord !" saith he, " if thou wilt spare me I will praise thee. If I die, then must my mortal praise at least be suspended ; and if I perish in hell, then thou wilt never have any thanksgiving from me. Songs of gratitude cannot rise from the flaming pit of hell. True, thou wilt doubtless be glorified, even in my eternal condemnation, but then, O Lord, I cannot glorify thee voluntarily ; and among the sons of men, there will be one heart the less to bless thee." Ah ! poor trembling sinners, may the Lord help you to use this forcible argument! It is for God's glory that a sinner should be saved. "When we seek pardon, we are not asking God to do that which will stain his banner, or put a blot on his escutcheon. He dclighteth in mercy. It is his peculiar, darling attribute. Mercy honours God. Do not we ourselves say, " Mercy blesseth him that gives, and him that takes?" And surely, in some diviner sense, this is true of God, who, when he gives mercy, glorifies himself.

6, 7. The Psalmist gives a fearful description of his long agony : " *lam weary with my groaning."* He had groaned till his throat was hoarse ; he had cried for mercy till prayer became a labour. God's people may groan, but they may not grumble. Yea, they must groan, being burdened, or they will never shout in the day of deliverance. The next sentence, we think, is not accurately translated. It should be, " *I shall make my led to sicim ecery night"* (when nature needs rest, and when I am most alone with my God). That is to say, my grief is fearful even now, but if God do not soon save me, it will not stay of itself, but will increase, until my tears will be so many, that my bed itself shall swim. A description rather of what he feared would be, than of what had actually taken place. May not our forebodings of future woe become arguments which faith may urge when seeking present mercy ? " *I water my couch with my tears. Mine eye is consumed because of grief; it waxeth old because of all mine enemies."* As an old man's eye grows dim with years, so, says David, my eye is grown red and feeble through weeping. Conviction sometimes has such an effect upon the body, that even the outward organs are made to suffer. May not this explain some of the convulsions and hysterical attacks which have been experienced under convictions in the revivals in Ireland. Is it surprising that some should be smitten to the earth, and begin to cry aloud ; when we find that David himself made his bed to swim, and grew old while he was under the heavy hand of God ? Ah ! brethren, it is no light matter to feel one's self a sinner, condemned at the bar of God. The language of this Psalm is not strained and forced, but perfectly natural to one in so sad a plight,

8 Depart from me, all ye workers of iniquity ; for the Lord hath heard the voice of my weeping.

9 The Lord hath heard my supplication ; the Lord will receive my prayer.

10 Let all mine enemies be ashamed and sore vexed : let them return *and* be ashamed suddenly.

8. Hitherto, all has been mournful and disconsolate, but nowl

" Tour harps, ye trembling saints,
Down from the willows take."

Ye must have your times of weeping, but let them be short. Get ye up, get ye up, from your dunghills ! Cast aside your sackcloth and ashes ! Weeping may endure for a night, but joy cometh in the morning

David has found peace, and rising from his knees he begins to sweep his house of the wicked. " *Depart from me, all ye workers of iniquity."* The best remedy for us against an evil man is a long space between us both. ' Get ye gone ; I can have no fellowship with you." Repentance is a practical thing. It is not enough to bemoan the desecration of the temple of the heart, we must scourge out the buyers and sellers, and overturn the tables of the money changers. A pardoned sinner *mil Jwte the sins* which cost the Saviour his blood. Grace and tin are quarrelsome neighbours, and one or the other must go to the wall.

" *For the Lord hath heard the voice of my weeping.'*1" What a fine Hebraism, and what grand poetry it is in English ! " He hath heard the voice of my weeping." Is there a voice in weeping? Does weeping speuk ? In what language doth it utter its meaning ? Why, in that universal tongue which is known and understood in all the earth, and even in heaven above. When a nian weeps, whether he be a Jew or Gentile, Barbarian, Scythian, bond or free, it has the same meaning in it. Weeping is the eloquence of sorrow. It is an unstammering orator, needing no interpreter, but understood of all. Is it not sweet to believe that our tears are understood even when words fail ? Let us learn to think of tears as liquid prayers, and of weeping as a constant dropping of importunate intercession which will wear its way right surely into the very heart of mercy, despite the stony difficulties which obstruct the way. My God, I will " weep" when I cannot plead, for thou nearest the voice of my weeping.

9. " *The Lord hath heard my supplication.*" The Holy Spirit had wrought into the Psalmist's mind the confidence that his prayer was heard. This is frequently the privilege of the saints. Praying the prayer of faith, they are often infallibly assured that they have prevailed with God. We read of Luther that, having on one occasion wrestled hard with God in prayer, he came leaping out of his closet crying, " *Vicimus, vicimvs ;*" that is, "We have conquered, we have prevailed with God." Assured confidence is no idle dream, for when the Holy Ghost bestows it upon us, wo know its reality, and could not doubt it, even though all men should deride our boldness. " *The Lord will receive my prayer.*'- Here is past experience used for future encouragement. *lie hath, he will.* Note this, O believer, and imitate its reasoning.

10. *"Let all mine enemies be ashamed and sore vexed."* This is rather a prophecy than an imprecation, it may be read in the future, "All my enemies shall be ashamed and sore vexed." *They nhall return and be ashamed instan- tanafUsly,*|in a moment ;|their doom shall come upon them suddenly. Death's day is doom's day, and both are sure and may be sudden. The Romans were wont to say, "The feet of the avenging Deity are shod with wool." With noiseless footsteps vengeance nears its victim, and sudden and overwhelming shall be its destroying stroke. If this were an imprecation, we must remember that the language of the old dispensation is not that of the new. We pray/or our enemies, not *against* them. God have mercy on them, and bring them into the right way.

Thus the Psalm, like those which precede it, shews the different estates of the godly and the wicked. O Lord, let us be numbered *with* thy people, both Ijgw and for ever I

3

SECTION 3

EXPLANATORY NOTES AND QUAINT SAYINGS.

Whole Psalm.|David was a man that was often exercised with sickness and troubles from enemies, and in all the instances almost that we meet with in the Psalms of these his afflictions, we may observe the outward occasions of trouble brought him under the suspicion of God's wrath and his own iniquity ; so that he was seldom sick, or persecuted, but this called on the disquiet of conscience, and brought his sin to remembrance ; as in this Psalm, which was made on the occasion of his sickness, as appears from verse eight, wherein he expresseth the vexation of his soul under the apprehension of God's anger ; all his other griefs running into this channel, as little brook?, losing themselves in a great river, change their name and nature. He that was at first only concerned for his sickness, is now wholly concerned with sorrow and smart under the fear and hazard of his soul's condition ; the like we may see in Psalm xxxviii. and many places more |*Richard Oilpin,* 1677.

Verse 1.|" Rebuke me not.'" God hath two means by which he reduceth his children to obedience ; his word, by which he rebukes them ; and his rod, by which he chastiseth them. The word precedes, admonishing them by his servants whom he hath sent in all ages to call sinners to repentance : of the which David himself saith, " Let the righteous rebuke me ;" and as a father cloth first rebuke his disordered child, so doth the Lord speak to them. But when men neglect the warnings of his word, then God, as a good father, takes up the rod and beats them. Our Saviour wakened the three disciples in the garden three times, but seeing that served not, he told them that Judas and his band were coming to awaken them whom his own voice could not waken.|*A. Symson*, 1(588.

Verge 1.|" *Jehovah,, rebuke me not in thine anger,'*1" etc. He does not altogether refuse punishment, for that would be unreasonable ; and to be without it, he judged would be more hurtful than beneficial to him ; but what he is afraid of is the wrath of God, which threatens sinners with ruin and perdition. To anger and indignation David tacitly opposes fatherly and gentle chastisement, and this last he was willing to bear.|-*John Calvin*, 1509|1564.

Vere 1.|" *O Lord, rebuke me not in thine anger."*
The anger of the Lord ? Oh. dreadful thought I
How can a creature frail as man endure
The tempest of his wrath ? Ah, whither flee
To 'scape the punishment he well deserves?
Flee to the cross I the great atonement there
Will shield the sinner, if he supplicate
For pardon with repentance true and deep,
And faith that questions not. Then will the frown
Of anger pass from off the face of God,
Like a black tempest cloud that hides the eun. *Anon.*

Verse 1.|" *Lord, rebuke me not in thine anger,'*1'1 etc. ; that is, do not lay upon me that thou hast threatened in thy law ; where anger is not put for the decree, nor the execution, but for the denouncing. So (Matt. iii. 11, and so Hos. xi. 9), " I will not execute the fierceness of mine anger," that is, I will not execute my wrath as I have declared it. Again, it is said, he executes punishment on the wicked ; he declares it not only, but executeth it, so anger is put for the exetru- ition of anger.|*Richard Stock*, 1641.

Verse 1.|" *Neither chasten me in thine hot displeasure."*
O keep up life and peace within,
If I must feel thy chastening rod 1
Yet kill not me, but kill my sin,
And let me know thou art my (.-].
O give my soul some sweet foretaste
Of that which I shall shortly see 1
Let faith and love cry to the last,
"Come, Lord, I trust myself with thcc!"

Richard Baxter, 1615|1681.

Verse 2.|"*Hate mercy upon me, O Lord.'*1" To fly and escape the anger of God, David sees no means in heaven or in earth, and therefore retires himself to God, even to him who wounded him that he might heal him. He flies not with Adam to the bush, nor with Saul to the witch, nor with Jonah to Tarshish ; but he appeals from an angry and just God to a merciful God, and from himself to himself. The woman who was condemned by King Philip, appealed from Philip being drunken to Philip being sober. But David appeals from one virtue, justice, to another, mercy. There may be appellation from the tribunal of man to the justice-seat of God ; but when thou art indicted before God's justice- seat, whither or to whom wilt thou go but to himself and his mercy-seat, which is the highest and last place of appellation ? "I have none in heaven but thee,

nor in earth besides thee." David, under the name of *mere;/,* includeth

all things, according to that of Jacob to his brother Esau, " I have gotten mercy, and therefore I have gotten all things." Desirest thou any thing at God's hands ? Cry for *mercy,* out of which fountain all good things will spring to thee.l*Archibald Symson.*

VerteZ.l" Far I am weal." Behold what rhetoric he useth to move God to cure him, " *I am weak,"'*1 an argument taken from his weakness, which indeed were a weak argument to move any man to show his favour, but is a strong argument to prevail with God. If a diseased person would come to a physician, and only lament the heaviness of his sickness, he would say, God help thee ; or an oppressed person come to a lawyer, and show him the estate of his action and ask his advice, that is a golden question ; or to a merchant to crave raiment, he will either have present money or a surety ; or a courtier favour, you must have your reward ready in your hand. But coming before God, the most forcible argument that ye can use is your necessity, poverty, tears, misery, unwortbiness, and confessing them to him, it shall be an open door to furnish

.you with all things that he hath The tears of our misery arc

forcible arrows to pierce the heart of our heavenly Father, to deliver us and pity our hard case. The beggars lay open their sores to the view of the world, that the more they may move men to pity them. So let us deplore our miseries to God, that he, with the pitiful Samaritan, at the sight of our wounds, may help us in due time.l*Archibald Symson.*

Verse 2.l" Heal me," etc. David comes not to take physic upon wantonness, but because the disease is violent, because the accidents are vehement ; Bo vehement, so violent, as that it hath pierced *ad ossa,* and *ad animam,* " *My bones are vexed, and my soul is tore trembled,"* therefore *"heal me;"* which is the reason upon which he grounds this second petition, *"Heal me, because my bones are vexed,"* etc.l*John Donne.*

Vent 2.l"My bones are vexed." The Lord can make the strongest and most insensible part of man's body sensible of his wrath when he,pleaseth to touch him, for here David's bones are vexed.l*David Dicknon.*

*Verse 2.l*The term *"bones"* frequently occurs in the Psalms, and if we examine we shall find it used in three different senses. (1.) It is sometimes applied literally to our blessed Lord's human body, to the body which hung upon the cross, as, "They pierced my hands and my feet; I may tell all my bones." (2.) It has sometimes also a further reference to his mystical body the church. And then it denotes all the members of Christ's body that stand firm in the faith, that cannot be moved by persecutions, or temptations, however severe, as, " All my bones shall say, Lord, who is like unto thee ?" (8.) In some passages the term bones is applied to the soul, and not to the body, to the inner man of the individual Christian. Then it implies the strength and fortitude of the soul, the determined courage which faith in God gives to the righteous. This is the sense in which it is used in the second verse of Psalm vi., " *O Lord, heal me; for my bones are vexed.*"\Augustine, Ambrose, and Chrytostom ; quoted by F. H. Dvnwett, B.A., ta "Parochial Lecture on the Ptalmt," 1855.

Verse 3.l" My soul." Yokefellows in sin are yokefellows in pain; the soul is punished for informing, the body for performing, and as both the informer and performer, the cause and the instrument, so shall the stirrer up of sin and the executor of it be punished.-\John Donne.

Verse 3.l" 0 Lord, hate Jong?" Out of this we have three things to observe ; first, that there is an appointed time which God hath measured for the crosses of all his children, before which time they shall not be delivered, and for which they must patiently attend, not thinking to prescribe time to God for their delivery, or limit the Holy One of Israel. The Israelites remained in Egypt till the complete number of four hundred and thirty years were accomplished. Joseph was three years and more in the prison till the appointed time of his delivery came. The Jews remained seventy years in Babylon. 80 that as the physician appointcth certain times to the patient, both wherein he must fast, and be dieted, and wherein he must take recreation, so God knoweth the convenient times both of our humiliation and exaltation. Next, see the impatiency of our nature in our miseries, our flesh still rebelling against the Spirit, which oftentimes forgetteth itself so far, that it will enter into reasoning: with God, and quarrelling with him, as we may read of Job, Jonas, etc., ana here also of David. Thirdly, albeit the Lord delay his coming to relieve his saints, yet hath he great cause if we could ponder it; for when we were in the heat of our sins, many times he cried by the mouth of his prophets and servants, " O fools, how long will you continue in your folly ?" And we would not hear ; and therefore when we are in the heat of our pains, thinking long, yea, every day a year till we be delivered, no wonder it is if God will not hear ; let us consider with ourselves the just dealing of God with us ; that as he cried and we would not hear, so now we cry, and he will not hear.l.4. *Symson.*

Verse 3.l" 0 Lord, how longV As the saints in heaven have their *usque gto,* how long, Lord, holy and true, before thou begin to execute judgment J So, the saints on earth have their *usque quo.* How long, Lord, before thou take off the execution of this judgment upon us ? For, our deprecatory prayers are not mandatory, they are not directory, they appoint not God his ways, nor his times ; but as our postulatory prayers are, they also are submitted to the will of God, and have all in them that ingredient, that herb of grace, which Christ put iato his own prayer, that *veruntamen, yet nit my will, but thy will be fulfilled;* and they have that ingredient which Christ put into our prayer, *fiat, toluntan, thy will be done in earth as it is in heaven ;* in heaven there is no resisting of his will ; yet in heaven there is a soliciting, a hastening, an accelerating of the judgment, and the glory of the resurrection ; so though we resist not his corrections here upon earth, we may humbly present to God the sense which we have of his displeasure, for this sense and apprehension of his corrections is one of the principal reasons why he sends them ; he corrects us therefore that we might be sensible of his corrections ; that when we, being humbled unier his hand, have said with his prophet, li / *will bear the wrath of the Lord because I have sinned against Aim"* (Mic. vii. 9), he mav be pleased to say to his correcting angel, as he did to his destroying angel, *This is enough,* and so burn his rod now, as he put up his sword then.I*John Donne.*

Verse 4.I" Return. 0 Lord, deliver my soul," etc. In this his besieging of God, he brings up his works from afar off, closer ; he begins in this Psalm, at a deprecatory prayer ; he asks nothing, but that God would do nothing, that he would forbear himI*rebuke me not, correct me not.* Now, it costs the king less to give a pardon than to give a pension, and less to give n reprieve than to give a pardon, and less to connive, not to call in question, than cither reprieve, pardon, or pension ; to forbear is not much. But then as the mathematician said, that he could make an engine, a screw, that should move the whole frame of the world, if he could have a place assigned him to fix that engine, that screw upon, that so it might work upon the world ; so prayer, when one petition hath taken hold upon God, works upon God, moves God, prevails with God,entirely for all. David (hen having got this ground, this footing in God, he brings his works closer ; he comes from the deprecatory to a postulatory prayer ; not only that God would do nothing against him, but that he would do something for him. God hath suffered man to see *Arcana imperil,* the secrets of his state, how he governsIhe governs by precedent ; by precedents of his predecessors, he cannot, he hath none ; by precedents of other gods he cannot, there are none ; and yet he proceeds by precedents, by his own precedents, he does as he did befoj'e, *halenti dat,* to him that hath received he gives more, and is willing to be wrought and prevailed upon, and pressed with his own example. And, as though his doing good were but to learn how to do good better, still he writes after his own copy, and *nulla dies sine linea.* He writes something to us, that is, he doth something for us every day. And then, that which is not often seen in other masters, his copies are better than the originals ; his latter mercies larger than his former ; and in this postulatory prayer, larger than the deprecatory, enters our text, " *Return, 0 Lard; deliver my soul: 0 save me,"* etc.I*John Donne.*

Verse 5.I" Ffr in death there is no remembrance of thee, in the grave who will gite thte thanfa?" Lord, be thou pacified and reconciled- to me .... for shouldst thou now proceed to take away my life, as it were a most direful condition for me to die before I have prophiate'd thee, so I may well demand what increase of glory or honour will it bring unto thee ? Will it not be infinitely more glorious for thee to spare me, till by true contrition 1 may regain thy favour ?Iand then I may live to praise and magnify thy mercy and thy grace : thy mercy in pardoning so great a sinner, and then confess thee by vital actions of all holy obedience for the future, and so demonstrate the power of thy grace which hath wrought this change in me; neither of which will be done by destroying me, but only thy just judgments manifested in thy vengeance on sinners.I*Henry Hammond, D.D., 1659.*

Verne 6.I" I fainted in my mourning.'1" It may seem a marvellous change in David, being a man of such magnitude of mind, to be thus dejected and cast down. Prevailed he not against Goliath, against the lion and the bear, through fortitude and magnanimity ? But now he is sobbing, sighing, and weeping as a child ! The answer is easy ; the diverse persons with whom he hath to do occasioneth the same. When men and beasts are his opposites, then he is more than a conqueror ; but when he hath to do with God against whom he sinned, then he is less than nothing.

Verge 0.l" *I caused my bed to swim."* Showers be better than dews,

yet it is sufficient if God at least hath bedewed our hearts, and hath given us some sign of a penitent heart. If we have not rivers of waters to pour forth with David, neither fountains flowing with Mary Magdalen, nor as Jeremy, desire to have a fountain in our head to weep day and night, nor with Peter weep bitterly ; yet if we lament that we cannot lament, and mourn that we cannot mourn : yea, if we have the smallest sobs of sorrow and tears of compunction, if they be true and not counterfeit, they will make us acceptable to God ; for as the woman with the bloody issue that touched the hem of Christ's garment, was no less welcome to Christ than Thomas, who put his fingers in tile print of the nails ; so, God looketh not at the quantity, but the sincerity of our repentance.

Verge 6.l" *My ted."* The place of his sin is the place of his repentance, and so it. should be ; yea, when we behold the place where we have offended, we should be pricked in the heart, and there again crave him pardon. As Adam sinned in the garden, and Christ sweat bloody tears in the garden. "Examine your hearts upon your beds, and convert unto the Lord;" and whereas ye have stretched forth yourselves upon your bed to devise evil things, repent there and make thenj sanctuaries to God. Sanctify by your tears every place which ye have polluted by sin. And let us seek Christ Jesus on our ownbed, with the spouse in the Canticles, who saith, " By night on my bed I sought him whom my soul lovcth."|*Archibald Symson.*

Verse 6.l" *I water my couch with tears.'"* Not only I *wash,* but also I *voter.* The faithful sheep of the great Shepherd go up from the *washing* place, every one bringeth forth twins, and none barren among them. Cant. iv. 2. For so Jacob's sheep, having conceived at the watering troughs, brought forth strong and party-coloured lambs. David likewise, who before had erred and strayed liko a lost sheep making here his bed a washing-place, by Bo much the less is barren in obedience, by how much the more he is fruitful in repentance. In Solomon's temple stood the caldrons of brass, to wash the flesh of those beasts which were to bo sacrificed on the altar. Solomon's father maketh a water of his tears, a caldron of his bed, an altar of his heart, a sacrifice, not of the flesh of unreasonable beasts, but of his own body, a living sacrifice, which is his reasonable serving of God. Now the Hebrew word here used signifies properly, to cause to swim, which is more than simply to wash. And thus the Geneva translation readeth it, I cause my bed every night to swim. So that as the priests used to swim in the molten sea, that they might be pure and clean, against they performed the holy rites and services of the temple, in like manner the princely prophet washeth his bed, yea, he swimmeth in his bed, or rather he causeth his bed to swim in tears, as in a sea of grief and penitent sorrow for his sin.|*Thomas Playfere,* 1604.

Verse 6.l" *I water my couch with my tears."* Let us water our bed every night with our tears. Do not only blow upon it with intermissive blasts, for then like fire, it will resurge and flame the more. Sin is like a stinking candle newly put out, it is soon lighted again. It may receive a wound, but fike a dog it will easily lick itself whole ; a little forbearance multiplies it like Hydra's heads. Therefore, whatsoever aspersion the sin of the day has brought upon us, let the tears of the night wash away.|*Thomas Adams.*

Verses 6, 7. |Soul-trouble is attended usually with great pain of body too, and Bo a man is wounded and distressed in every part. There is no soundness in my flesh, because of thine anger, says David. " The arrows of the Almighty are within me, the poison whereof drinketh up my spirit." Job vi. 4. Sorrow of heart contracts the natural spirits, making all their motions slow and feeble ; and the poor afflicted body does usually decline and waste away ; and, therefore, saith Heman, " My soul is full of troubles, and my life draweth nigh unto the grave." In this inward distress we find our strength decay and melt, even as wax before the fire ; for sorrow darkeueth the spirits, obscures the judgment, blinds the memory, as to all pleasant things, and beclouds the lucid part of the mind, causing the lamp of life to burn weakly. In this troubled condition the person cannot be without a countenance that is pale, and wan, and dejected, like one that is seized with strong fear and consternation ; all his motions arc sluggish, and no sprightliness nor activity remains. A merry heart doth good, like a medicine ; but a broken spirit drieth the bones. Hence come those frequent complaints in Scripture : My moisture is turned into the drought of the summer : I am like a bottle in the smoke ; my soul cleaveth unto the dust : my face is foul with weeping, and on my eyelid is the shadow of death. Job. xvi. 16, xxx. 17, 18|19. My bones arc pierced in me, in the night season, and my sinews take no rest; by the great force of my disease is my garment changed. He hath cast me into the mire, and I am become like dust and nshes. Many times indeed the trouble of the soul does begin Irom the weakness and indisposition of the body. Long affliction, without any prospect of remedy, does, in process of time, begin to distress the soul itself. David was a man often exercised with sickness and the rage of enemies ; and in all the instances almost that we meet with in the Psalms, we may observe that the outward occasions of trouble brought him under an apprehension of the wrath of God for his sin. (Psalm vi. 1, 2 ; and the reasons given, verses 5 and 6.) All his griefs running into this most terrible thought, that God was his enemy. As little brooks lose themselves in a great river, and change their name and nature,it most frequently happens, that when our pain is long and sharp, and helpless and unavoidable, we begin to question the sincerity of our estate towards God, though at its first assault we hud few doubts or fears about it. Long weakness of body makes the soul more susceptible of trouble, and uneasy thoughts.| *Timothy Boger on Trouble of Mind.*

Yens'!.|" Mine eye is consumed." Many make those eyes which God hath given them, as it were two lighted candles to let them see to go to hell ; and for this God in justice" requiteth them, that seeing their minds are blinded by the lust of the eyes, the lust of the flesh, and the pride of life, God, I say, sendeth sickness to debilitate their eyes which were so sharp-sighted in the devil's service, and their lust now causeth them to want the necessary sight of their body.

Verge 7.|"Mine enemies." The pirates seeing an empty bark, pass by it; but if she be loaded with precious wares, then they will assault her. Ho, if a man have no grace within him, Satan passeth by him as not a convenient prey for him ; but being loaded with graces, as the love of God, his fear, and such other spiritual virtues, let him be persuaded that according as he knows what stuff is in him, so will he not fail to rob him of them, if in any case he may. *Archibald Symson.*

Verse 7.|That eye of his that had looked and lusted after his neighbour's wife is now dimmed and darkened with grief and indignation. He had wept himself almost blind. |*John Trapp.*

Verge 8.|" *Depart from* me," etc., *i.e.,* you may now go jour way ; for that which you look for, namely, my death, you shall not have at this present; *for the Lord hath heard the voice of my weeping, i.e.,* has graciously granted me that which with tears I asked of him. | *Thomas WUcocks.*

Verne 8.|" *Depart from me, all ye workers of iniquity.* " May not too much familiarity with profane wretches be justly charged upon church members ? 1 know man is a sociable creature, but that will not excuse saints as to their carelessness of the choice of their company. The very fowls of the air, and beasts of the field, love not heterogeneous company. " Bi rds of a feather flock together." I have been afraid that many who would be thought eminent, of a high stature in grace and godliness, yet see not ths vast difference there is between nature and regeneration, sin and grace, the old and the new man, seeing all company i- alike unto them.|*Lewis Stuckley's " Gospel Glass,"* 1607.

Verse 8.|" *The voice of my weeping.* " Weeping hath a voice, and os music upon the water sounds farther and more harmoniously than upon the land, so prayers, joined with tears, cry louder in God's ears, and make sweeter music than when tears are absent. When Antipater had written a large letter against Alexander's mother unto Alexander, the king answered him,"One tear from my mother will wash away all her faults." So it is with God. A penitent tear *it* an undeniable ambassador, and never returns from the throne of grace unsatisfied.|*Spencer's Things New and Old.*

Vcrte 8.|The wicked are called *"workers of iniquity,"* because they are free and ready to sin, they have a strong tide and beat of spirit to do evil, and they do it not to halves but thoroughly ; they do not only begin or nibble at the bait a little (as a good man often doth), but greedily swallow it down, hook and all; they are fully in it, and do it fully ; they make a work of it, and so are *vorters of iniguity."|Joseph Caryl.*

Verse 8.|Some may say, " My constitution is such that I cannot weep ; I may as well go to squeeze a rock, as think to get a tear." But if thou canst not weep for sin, canst thou grieve ? Intellectual mourning is best; there may be sorrow where there are no tears, the vessel may be full though it wants vent ; it is not so much the weeping eye God respects as the broken heart; yet I would be loath to stop their tears who can weep. God stood looking on Hezekiah's tears (Isaiah xxxviii. 5), "I have seen thy tears." David's tears made music in God's ears, " *The Lord hath heard the voice of my weeping.* " It is a sight fit for angels to behold, tears as pearls dropping from a penitent eye. | *T. Watson.*

Verse 8.|" *The Lord hath heard the voice of my veeping.* " God hears the voice of our looks, God hears the voice of our tears sometimes better than thu voice of our words ; for it is the Spirit itself that makes intercession for ns. Rom. viii. 26. *Oemitibus inenarrabililnu,* in those *groan,* and so in those *teart,* which we *cannot utter; ineloquacibut,* as Tertullian reads that place, devout, and simple tears, which cannot speak, speak aloud in the ears of God ; n.sy, tears which we cannot utter ; not only not utter the force of the tears, but not utter the very tears themselves. As God sees the water in the spring in the veins of the earth before it bubble upon the face of thu earth, so God sees tears in the heart of a rrwn before they blubber his face ; God hears the tears of that sorrowful soul, which for sorrow cannot shed tears. From this casting up of the eyes, and pouring out the sorrow of the heart at the eyes, at least opening God a window through which he may sec a wet heart through a dry eye ; from these overtures of repentance, which are as those imperfect sounds of words, which parent!) delight in, in their children, before they speak plain, a penitent sinner comes to a verbal and a more express prayer. To these prayers, these vocal and verbal prayers from David, God had given ear, and from this hearing of those prayers was David come to this thankful confidence, " *The Lord hath- heard, the Lord will hear.'* 1*John Donne.*

Verse 8.\What a strange change is here all on a sudden "Well might Luther say, " Prayer is the leech of the soul, that sucks out the venom and swelling thereof." " Prayer," saith another, " is an exorcist with God, and an exorcist against sin and misery." Bernard saith, " How oft hath prayer found me despairing almost, but left me triumphing, and well assured of pardon !" The same in effect saith David here, " Depart from me, all ye workers of iniquity ; for the Lord hath heard the voice of my weeping." What a word is that to his insulting enemies ! Avaunt ! come out! vanish ! These be words used to devils and dogs, but good enough for a Doeg or a Shimei. And the Son of David shall say the same to his enemies when he comes to judgment.\././.*, *Trapp.*

Verse 9.\" *The Lord hath heard my supplication,"* etc. The psalmist three times expresses his confidence of his prayers being heard and received, which may bo either in reference to his having prayed so many times for help, as tho apostle Paul did (2 Cor. xii. 8) ; and as Christ his antitype did (Matt. xxvi. 39, 42, 44) ; or to express the certainty of it, the strength of his faith in it, and the exuberance of his joy on account of it.*John Gill, D.D.,* 1697\1771.

Verse 10.\" *Let att mine enemies lie ashamed,'* 1" etc. If this were an imprecation, a malediction, yet it was medicinal, and had *rationem boni,* a charitable tincture and nature in it ; he wished the men no harm as men. But it is rather *pradictorium,* a prophetical vehemence, that if they will take no knowledge of God's declaring himself in the protection of his servants, if they would not consider that God had heard, and would hear, had rescued, and would rescue his children, but would continue their opposition against him, heavy judgments would certainly fall upon them ; their punishment should be certain, but the effect should bo uncertain ; for God only knows whether his correction shall

work upon his enemies to their mollifying, or to their obduration In the

second word, " *Let them be sore vexed,"* he wishes his enemies no worse than himself had been, for he had used the same word of himself before, *Ossa turbata, My bones are vexed;* and, *Anima turbata, My soul is vexed;* and considering that David had found this vexation to be his way to God, it was no malicious imprecation to wish that enemy the same physic that he had taken, who was more sick of the same disease than he was. For this is like a troubled sea after a tempest; the danger is past, but yet the billow is great still ; the danger was in the calm, in the security, or in the tempest, by misinterpreting God's corrections to our obduration, and to a remorseless stupefaction ; but when a man is come to this holy vexation, to be troubled, to be shaken with the sense of the indignation of God, the storm is past, and the indignation of God is blown over. Thatsoul is in a fair and near way of being restored to a calmness, and to reposed security of conscience that is come to this holy vexation.|*John Donne.*

Vene 10.|" Let all mine enemies [or *all mine enemies shall] be ashamed, and tore vexed,'*11 etc. Many of the mournful Psalms end in this manner, to instruct the believer that he is continually to look forward, and solace himself with beholding that day, when his warfare shall be accomplished ; when sin and sorrow shall be no more ; when sudden and everlasting confusion shall cover the enemies of righteousness ; when the sackcloth of the penitent shall be exchanged for a robe of glory, and every tear become a sparkling gem in his crown ; when to sighs and groans shall succeed the songs of heaven, set to angelic harps, and faith shall be resolved into the vision of the Almighty.|*George Borne.*

HINTS TO THE VILLAGE PREACHER.

Vene .|A sermon, for afflicted souls. I. God's twofold dealings. (1) *Rebuke,* by a telling sermon, a judgment on another, K slight trial in our own person, or a solemn monition in our conscience by the Spirit. (2) *Chastening.* This follows the other when the first is disregarded. Pain, losses, bereavements, melancholy, and other trials. II. The evils in them to be most dreaded, anger and hot displeasure. III. The means to avert these ills. Humiliation, confession, amendment, faith in the Lord, etc.

*Verse 1.|*The believer's greatest dread, the anger of God. What this fact reveals in the heart ? Why it is so ? What removes the fear ?

*Verse 2.|*The *argumentum ad miserifordiam.*

Vene 2.|First sentence|Divine liealing. 1. What precedes it, *my lones are vexed.* 2. How it is wrought. 3. What succeeds it.

*Verse 3.|*The impatience of sorrow ; its sins, mischief, and cure.

*Verse 3.|*A fruitful topic may be found in considering the question, How long will God continue afflictions to the righteous ?

Verted.|"Return, O Lord."" A prayer suggested by a sense of the Lord's absence, excited by grace, attended with heart searching and repentance, backed by pressing danger, guaranteed as to its answer, and containing a request for all mercies.

*Verte 4.|*The prayer of the deserted saint. 1. *His state:* his soul is evidently in bondage and danger ; 2. *His hope:* it is in the Lord's *return.* 3. *His plea :* mercy only.

*Verte 5.|*The final suspension of earthly service considered in various practical aspects.

*Vene 5.|*The duty of praising God while we live.

*Verse 6.|*Saints' tears in quality, abundance, influence, assuagement, and final end.

*Verte 7.|*The voife of weeping. What it is.

*Verte 8.|*The pardoned sinner forsaking his bad companions.

*Vene 9.|*Pas-t answers the ground of present confidence. He *hath-,* he *will.*

*Verte 10.|*The shame reserved for the wicked.

WORKS UPON THE SIXTH PSALM.

A Qodly and Fruitful! Exposition on the Sift Psalme, the First of the Peni- tentials ; in a tacred Sejitenarie ; or, a Qodly and Fruitfutt Exposition on the Seven Psalmes of Repentance. By Mr. Archibald Symson, late Pastor of the Church at Dalkeeth in Scotland. 1638.

Sermons on the Penitential Psalmi, in " The Works of John Donne, D.D., Dean of St. Paul's," 1621|1631. Edited by Henry Alford, M.A. In six volumes. 1839.

On Verse 6. *The Sick Man's Couch; a Sermon preached before the most noble P'ince Henry, at Greenwich, Mar.* 12., *ann.* 1604. By Thomas Playfkhe, &c., in Playfere's Sermons.

PSALM VII.

Title.|"Shiggaion of David, which he sang unto the Lord, concerning the words of Cosh the Benjamite."|" *tfhiggaion of David." As far as we can gather from the observations of learned men, and from a comparison of this Psalm with the only other Sliig- gaion inthe Wordof God, (Hab.* iii.,) *this title seems to mean " variable songs," with which also the idea of solace and pleasure is associated. Truly our life-psalm is composed of variable verses; one stanza rolls along icith the sublime metre of triumph, but another limps irith the bmken rhythm of complaint. There is much bass in the saint's music here below. Our experience is as variable as the taealher in Em/land.*

fVom the title we learn the occasion of the composition of this song. It appears probable that Cash the Benjamite had accused David to Saul of treasonable conspiracy against his royal authority. This the king would be ready enough to credit, both from his jealousy of Dacid, and from the relation which most probably existed between himself, the son of Kish, and this (,'itsh, or Kish, the Benjamite. He who is near the throne can do more injury to a subject than an ordinary slanderer.

This may be called the Sono Op The Slandebed Saint. *Even this sorest of evils may furnish occasion for a Psalm. Whai a blessing would it be if we could turn even the most disastrous event into a theme for song, and so turn the tables upon our great enemy. Let us learn a lesson from Luther, who once said," David made Psalms; we also will make Psalms, and sing them as well as we can to the honour of our Lord, and to spite and mock the devil."*

Division.|*In the first and second verses the danger is stated, and prayer offered. Tlten the Psalmist most solemnly avows his innocence. (3,* 4, 6.) *The Iiord is pleaded with lo arist to judgment* (6, 7). *Tfie Lord, sitting upon his throne, hears the renewed appeal of the Slandered .Supplicant (8,* 9). *The Lord clears his servant, and threatens the wicked* (10, 11, 12, 13). *The slanderer is seen in vision bringing a curse upon his own head,* (14, 15, 16,) *white Dacid retires from trial singing a hymn of praise to his righteous God. We have here a nolrle sermon upon that text: "No weapon that is formed against thee shall prosper, and every tongue that riseth against thee in judgment thou shall condemn."*

EXPOSITION.

OLORD my God, in thee do I put my trust : save me from all them that persecute me, and deliver me :

2 Lest he tear my soul like a lion, rending *it* in pieces, while *there is* none to deliver.

David appears before God to plead with him against the Accuser, who had charged him with treason and treachery. The case is here opened with an avowal of confidence in God. Whatever may be the emergency of our condition we shall never find it amiss to retain our reliance upon our God. " *O Lord my God,"'* mine by a special covenant, sealed by Jesus' blood, and ratified in my own soul by a sense of union to thee ; " *in thee,"* and in thee only, " *do I put my trust,"* even now in my sore distress. I shake, but my rock moves not. It is never right to distrust God, and never vain to trust him. And now, with both di.ine relationship and holy trust to strengthen him, David utters the burden of his desire|" *tate me from all them that persecute me."* His pursuers were very many, and any one of them cruel enough to devour him ; he cries, therefore, for salvation from them *aU*. We should never think our prayers complete until we *ask* for preservation from *all* sin, and all enemies. " *And deliver me,"* extricate me from their snares, acquit me of their accusations, give a true and just deliverance in this trial of my injured character. See how clearly his case is stated ; let us see to it, that we know what we would have when we are come to the throne of mercy. Pause a little while before you pray, that you may not offerthe sacrifice of fools. Get a distinct idea of your need, and then you can pray with the more fluency of fervency.

" *Lest he tear my soul."* Here is the plea of fear co-working with the plea of faith. There was one among David's foes mightier than the rest, who had both dignity, strength, and ferocity, and was, therefore, " *lite a lion."* From this foe he urgently seeks deliverance. Perhaps this was Saul, his royal enemy ; but in our own case there is one who goes about like a lion, seeking whom he may devour, concerning whom we should ever cry, " Deliver us from the Evil One." Notice the vigour of the description|" *rending it in pieces, while there is none to deliver.'*1" It is a picture from the shepherd-life of David. WTien the fierce lion had pounced upon the defenceless lamb, and had made it his prey, he would rend the victim in pieces, break all the bones, and devour all, because no shepherd was near to protect the lamb or rescue it from the ravenous beast. This is a soul-moving portrait of a saint delivered over to the will of Satan. This will make the bowels of Jehovah yearn. A father cannot be silent when a child is in such peril. No, he will not endure the thought of his darling in the jaws of a lion, he will arise and deliver his persecuted one. Our God is very pitiful, and he will surely rescue his people from so desperate a destruction. It will be well for us here to remember that this is a description of the danger to which the Psalmist was exposed from slanderous tongues. Verily this is not an overdrawn picture, for the wounds of a sword will heal, but the wounds of the tongue cut deeper than the flesh, and are not soon cured. Slander leaves a slur, even if it be wholly disproved. Common fame, although notoriously a common liar, has very many believers. Once let an ill word get into men's mouths, and it is not easy to get it fully out again. The Italians say that good repute is like the cypress, once cut, it never puts forth leaf again ; this is not true if our character be cut by a stranger's hand, but even then it will not soon regain its former verdure. Oh, 'tis a meanness most detestable to stab a good man in his reputation, but diabolical hatred observes no nobility in its mode of warfare. We must be ready for this trial, for it will surely come upon us. If God was slandered in Eden, we shall surely be maligned in this land of sipners. Gird up your loins, ye children of the resurrection, for this fiery trial awaits you all.

3 O Lord my God, if I have done this ; if there be iniquity in my hands ;

4 If I have rewarded evil unto him that was at peace with me ; (yea, I have delivered him that without cause is mine enemy :)

5 Let the enemy persecute my soul, and take *it;* yea, let him tread down my life upon the earth, and lay mine honour in the dust. Selah.

The second part of this wandering hymn contains a protestation of innocence, and an invocation of wrath upon his own head, if he were not clear from the evil imputed to him. So far from hiding treasonable intentions in his hands, or ungratefully requiting the peaceful deeds of a friend, he had even suffered his enemy to escape when he had him completely in his power. Twice had he spared Saul's life ; once in the cave of Adullam, and again when he found him sleeping in the midst of his slumbering camp ; he could, therefore, with a clear conscience, make his appeal to heaven. He needs not fear the curse whose soul is clear of guilt. Yet is the imprecation a most solemn one, and only justifiable through the extremity of the occasion, and the nature of the dispensation under which the Psalmist lived. *We* are commanded by our Lord Jesus to let our yea be yea, and our nay, nay; "for whatsoever is more than this cometh of evil." If we cannot be believed on our word, we are surely not to be trusted on our oath ; for to a true Christian his simple word is as binding as another man's oath. Especially beware, O unconverted men ! of trifling with solemn imprecations. Remember the woman at Devizes, who wished she might die ifshe had not paid her share in a joint purchase, and who fell dead there and then with the money in her hand.

Selah. David enhances the solemnity of this appeal to the dread tribunal of God by the use of the usual pause.

From these verses we may learn that no innocence can shield a man from the calumnies of the wicked. David had been scrupulously careful to avoid any appearance of rebellion against Saul, whom he constantly styled " the Lord's anointed ;" but all this could not protect him from lying tongues. As the shadow follows the substance, so envy pursues goodness. It is only at the tree laden with fruit that men throw stones. If we would live without being slandered we must wait till we get to heaven. Let us be very heedful not to believe the flying rumours which are always harassing gracious men. If there are no believers in lies there will be but a dull market in falsehood, and good men's characters will be safe. Ill-will never spoke well. Sinners have an ill- will to saints, and therefore, be sure they will not speak well of them.

6 Arise, O LORD, in thine anger, lift up thyself because of the rage of mine enemies : and awake for me *to* the judgment *that* thou hast commanded.

J So shall the congregation of the people compass thee about : for their sakes therefore return thou on high.

"We now listen to a fresh prayer, based upon the avowal which he has just made. We cannot pray too often, and when our heart is true, we shall turn to God in prayer as naturally as the needle to its pole.

*"Arise, 0 Lord, in thim anger.'*1" His sorrow makes him view the Lord as a judge who had left the judgment-seat and retired into his rest. Faith would move the Lord to avenge the quarrel of his saints. " *Lift vp thyself because of the rage of mine enemies"*1la still stronger figure to express his anxiety that the Lord would assume his authority and mount the throne. Stand up, O God, rise thou above them all, and let thy justice tower above their villainies. " *Awake for me to the judgment that thou host commanded."* This is a bolder utterance still, for it implies sleep as well as inactivity, and can only be applied to God in a very limited sense. He never slumbers, yet doth he often seem to do so ; for the wicked prevail, and the saints are trodden in the dust.

God's silence is the patience of longsuffering, and if wearisome to the saints, they should bear it cheerfully in the hope that sinners may thereby be led to repentance.

" *So shall the congregation of the people compass thee about.*'1 Thy saints shall crowd to thy tribunal with their complaints, or shall surround it with their solemn homage : *"for their takes therefore return thou on high."* As when a judge travels at the assizes, all men take their cases to his court that they may be heard, so will the righteous gather to their Lord. Here he fortifies himself in prayer by pleading that if the Lord will mount the throne of judgment, multitudes of the saints would be blessed as well as himself. If I be too base to be remembered, yet "/or *their sakes,",* for the love thou bearest to thy chosen people, come forth from thy secret pavilion, and sit in the gate dispensing justice among the people. When my suit includes the desires of all the righteous it shall surely speed, for " shall not God avenge his own elect ?"

8 The LORD shall judge the people : judge me, O LORD, according to my righteousness, and according to mine integrity *that* is in me.

9 Oh let the wickedness of the wicked come to an end ; but establish the just : for the righteous God trieth the hearts and reins.

If I am not mistaken, David has now seen in the eye of his mind the Lord ascending to his judgment-seat, and beholding him seated there in royal state,he draws near to him to urge hia suit anew. In the last two verses he besought Jehovah to arise, and now that he is arisen, he prepares to mingle with "the congregation of the people" who compass the Lord about. The royal heralds proclaim the opening of the court with the solemn words, " *The Lord shall judge the people."* Our petitioner rises at once, and cries with earnestness and humility, *"Judge me, 0 Lord, according to my righteousness, and according to mine integrity that is in me."* His hand is on an honest heart, and his cry is to a righteous Judge. He sees a smile of complacency upon the face of the Kiug, and in the name of all the assembled congregation he cries aloud, " *Oh let the wickedness of the wicked come to an end; but establish the* JuJ." Is not this the universal longing of the whole company of the elect? When shall we be delivered from the filthy conversation of these men of Sodom ? When shall we escape from the filthiness of Mesech and the blackness of the tents of Kedar ?

What a solemn and weighty truth is contained in the last sentence of the ninth verse ! How deep is the divine knowledge!l" *he trieth."* How strict, how accurate, how intimate his search !l" *he trieth the hearts,'*1' the secret thoughts, *"and reins,"* the inward affections. "All things are naked and opened to the eyes of him with whom we have to do."

10 My defence *is* of God, which saveth the upright in heart.

11 God judgeth the righteous, and God is angry *with the wicked* every day.

12 If he turn not, he will whet his sword ; he hath bent his bow, and made it ready.

13 He hath also prepared for him the instruments of death ; he ordaineth his arrows against the persecutors.

The judge has heard the cause, has cleared the guiltless, and uttered his voice against the persecutors. Let us draw near, and learn the results of the great assize. Yonder is the slandered one with his harp in hand, hymning the justice of his Lord, and rejoicing aloud in his own deliverance. " *My defence is of God, which sacel.h the upright in heart."* Oh, how good to have a true and *iipright* heart. Crooked sinners, with all their craftiness, are foiled by the upright in heart. God defends the right. Filth will not long abide on the pure white garments of the saints, but shall be brushed off by divine, providence, to the vexation of the men by whose base hands it was thrown upon the godly. When God shall try our cause, our sun has risen, and the sun of the wicked is set for ever. Truth, like oil, is ever above, no power of our enemies can drown it; we shall refute their slanders in the day when the trumpet wakes the dead, and we shall shine in honour when lying lips are put to silence. O believer, fear not all that thy foes can do or say against thee, for the tree which God plants no winds can hurt. " *God judgeth the righteous,"* he hath not given thee up to be condemned by the lips of persecutors. Thine enemies cannot sit on God's throne, nor blot thy name out of his book. Let them alone, then, for God will find time for his revenges.

" *God is angry with the wicked every any."* He not only detests sin, but is angry with those who continue to indulge in it. We have no insensible and stolid God to deal with ; he can be angry, nay, he is angry to-day and every day with you, ye ungodly and impenitent sinners. The best day that ever dawns on a sinner brings a curse with it. Sinners may have many feast days, but no safe days. From the beginning of the year even to its ending, there is not an hour in which God's oven is not hot, and burning in readiness for the wicked, who shall be as stubble.

" *If he tnrn not, lie will whet his iword."* What blows are those which will be dealt by that long uplifted arm ! God's sword has been sharpening upon the revolving stone of our daily wickedness, and if we will not repent, it will speedily cut us in pieces. Turn or burn is the sinner's only alternative. " *//;bath 'bent Jii 'bow and made it ready."* Even now the thirsty arrow longs to wet itself with the blood of the *persecutor.* The bow is bent, the aim is taken, the arrow is fitted to the string, and what, O sinner, if the arrow should be let fly at thee even now ! Remember, God's arrows never miss the mark, and are, every one of them, "instruments of death." Judgment may tarry, but it will not come too late. The Greek proverb saith, "The mill of God grinds late, but grinds to powder."

14 Behold, he travaileth with iniquity, and hath conceived mischief, and brought forth falsehood.

15 He made a pit, and digged it, and is fallen into the ditch *ufhich* he made.

16 His mischief shall return upon his own head, and his violent dealing shall come down upon his own pate.

In three graphic pictures we see the slanderer's history. A woman in travail fuinishes the first metaphor. *"He trataileth with iniquity."* He is full of it, pained until he can carry it out, he longs to work his will, he is full of pangs until his evil intent is executed. " *He Jiath, conceived mucfiief."* This is the original of his base design. The devil has had doings with him, and the virus of evil is in him. And now behold the progeny of this unhallowed conception. The child is worthy of its father, his name of old was " the father of lies," and the birth doth not belie the parent, for *Tie brought forth falsehood.* Thus, one figure is carried out to perfection ; the Psalmist now illustrates his meaning by another, taken from the stratagems of the hunter. " *Hemadeapit, and digged it."* He was cunning in his plans, and industrious in his labours. He stooped to the dirty work of digging. He did not feiir to soil his own hands, he was willing to work in a *ditch* if others might fall therein. What mean things men will do to wreak revenge on the godly. They hunt for good men, as if they were brute beasts ; nay, they will not give them the fair chase afforded to the hare or the fox, but must secretly entrap them, because they can neither run them down nor shoot them down. Our enemies will not meet us to the face, for they fear us as much as they pretend to despise us. But let us look on to the end of the scene. The verse says, he *"it fallen into the ditch which he made."* Ah ! there he is, let us laugh at his disappointment. Lo t he is himself the beast, he has hunted his own soul, and the chase has brought him a goodly victim. Aha, aha, so should it ever be. Come hither and moke merry with this entrapped hunter, this biter who has bitten himself. Give him no pity, for it will be wasted on such a wretch. He is but rightly and richly rewarded by being paid in his own coin. He cast forth evil from his mouth, and it has fallen into his bosom. He has set his own house on fire with the torch which he lit to burn a neighbour. He sent forth a foul bird, and it has come back to its nest. The rod which he lifted on high, has smitten his own back. He shot an arrow upward, and it has *"returned upon his own head."* He hurled a stone at another, and it has *"comedown, upon his own pate.'*1'1 Curses are like young chickens, they always come home to roost. Ashes always fly back in the face of him that throws them. " As he loved cursing, so let it come unto him." (Ps. cix. 17.) How often has this been the case in the histories of both ancient and modern tiroes. Men have burned their own fingers when they were hoping to brand their neighbour. And if this does not happen now, it will hereafter. The Lord has caused dogs to lick the blood of Ahab in the midst of the vineyard of Naboth. Sooner or later the evil deeds of persecutors have always leaped back into their arms. So will it be in the last great day, when Satan's fiery darts shall all be quivered in his own heart, and all his followers shall reap the harvest which they themselves have sown.

17 I will praise the Lord according to his righteousness : and will sing praise to the name of the LORD most high.

We conclude with the joyful contrast. In this all these Psalms are agreed ; they all exhibit the blessedness of the righteous, and make its colours the more Blowing by contrast with the miseries of the wicked. The bright jewel sparkles in a black foil. *Praise* is the occupation of the godly, their eternal work, and their present pleasure. *Singing* is the fitting embodiment for praise, and therefore do the saints make melody before the Lord Most High. The slandered one is now a singer : his harp was unstrung for a very little season, and now we leave him sweeping its harmonious chords, and flying on their music to the third heaven of adoring praise.

EXPLANATORY NOTES AND QUAINT SAYINGS.

Title.|"Shiggaion," though some have attempted to fix on it, a reference to the moral aspect of the world as depicted in this Psalm, is in all probability to be taken as expressing the *nature of the composition.* It conveys the idea of something *erratic* (HJEf, to wander) in the style ; something not so calm as other Psalms ; and hence *Ewald* suggests, that it might be rendered, " a confused ode," a Dithyramb. This characteristic of excitement in the style, and a kind of disorder in the sense, suits Habakkuk iii. 1, the only other place where the word occurs.|*Andrew A. Sonar.*

Whole Psalm.|Whatever might be the occasion of the Psalm, the real subject seems to be the Messiah's appeal to God against the false accusations of his enemies ; and the predictions which it contains of the final conversion of the whole world, and of the future judgment, are clear and explicit.|*Samuel Hartley, LL.D.,* 1733|1806.

Verne 1.|" *0 Lwd, my God, in thee do I put my trust.* " This is the first instance in the Psalms where David addresses the Almighty by the united names Jehovah and my God. No more suitable words can be placed at the beginning of any act of prayer or praise. These names show the ground of the confidence afterwards expressed. They "denote at once supreme reverence and the most endearing confidence. They convey a recognition of God's infinite perfections, and of his covenanted and gracious relations."|*William S. Plumer.*

Verse 2.|" *Lett Tie tear my soul like a lion,* " etc. It is reported of tigers, that they enter into a rage uppn the scent of fragrant spices ; so do ungodly men at the blessed savour of godliness. I have read of some barbarous nations, who, when the sun shines hot upon them, they shoot up their arrows ajrainst it; so do wicked men at the light and heat of godliness. There is a natural antipathy between the spirits of godly men and the wicked. Genesis iii. 15. " I will put enmity between thy seed and her seed."|*Jeremiah Burroughs,* 1660.

Verse 3.|" *0 Lord, my Qod, if I have done this, if there le iniquity in my 7iand.* " In the primitive times the people of God were then a people under great reproach. What strange things does Tertullian tell us they reproached them withal; as that in their meetings they made Thyestes suppers, who invited his brother to a supper, and presented him with a dish of his own flesh. They charged them with uncleanness because they met in the night (for they durst not meet in the day), and said, they blew out the candles when they were together, and committed tilthiness. They reproached them for ignorance, saying, they were all unlearned ; and therefore the heathens in Tertullian's time used to paint the God of the Christians with an ass's head, and a book in his hand, to signify that though they pretended learning, yet they were an unlearned, silly people, rude and ignorant. Bishop Jewel in his sermon upon.Luke si. 5, cites this out of Tertullian, and applies it to his time :|" Do not our adversaries do the like," saith he, " at this day, against all those that profess the gospel of Christ ? Oh, say they, who are they that favour this way ? they are none but shoemakers, tailors, weavers, and such as were never at the university ;" they are the bishop's own words. He cites likewise Tertullian a little after, saying, that the Christians were accounted the public enemies of the State. And Josephus tells us of Apollinaris, speaking concerning the Jews and Christians, that they were more foolish than any barbarian. And Paul us Fagius reports a story of an Egyptian, concerning the Christians, who said, " They were a gathering together of a most filthy, lecherous people,;" and for the keeping of the Sabbath, he says, "they had a disease that was upon them, and they were fain to rest the seventh day because of that disease." Ano! so in Augustine's time, he bath this expression, "Any one that begins to be godly, presently he must prepare to suffer reproach from the tongues of adversaries ;" and this was their usual manner of reproach, " TVhat shall we have of you, an Eli as ? a Jeremy?" And Nazianzen, in one of his orations says, " It is ordinary to reproach, that I cannot think to go free myself." And so Athanasius, they called him Sathanasius, because he was a special instrument against the Arians. And Cyprian, they called him Coprian, one that gathers up dung, as if all the excellent things that he had gathered in his works were but dung.|*Jeremiah Burroughs.*

Vertc 3.|" *If I have done this ; if there be iniquity in my hands."* I deny not but you may, and ought to be sensible of the wrong done to your name, for as " a good name is a precious ointment" (Cant. i. 3), so to have an evil name is a great judgment; and therefore you ought not to be insensible of the wrong done to your name by slanders and reproaches, saying, " Let men epeak of me what they please, I care not, so long as I know mine own innocency," for though the- testimony of your own innocency be a ground of comfort unto you, yet your care must be not only to approve yourselves unto God, but also unto men, to be as careful of your good names as possibly ye can ; but yet you are not to manifest any distemper or passion upon the reproachful speeches of others against you.|*Thomas Qouge,* 1660.

Verse 3.|It is a sign that there is some good in thee if a wicked world abuse thee. " *Quid malifecir'* I said Socrates, what evil have I done that this bad man commends me ? The applause of the wicked usually denotes some evil, and their censure imports some good. | *Thomas Watson.*

Verse 3.|" *If there lie iniquity in my hands."* Injustice is ascribed to the *hnnd,* not because injustice is always, though usually it be, done by the hand. With the hand men take away, and with that men detain the right of others. David speaks thus (1 Chron. xii. 17), " Seeing there is no wrong in mine hands ;" that is, I have done no wrong.|*Joseph Caryl.*

Verses 3, 4.|A good conscience is a flowing spring of assurance. " For our rejoicing is this, the testimony of our conscience, that in simplicity and godly sincerity, not with fleshly wisdom, but by the grace of God, we have had our conversation in the world, and more abundantly to you-ward." 2 Cor. i. 12. " Beloved, if our heart condemn us not, then have we confidence towards God." 1 John iii. 21. A good conscience has sure confidence. He who has it sits in the midst of all combustions and distractions, Noah-like, all sincerity and serenity, uprightness and boldness. What the probationer disciple said to our Saviour, "Master, I will follow thee whithersoever thou goest," that a good conscience says to the believing soul ; I will stand by thee ; I will strengthen thee : I will uphold thee ; I will be a comfort to thee in life, and a friend to thee in death. " Though all should leave thee, yet will I never forsake thee."| *Thomas Brooks.*

Verse 4.|" *Tea, I hate delivered him that without cause is mine enemy."* Meaning Saul, whose life he twice preserved, once in Engedi, and again when he slept on the plain.|*John Gill.*

Verse 4.|" *If I have rewarded nil unto him that vxu at peace with me.'* I To do evil for good, is human corruption ; to do good for good, is civil retribution ; but to do good for evil, is Christian perfection. Though this be not the grace of nature, yet it is the nature of grace.| *William Seeker.*

Verse 4.|Then is grace victorious, and then hath a man a noble and brave spirit, not when he is overcome by evil (for that argueth weakness), but when he can overcome evil. And it is God's way to shame the party that did the wrong, and to overcome him too ; it is the best way to get the victory over him. When David had Saul at an advantage in the cave, and cut off the lap of his garment, and did forbear any act of revenge against him, Saul was melted, and said to David, " Thou art more righteous than I." 1 Sam. zxiv. IT. Though he had such a hostile mind against him, and chased and pursued him up and down, yet when David forebore revenge when it wan in his power, it overcame him, and he falls a-weeping.I*Thomas Manton.*

*Verm 5.*I" *Let him tread down my life upon the earth.*'1" The allusion here is to the manner in which the vanquished were often treated in battle, when they were rode over by horses, or trampled by men in the dust. The idea of David is, that if he was guilty he would be willing that his enemy should triumph over him, should subdue him, should treat him with the utmost indignity and scorn.I*Albert Barnes, in loc.*

*Verse 5.*I*"Mine honour in the dust."* When Achilles dragged the body of Hector in the dust around the walls of Troy, he did but carry out the usual manners of those barbarous ages. David dares in his conscious innocence to imprecate such an ignominious fate upon himself if indeed the accusation of the black Benjamite be true. He had need have a golden character who dares to challenge such an ordeal.I*O. H. 8.*

*Verse 6.*I" *The judgment which thou hast ordained.*'1" In the end of the verse he shows that he asks nothing but what is according to the appointment of God. And this is the rule which ought to be observed by us iu our prayers ; we should in everything conform our requests to the divine will, as John also instructs us. 1 John iv. 14. And, indeed, we can never pray in faith unless we attend, in the first place, to what God commands, that our minds may not rashly and at random start aside in desiring more than we are permitted to desire and pray for. David, therefore, in order to pray aright, reposes himself on the word and promise of God ; and the import of his exercise is this : Lord, I am not led by ambition, or foolish headstrong passion, or depraved desire, inconsiderately to ask from thee whatever is pleasing to my flesh ; but it is the clear light of thy word which directs me, and upon it 1 securely depend.I *John Calvin.*

*Verse 7.*I" *The congregation of the people:"* either, 1. A great number of 411 sorts of people, who shall observe thy justice, and holiness, and goodness in ipleading my righteous cause against my cruel and implacable oppressor. Or rather, 2. The whole body of thy people Israel, by whom both these Hebrew words are commonly ascribed in Holy Scripture. " *Compass thee about;"*" they will, and I, as their king and ruler in thy stead, will take care that they shall come from all parts and meet together to worship thee, which in Saul's time they have grossly neglected, and been permitted to neglect, and to offer to thee praises and sacrifices for thy favour to me, and for the manifold benefits which they shall enjoy by my means, and under my government. " *For their sake* I' *or, for its sake, i.e.,* for the sake of thy congregation, which now is woefully dissipated and oppressed, and has in a great measure lost all administration of justice, and exercise of religion. " *Return thou on high,*'1'1 or, *return to thy high place, i.e.* to thy tribunal, to sit there and judge my cause. An allusion to earthly tribunals, which generally are set up on high above the people. 1 Kings x. 19.I*Matthew Pool,* 1624I1079.

4

SECTION 4

Verge 9.|Believers ! let not the terror of that day dispirit yon when you meditate upon it ; let those who have slighted the Judge, and continue cm niiies to him and the way of holiness, droop and hang down their heads when 1h(-y think of his coming ; but lift ye up your heads with joy, for the last day will be your best day. The Judge is your Head and Husband, your Redeemer, and your Advocate. Ye must appear before the judgment-seat ; but ye shall not come into condemnation. His coming will not be against you, but for you. It is otherwise with unbelievers, a *neglected Saviour* will be a *severe Judge.*| *Thomas Boston,* 1676|1732.

Verge 9.|" *The righteous Ood trieth the hearts and reins.*" As common experience shows that the workings of the mind, particularly the passions of joy, grief, and fear, have a very remarkable effect on the *reins* or *kidneys* (see Prov. xxiii. 16 ; Psalm Ixxiii. 21), so from their retired situation in the body, and their being hid in fat, they are often used to denote the most secret workings and affections of the soul. And to "see or examine the *reins,*" is to see or examine those most secret thoughts or desires of the soul.|*John Parkhtirst,* 1762.

Verge 9 (last clause).|" *The righteous Ood trieth the hearts and reins.*"

" I tbat alone am Infinite, can try
How deep within itself thine heart doth He.
Thy seamen's plummet can bnt reach the ground,
I Jnid that which thine heart itself ne'er found."

Francis Quarles, 1592l1644.

Verse 0.l" The heart," may signify the cogitations, and the " *reins"* the affec-
tions.l*Henry Ainnaorth.*

rente 10.l" *Jfy defence it of God."* Literally, " *My shield is vpon God,"* like Psalm
Ixii. 8, "My salvation is *vpon Ood."* The idea maybe taken from the armour-bearer,
ever ready at hand to give the needed weapon to the warrior. *Andrew A. Honor.*

Verge 11.l" *Ood judgeth the righteous,"* etc. Maiiy learned disputes have arisen as
to the meaning of this verse ; and it must be confessed that its real import is by no
means easily determined : without the words written in italics, which are not iu the
original, it will read thus, " God judgeth the righteous, and God is angry every day."
The question still will be, is this a good rendering ? To this question it mny be replied,
that there is strong evidence for a contrary one. Ainsworth translates it, " God *is* a
just judge ; and God angrily threateneth every day." With this corresponds the reading
of Coverdale's Bible, " God is a righteous judge, and God is ever threatening." In
King Edward's Bible, of 1549, the reading is the same. But there is another class of
critics who adopt quite a different view of the text, and apparently with much colour
of argument. Bishop Horsley reads the verse, " God is a righteous judge, although
he is not angry every day." Ih this rendering he seems to have followed most of the
ancient versions. The Vulgate reads it, " God is a judge, righteous, strong, and patient;
will he be angry every day ?" The Septuagint reads it, " God is a righteous judge,
strong, and longsuffering ; not bringing forth his anger every day." The Syriac has it,"
God is the judge of righteousness ; he is not angry every day." In this view of the text
Dr. A. Clarke agrees, and -[::– it as his opinion that the text was first corrupted by the
Chaldeb. This learned divine proposes to restore the text thus, " /K, *el,* with the vowel
point *t&eri,* signifies God ; *i,, al,* the same letters, with the point *pathach,* signifies
not." There is by this view of the original no repetition of the divine name in the verse,
so that it will simply read, as thus restored, " God is a righteous judge, and is Not
angry every day." The text at large, as is intimated in the Vot-gate, Septuagint, and
some other ancient versions, conveys a strong intimation of the longsuffering of God,
whose hatred of sin isunchangeable, *it* whose anger against transgressors is marked
by infinite patience, and does not burst forth in vengeance every day.il*John Morison,
in ' An Exposition of the Book of Psalms,"* 1829.

Verte 11.l" *God it angry.'*1'1 The original expression hee is very forcible. The true
idea of it appears to be, to *froth* or *foam at the mouth* with indignation. *Richard Mant,
D.D.,* 1824.

Verses 11, 12.lGod hath set up his royal standard in defiance of all the sons and
daughters of apostate Adam, who from his own mouth are proclaimed rebels and
traitors to his crown and dignity ; and as against such he hath taken the field, as with
fire and sword, to be avenged on them. Yea, he gives the world sufficient testimony of
his incensed wrath, by that of it which is revealed from heaven daily in the judgments

executed upon sinners, and those many but of a span long, before they can show what nature they have by actual sin, yet crushed to death by God's righteous foot, only for the viperous kind of which they come. At every door where sin sets its foot, there the wrath of God meets us. Every faculty of soul, and member of body, are used as a weapon of unrighteousness against God ; so every one hath its portion of wrath, even to the tip of the tongue. As man is sinful all over, so is he cursed all over. Inside and outside, soul and body, is written all with woes and curses, so close and full, that there is not room for another to interline, or add to what God hath written.| *William OurnaU.*

Verses 11|13.|The idea of God's righteousness must have possessed great vigour to render euch a representation possible. There are some excellent remarks upon the ground of it in Luther, who, however, too much overlooks the fact, that the psalmist presents before his eyes this form of an angry and avenging God, primarily with the view of strengthening by its consideration his own hope, and pays too little regard to the distinction between the psalmist, who only indirectly teaches what he described as part of his own inward experience, and the prophet: "The prophet takes a lesson from a coarse huma a similitude, in order that he might inspire terror unto the ungodly. For he speaks against stupid and hardened people, who would not apprehend the reality of a divine judgment, of which he had just spoken ; but they might possibly be brought to consider this by greater earnestness on the part of man. Now, the prophet is not satisfied with thinking of the sword, but he adds thereto the bow ; even this does not satisfy him, but he describes how it is already stretched, and aim is taken, and the arrows are applied to it as here follows: 80 hard, stiff-necked, and unabashed are the ungodly, that however many threatenings may be urged against them, they will still remain unmoved. But in these words he forcibly describes how God's anger presses hard upon the ungodly, though they will never understand this until they actually experience it. It is also to be remarked here, that we have had so frightful a threatening and indignation against the ungodly in no Psalm before this ; neither has the Spirit of God attacked them with so many words. Then in the following verses, he also recounts their plans and purposes, shows how these shall not be in vain, but shall return again upon their own head. So that it clearly and manifestly appears to all those who suffer wrong and reproach, as a matter of consolation, that God hates such revilers and slanderers above all other characters."|*E. W. Hengstenberg, in lac.,* 1845.

Verse 12.|" *If he turn not,'"* etc. How few do believe what a quarrel Go hath with wicked men ? And that not only with the loose, but the formal and hypocritical also ? If we did we would tremble as much to be among them as to be in a house that is falling ; we would endeavour to " save" ourselves " from this untoward generation." The apostle would not so have adjured them, sci charged, so entreated them, had he not known the danger of wicked company. " *Ooil is angry with the vnclced every day* ;" *his low is bent, the arrows are on the string;* the instruments for their ruin are all prepared. And i.'t it safe to be there where the arrows of God are ready to fly about our eara ?How -was the apostle afraid to be in the bath with Cerlnthus ! " Depart," saith God by Moses, " from the tents of Korah, Dathan, and Abiram, lest ye be consumed in all their sins." How have the baskets of good figs suffered with the bad ! Is it not prejudicial to the gold to be with the dioss? Lot had bctn ruined by his neighbourhood to the Sodomites if God had not wrought wonderfully for his deliverance. Will you put God to work miracles to save you from your ungodly company ? It is dangerous being in the road with thieves whilst God's hue and cry of vengeance is at their backs. " A compHnion of fools shall be destroyed." The very beasts may instruct you to consult better for your security : the very deer are afraid of a wounded chased deer, and therefore for their preservation thrust him out of their company.*lLewis StucMey.*

Vense 12.l"If Tie turn not, he will whet his sword,'1'1 etc. The whetting of the sword is but to give n keener edge that it may cut the deeper. God is silent as long as the sinner will let him ; but when the sword is whet, it is to cut ; and when the bow is bent, it is to. kill ; and woe be to that man who is the butt.l *William Seeker.*

Verse 13.l"He hath also prepared for him the instruments of death; he ordaineth his arrows against the persecutors." It is said that God hath ordained his arrows against the persecutors ; the word signifies such as burn in anger and malice against the godly ; and the word translated *ordained,* signifies God hath wrought his arrows ; he doth not shoot them at random, but he works them against the wicked. Illiricus hath a story which may well be a commentary upon this text in both the parts of it. One Felix, Earl of Wartenberg, one of the captains of the Emperor Charles V., swore in the presence of divers at supper, that before he died he would ride up to the spurs in the blood of the Lutherans. Here was one that burned in malice, but behold how God works his arrows against him ; that very night the hand of God so struck him, that he was strangled and choked in his own blood ; so he rode not, but bathed himself, not up to the spurs, but up to the throat, not in the blood of the Lutherans, but in his own blood before he died.l*Jeremiah Burroughs.*

Verse 13.l" He ordaineth his arrows.'1'1 This might more exactly be rendered, " He maketh his arrows burning." This image would seem to be deduced from the use of fiery arrows.l*John Kitto,* 1804l1854.

Verte 14.l" Behold he travaileth with iniquity," etc. The words express the *conception, birth, carriage* and *miscarriage,* of a *plot* against David. In which you may consider :l(1.) What his *enemies* did. (2.) What *Ood* did. (8.) What *we all* should do : his enemies' *intention,* God's *prevention,* and our *duty ;* his enemies' intention, *he travaileth with iniquity, and conceireth mischief;* God's prevention, *he brought forth a lie;* our duty, *Behold* Observe the aggravation of the sin, *he conceweth.* He was not put upon it, or forced into it : it was voluntary. The more liberty we have not to sin, makes our sin the greater. He did not this in passion, but in cold blood. The less will, less sin.l*Richard Sills.*

Verse 14.l" He travaileth with iniquity, and hath conceited mischief." All note that conceiving is before travailing, but here travailing, as a woman in labour, gocth first ; the reason whereof is, that the wicked are so hotly set upon the evil which they maliciously intend, that they would be immediately acting of it if they could tell how, even before they have conceived by what means ; but in fine they bring forth but a lie, that is, they find that their own heaita lied to them, when they promised good success, but they had evil. For their haste to perpetrate mischief is intimated in the word rendered *"persecutors"* (verse 13), which properly signifieth *ardentes, burning;* that is, with a desire to do mischiefland this admits of no delay. A notable common-place, both setting forth the evil case of the wicked, especially attempting anything against the righteous, to move them to repentance|for thou hast God for thine enemy warring against thee, whose force thou canst not resist|and the greedy desire of the wicked to be evil, but their conception shall all prove abortive.|*J. Mayer, in loe.Verts* 14.|" *And hath brought forth fabehood."* Ever; sin is a lie.|*Augustine. Verte* 14. Earth's entertainment are like those of Joel,

Her left band brings me milk, her right, a nail."
Thomas Fuller.

Venn 14, 15.|" *They hat digged a pit far* ta"|and that low, unto hell| " *and are /alien into it themtdtet."*

" No joster law can be (Jerked or made.
Than tbat tin's agente fall by their own trade."

The order of hell proceeds with the same degrees ; though it (five a greater portion, yet still a just proportion, of torment. These wretched guests were too busy with the waters of sin ; behold, now they are in the depth of a pit, " where no water is." Dives, that wasted so many tuns of wine, cannot now procure water, not a pot of water, not a handful of water, not a drop of water, to cool his tongue. *Detideracit guttam, qui non dedit micam.* A just recompense ! He would not give a crumb ; he shall not have a drop. Bread hath no smaller fragment than a crumb, water no less fraction than a drop. As he denied the least comfort to Lazarus living, so Lazarus shall not bring him the least comfort dead. Thus the pain for sin answers the pleasure of sin. . . . Thus damnable sins shall have semblable punishments ; and as Augustine of the

tongue, so we may say of any member If it will not serve God in
action, it shall serve him in passion.|*Thomas Adam.*

Verse 15.|" *Bemadeapit, and digged it."* The practice of making pitfalls was an-ciently not only employed for ensnaring wild beasts, but was also a stratagem used against men by the enemy, in time of war. The idea, therefore, refers to a man who, having made such a pit, whether for man or beast, and covered it over so as completely to disguise the danger, did himself inadvertently tread on his own trap, and fall into the pit he had prepared for another.|*Pictorial Bible.*

Verse 16.|That most witty of commentators, Old Master Trapp, tells the following notable anecdote, in illustration of this verse :|That was a very remarkable instance of Dr. Story, who, escaping out of prison in Queen Elizabeth's days, got to Antwerp, and there thinking himself out of the reach of Go.i's rod, he got commission under the Duke of Alva to search all ships coming thither for English books. But one Parker, an English merchant, trading to Antwerp, laid his snare fair (saith our chronicler), to catch this foul bird, causing secret notice to be given to Story, that in his ship were stores of heretical books, with other intelligence that might stand him in stead. The Canonist conceiving that all was quite sure, hasted to the ship, where, with looks very big upon the poor mariners, each cabin, chest, and corner above-board were searched, and some things found to draw him further on : so that the hatches must be opened, which seemed to be unwillingly done, and great signs of fear were showed by their faces. This drew on the Doctor to descend into the hold, where now in the trap the mouse might well gnaw, but could not get out, for the hatches were down, and the sails hoisted up, which, with a merry gale, were blown into England, where ere long he was arraigned, and condemned of high treason, and accordingly executed at Tyburn, as he had well deserven.

Verse 16.|The story of Phalaris's bull, invented for the torment of others,

and serving afterwards for himself, is notorious in heathen story

It was a voluntary judgment which Archbishop Cranmer inflicted on himself when he thrust that very hand into the fire, and burnt it, with which he had signed to the popish articles, crying out, " *Ok, my unworthy right hand.*1" but who will deny that the hand of the Almighty was also concerned in it I| *William Turner in " Divine Judgments by way of Retaliation,"* 1607.

Verse 17.|To bless God for mercies is the way to increase them ; to bless him for miseries is the way to remove them : no good lives so long as that which is thankfully improved ; no evil dies so soon as that which is patiently endured.| *William Dyer.*

Aug. Horn. 7.

HINTS TO THE VILLAGE PREACHER.

Verse 1.|The necessity of faith when we address ourselves to God.   Show the worthlessness of prayer without trust in the Lord.

Verses 1, 2.|Viewed as a prayer for deliverance from all enemies, especially Satan the lion.

Verte 3.|Self-vindication before men.   When possible, judicious, or serviceable. "With remaiks upon the spirit in which it should be attempted.

Verte 4.|" *The best revenge.*" Evil for good is devil-like, evil for evil is beast-like, good for good is man-like, good for evil is God-like.

Verte 6.|How and in what sense divine anger may become the hope of the righteous. Fire fought by fire, or man's anger overcome by God's anger.

Verse 1.|" The congregation of the people." 1.   Who they are.   2.   Why they congregate together with one another. 8.   Where they congregate. 4.   Why they choose such a person to be the centre of their congregation.

Verse 7.|The gathering of the saints around the Lord Jesus.

Verse 7 *(fast clause).*|The coming of Christ to judgment for the good of his saints.

Verse 8.|The character of the Judge before whom we all must stand.

Verse 9 *(first clause).*|(1) By changing their hearts ; or (2) by restraining their wills, (3) or depriving them of power, (4) or removing them.   Show the times when, the reasons why, such a prayer should be offered, and how, iu the first sense, we may labour for its accomplishment.

Verne 9. |This verse contains two grand prayers, and a noble proof that the Lord can grant them.

Verse 9.|The period of sin, and the perpetuity of the righteous.|*Matthew Ilenry.*

Verte 9.|" *Establish the just.*" By what means and in what sense the just are established, or, the true established church.

Verse 9 *(last clause).* |God's trial of men's hearts.

Verse 10.|" *Upright in heart.*" Explain the character.

Verse 10.|The believer's trust in God, and God's care over him.   Show the action of faith in procuring defence and protection, and of that defence upon our faith by strengthening it, etc.

Verse 11.|The Judge, and the two persons upon their trial.

Verte 11 *(second clause).*|God's present, daily, constant, and vehement anger, against the wicked.

Verse 12.|See " Spurgeon's Sermons," No. 106. " Turn or Burn."

Verses 14, 15, 16.|Illustrate by three figures the devices and defeat of persecutors.

Verse 17.|The excellent duty of praise.

Verse 17.|View the verse in connection with the subject of the Psalm, and show how the deliverance of the righteous, and the destruction of the wicked are themes for song.

PSALM VIII.

.|"To the Chief Musician npon Gittith, a Fsalin of David." *We are not dear upon the meaning of the word Oittith. Some think it refers to Goth, and may refer to a tune commonly sung there, or an instrument of music there invented, or a song of Obededom the Oittite, in wlioxe house the ark rested, or, better still, a song sung over Goliath of Goth. Others, tracingthe Hebrew to its root, conceive it to mean a song for the winepress, a joyful hymn f or tlietreaders of grapes. The term Giitith is applied to two other Psalms,* (lixii. and lxxxiv.) *both of which, being of a joyous character, it may be concluded, that where we find that word in the title, we may look for a hymn of delight.*

We may style this Psalm the Song of the Astronomer: let us go abroad and sing it beneath the starry heavens at eventide, for it is very probable that in such a position, it first occurred to the poet's mind. Dr. Chalmers says, " There is much in the scenery of a *nocturnal sky, to lift Hie soul to pious contemplation. That moon, and these stars, what are Viey f They are detached from the world, and they lift us above it. We feel withdrawn from the earth, and rise in lofty abstraction from this little theatre of human passions and human anxieties. The mind abandons itself to reverie, and is transferred in the ewtasy of its thought to distant and unexplored regions. It sees nature in the simplicity of her great elements, and it sees the God of nature invested with the high attributes of wisdom and majesty."*

Division. | *The first and last verses are a sweet song of admiration, in which the excellence of the name of God is extolled. Tlie intermediate verses are made up of holy wonder at the Lord?s greatness in creation, and at his condescension towards man. Poole, in his annotations, has well said, " It is a great question among interpreters, whether this Psalm speaks of man in general, and of the honour which God puts upon him in his creation ; or only of* the man Christ Jesus. *Possibly both may be reconciled and put together, and the controversy, if rightly stated, may be ended, for the scope and business of this Psalm seems plainly to be t⁄iis : to display and celebrate the great love and kindness of God to mankind, not only in his creation, but especially in his redemption by Jesus Christ, whom, as he Vms man, he advanced to the honour and dominion here mentioned, that he might carry on his great and glorious work. Ho Christ* is the principal subject of this Psalm, and it is interpreted of him, both by our Lord himself *(Matt.* xxi. 16), *and by his holy apostle (I (Jor.* rv. 27 ; *Heb.* ii. 6, 7).

EXPOSITION.

LORD our Lord, how excellent *is* thy name in all the earth ! who hast set thy glory above the heavens.

Unable to express the glory of God, the Psalmist utters a note of exclamation. O Jehovah our Lord I We need not wonder at this, for no heart can measure, 4no tongue can utter, the half of the greatness of Jehovah. The whole creation is full of his glory and radiant with the excellency of his power ; his goodness and his wisdom are manifested on every hand. The countless myriads of terrestrial beings, from man the head, to the creeping worm at the foot, are all supported and nourished by the Divine bounty. The solid fabric of the universe leans upon his eternal arm. Universally is he present, and everywhere is his name excellent. God worketh ever and everywhere. There is no *place* where God ia not. The miracles of his power await us on all sides. Traverse the silent valleys where the rocks enclose you on either side, rising like the battlements of heaven till you can see but a strip of the blue sky far overhead ; you may be the only traveller who has passed through that glen ; the bird may start up affrighted, and the moss may tremble beneath the first tread of human foot; but God is there in a thousand wonders, upholding yon rocky barriers, fillingthe fl6wenrups with their perfume, and refreshing the lonely pines with the breath of his mouth. Descend, if you will, into the lowest depths of the ocean, where undisturbed the water sleeps, and the very sand is motionless in unbroken quiet, but the glory of the Lord is there, revealing its excellence in the silent palace of the sea. Borrow the wings of the morning and fly to the uttermost parts of the sea, but God is there. Mount to the highest heaven, or dive into the deepest hell, and God is in both hymned in everlasting song, or justified in terrible vengeance. Everywhere, and in every place, God dwells and is manifestly at work. Nor on earth alone is Jehovah extolled, for his brightness shines forth in the firmament above the earth. His glory exceeds the glory of the starry heavens ; above the region of the stars he hath set fast his everlasting throne, and there he dwells in light ineffable. Let us adore him "who alone spreadeth out the heavens, and treadeth upon the waves of the sea ; who maketh Arcturus, Orion, and Pleiades, and the chambers of the south." (Job ix. 8, 9.) We can scarcely find more fitting words than those of Nehenfiah, " Thou, even thou, art Lord alone ; thou hast made heaven, the heaven of heavens, with all their host, the earth, and all things that are therein, the seas, and all that is therein, and thou preservest them all; and the host of heaven worshippeth thee." Returning to the text we are led to observe that this psalm is addressed to God, because none but the Lord himself can fully know his own glory. The believing heart is ravished with what it sees, but God only knows the glory of God. What a sweetness lies in the little word *our,* how much is God's glory endeared to us when we consider our interest in him as our Lord. *How excellent is thy name !* no words can express that excellency ; and therefore it is left as a note of exclamation. The very *name* of Jehovah is excellent, what must his person be. Note the fact that even the heavens .cannot contain his glory, it is set *above the heavens,* since it is and ever must be too great for the creature to express. When wandering amid the Alps, we felt that the Lord was infinitely greater than all his grandest works, and under that feeling we roughly wrote these few lines :l

Tet in all these how great soe'er they be,
We see not Him. The glass Is all too dense
And dark, or else our earthborn eyes too dim.

Ton Alps, that lift their heads above the clouds
And hold familiar converse with the stars,
Are dust, at which the balance treroblcth not,
Compared with His divine immensity.
The snow-crown'd summits fail to s-et Him forth,
Who dwelleth in Eternity, and bears
Alone, the name of High and Lofty One.
Depths unfathomed are too shallow to express
The wisdom and the knowledge of the Lord.
The mirror of the creatures has no space
To bear the image of the Infinite.
'Tis true the Lord hath fairly writ his name,
And set his seal upon creation's brow.
But as the skilful potter much excels
The vessel which he fashions on the wheel,
E'en so, but in proportion greater far,
Jehovah's self transcends his noblest works.
Earth's ponderous wheels would break, her axles inap.
If freighted with the load of Deity.
Space is too narrow for the Eternal's rest,
And time too short a footstool for his throne.
E'en avalanche and thunder lack a voice,
To utter the full volume of his praise.
How then can I declare him ? Where are words
"With which my glowing tongue may speak his name ?
Silent I bow, and humbly I adore.

2 Out of the mouth of babes and sucklings hast thou ordained strength because of thine enemies, that thou mightest still the enemy and the avenger.

Nor only in the heavens above is the Lord seen, but the earth beneath is telling forth his majesty. In the sky, the massive orbs, rolling in their stupendous grandeur, are witnesses of his power in great things, while here below, the lisping utterances of babes are the manifestations of his strength in little ones. How often will children tell us of a God whom we have forgotten ! How doth their simple prattle refute those learned fools who deny the being of God ! Many men have been made to hold their tongues, while sucklings have borne witness to the glory of the God of heaven. It is singular how clearly the history of the church expounds this verse. Did not the children cry " Ho- sannah !" inthe temple, when proud Pharisees were silent and contemptuous ? and did not the Saviour quote these very words as a justification of their infantile cries ? Early church history records many amazing instances of the testimony of children for the truth of God, but perhaps more modern instances will be the most interesting. Fox tells us, in the Book of Martyrs, that when Mr. Lawrence was burnt in Colchester, he was carried to the fire in a chair, because, through the cruelty of the Papists, he could not stand upright, several young children came about the fire, and cried, as well as they could speak, "Lord, strengthen thy servant, and keep thy promise." God answered their prayer, for Mr. Lawrence died as firmly and calmly as any one could wish to breathe his last. When one of the Popish chaplains told Mr. Wishart, the great Scotch martyr, that he had a devil in him, a child that stood by cried out," A devil cannot speak such words as yonder man speaketh." One more instance is still nearer to our time. In a postscript to one of his letters, in which he details his persecution when first preaching in Moorfields, Whitfield says, " I cannot help adding that several little boys and girls, who were fond of sitting round me on the pulpit while I preached, and handed to me people's notes|though they were often pelted with eggs, dirt, &c., thrown at me|never once gave way ; but on the contrary, every time I was struck, turned up their little weeping eyes, and seemed to wish they could receive the blows for me. God make them, in their growing years, great and living martyrs for him who, out of the mouths of .babes and sucklings, perfects praise 1" He who delights iu the nong8 of angels is pleased to honour himself in the eyes of his enemies by the praises of little children. What a contrast between the glory above the heavens, and the mouths of babes and sucklings ! yet by both the name of God is made excellent.

3 When I consider thy heavens, the work of thy fingers, the moon and the stars, which thou hast ordained ;

4 What is man, that thou art mindful of him ? and the son of man, that thou visitest him ?

At the close of that excellent little manual entitled "The Solar System," written by Dr. Dick, we find an eloquent passage which beautifully expounds tho text : | A survey of the solar system has a tendency to moderate the pride of man and to promote humility. Pride is one of the distinguishing characteristics of puny man, and has been one of the chief causes of all the contentions, wars, devastations, systems of slavery, and ambitious projects which have desolated and demoralized our sinful world. Yet there is no disposition more incongruous to the character and circumstances of man. Perhaps there are no rational beings throughout the universe among whom pride would appear more unseemly or incompatible than in man, considering the situation in which he is placed. He is exposed to numerous degradations and calamities, to the rage of storms and tempests, the devastations of earthquakes and volcanoes, the fury of whirlwinds, and the tempestuous billows of the ocean, to the ravages of thesword, famine, pestilence, and numerous diseases ; and at length he must sink into the grave, and his body must become the companion of worms ! The most dignified and haughty of the sons of men are liable to these and similar degradations as well as the meanest of the human family. Yet, in such circumstances, man|that puny worm of the dust, whose knowledge is so limited, and whose follies are so numerous and glaring|has the effrontery to strut in all the haughtiness of pride, and to glory in his shame.

When other arguments and motives produce little effect on certain minds, no considerations seem likely to have a more powerful tendency to counteract this deplorable propensity in human beings, than those which are borrowed from the objects connected with astronomy. They show us what an insignificant being| what a mere atom, indeed, man appears amidst the immensity of creation ! Though he is an object of the paternal care and mercy of the Most High, yet be is but as a grain of sand to the whole earth, when compared to the countless myriads of beings that people the amplitudes of creation. What is the whole of this globe on which we dwell compared with the solar system, which contains a mass of matter ten thousand times greater ? What is it in comparison of the hundred millions of suns and worlds which by the telescope have been descried throughout the starry regions ? What, then, is a kingdom, a province, or a baronial territory, of which we are as proud as if we were the lords of the universe And for which we engage in so much devastation and carnage ? What are they, when set in competition with the glories of the sky ? Could we take our station on the lofty pinnacles of heaven, and look down on this scarcely distinguishable speck of earth, we should be ready to exclaim with Seneca, "Is it to this little spot that the great designs and vast desires of men are confined ? Is it for this there is so much disturbance of nations, so much carnage, and so many ruinous wars ? Oh, the folly of deceived men, to imagine great kingdoms in the compass of an atom, to raise armies to decide a point of earth with the sword I" Dr. Chalmers, in his Astronomical Discourses, very truthfully says, " We gave you but a feeble image of our comparative insignificance, when we said that the glories of an extended forest would suffer no more from the fall of a single leaf, than the glories of this extended universe would suffer though the globe we tread upon, ' and all that it inherits, should dissolve.' "

5 For thou hast made him a little lower than the angels, and hast crowned him with glory and honour.

6 Thou madest him to have dominion over the works of thy hands ; thou hast put all *things* under his feet :

7 All sheep and oxen, yea, and the beasts of the field ;

8 The fowl of the air, and the fish of the sea, *and whatsoever* passeth through the paths of the sea.

These verses may set forth man's position among the creatures before he fell; but as they are, by the apostle Paul, appropriated to man as represented by the Lord Jesus, it is best to give most weight to that meaning. In order of dignity, man stood next to the angels, and a little lower than they ; in the Lord Jesus this was accomplished, for he was made a little lower than the angels by the suffering of death. Man in Eden had the full command of all creatures, and they came before him to receive their names as an act of homage to him as the vicegerent of God to them. Jesus in his glory, is now Lord, not only of all living, but of all created things, and, with the exception of him who put all things under him, Jesus is Lord of all, and his elect, in him, are raised to a dominion wider than that of the first Adam, as shall be more clearly seen at his coming. Well might the Psalmist wonder at the singular exaltation of man in the scale of being, when he marked his utter nothingness in comparison with tne starry universe.

Thou modest him a little lower than the angels|a little lower in nature, since they are immortal, and but a little, because time is short; and when that is over,saints are no longer lower than the angels. The margin reads it, " A little while inferior to." *Thou erownest him.* The dominion that God has bestowed on man is a great *glory and honour* to him ; fur all dominion is honour, and the highest is that which wears the crown. A full list is given of the subjugated creatures, to show that all the dominion lost by sin is restored in Christ Jesus. Let none of us permit the possession of any earthly creature to be a snare to us, but let us remember that we are to reign over them, and not to allow them to reign over us. Under our feet we must keep the world, and we must shun that base spirit which is content to let worldly cares and pleasures sway the empire of the immortal soul.

9 O LORD our Lord, how excellent is thy name in all the earth !

Here, like a good composer, the poet returns to his key-note, falling back, as it were, into his first state of wondering adoration. What he started with as a proposition in the first verse, he closes with as a well proven conclusion, with a sort of *quod erat demonstrandum.* O for grace to walk worthy of that excellent name which has been named upon us, and which we are pledged to magnify :

EXPLANATORY NOTES AND QUAINT SAYINGS.

Title.|" Gittith, " was probably a musical instrument used at their rejoicings after the vintage. The vintage closed the civil year of the Jews, and this Psalm directs us to the latter-day glory, when the Lord shall be King over all the earth, having subdued all his enemies. It is very evident that the vintage was adopted as a figurative representation of the final destruction of all God's enemies. Isaiah Ixiii. 1|6 ; Rev. xix. 18|20. The ancient Jewish interpreters so understood this Psalm, and apply it to the mystic vintage. We may then consider this interesting composition as a prophetic anticipation of the kingdom of Christ, to be established in glory and honour in the " world to come," the habitable world. Heb. ii. 5. We see not yet all things put under his feet, but we are sure that the Word of God shall be fulfilled, and every enemy, Satan, death, and hell, shall be for ever subdued and destroyed, and creation itself delivered from the bondage of corruption into the glorious liberty of the children of God. Rom. viii. 17|23. In the use of this Psalm, then, we anticipate that victory, and in the praise we thus celebrate, we go on from strength to strength, till, with him who is our glorious Head, we appear in Zion before God.|*W. Wilson, D.D., in loc.*

*Whole Psalm.|*Now, consider but the scope of the Psalm, as the apostle quoteth it to prove the world to come. Heb. ii. Any one that reads the Psalm would think that the psalmist doth but set forth old Adam in his kingdom, in his paradise, made a little lower than the angels|for we have spirits wrapped up in flesh and blood, whereas they are spirits simply|a degree lower, as if they were dukes, and we marquises ; one would think, I say, that this were all his meaning, and that it is applied to Christ but by way of allusion. But the truth is, the apostle bringeth it in to prove and to convince these Hebrews, to whom he wrote, that that Psalm was meant of Christ, of that man whom they expected to be the Messiah, the Man Christ Jesus. And that he doth it, I prove by the sixth verse| it is the observation that Beza hath|" One in a certain place," quoting David, *6itjjLa.prvpa.ro,* hath testified ; so we may translate it, hath testified it, *etiam atque etiam,* testified most expressly ; he bringeth an express proof for it that it was meant of the Man Christ Jesus ; therefore it is not an allusion. And indeed it was Beziv that did first begin that interpretation that I read of, and himself

5

SECTION 5

therefore doth excuse it and make an apology for it, that he diverteth out of the common road, though since many others have followed him.

Xow the scope of the Psalm *is* plainly this : in Rom. v. 14, you read that Adam -was a type of him that was to come. Now in Psalm viii., you find there Adam's -world, the type of a world to come ; he was the first Adam, and had a world, so the second Adam hath a world also appointed for him ; there is his oxen and his sheep, and the fowls of the air, whereby are meant other things, devils perhaps, and wicked men, the prince of the air ; as by the heavens there, the angels, or the apostles rather|" the heavens declare the glory of God ;" that is applied to the apostles, that were preachers of the gospel.

To make this plain to you, that that Psalm where the phrase is used, " All things under his feet," and quoted by the apostle in Eph. i. 22|therefore it 5s proper|was not meant of man in innocency, but of the Messiah, the Lord Jesus Christ; and therefore, answerably, that the world there is not this world, but a world on purpose made for this Messiah, as the other was for Adam.

First, it was not meant of man in innocency properly and principally. Why ? Because in the first verse he saith, " Out of the mouths of babes and sucklings hast thou ordained strength." There were no babes in the time of Adam's innocency, he fell before there were any. Secondly, he addeth, " That thou mightest still the enemy and the avenger ;" the devil that is, for he showed himself the enemy there, to be a manslayer from the beginning. God would use man to still him ; alas ! he overcame Adam presently. It must be meant of another therefore, one that is able to still this enemy and avenger.

Then he saith, " How excellent is thy name in all the earth ! who hast set thy glory above the heavens." Adam had but paradise, he never propagated God's name over all the earth ; he did not continue so long before he fell as to beget sons ; much less did he found it in the heavens.

Again, verse 4, "What is man, and the son of man ?" Adam, though he was man, yet he was not the son of man ; he is called indeed, " the son of God " (Luke iii. 38), but he was riot *jttius fuiminis.* I remember Ribera urgeth that.

But take an argument the apostle, himself useth to prove it. This man, saith he, must have all subject to him ; all but God, saith he ; he must have the angels subject to him, for he hath put all principalities and powers under his feet, saith he. This could not be Adam, it could not be the man that had this world in a state of innocency ; much less had Adam all under his feet. No, my brethren, it was too great a vassalage for Adam to have the creatures thus bow to him. But they are thus to Jesus Christ, angels and all; they are all under his feet, he is far above them.

Secondly, it is not meant of man fallen, that is as plain ; the apostle himself saith so. " We see not," saith he, " all things subject unto him." Some think that it is meant as an objection that the apostle answereth ; but it is indeed to prove that man fallen cannot be meant in Psalm viii. Why 9 Because, saith he, we do not see anything, all things at least, subject unto him ; you have not any one man, or the whole race of man, to whom all things have been subject; the creatures are sometimes injurious to him. We do not see him, saith he ; that is, the nature of man in general considered. Take all the monarchs in the world, they never conquered the whole world ; there was never any one man that was a sinner that had all subject to him. " But we see,1' saith he|mark the opposition|"but we see Jesus," that Man, " crowned with glory and honour;" therefore, it is this Man, and no man else ; the opposition implieth it." . . . . So now it remaineth, then, that it is only Christ, God-man, that is meant in Psalm viii. And indeed, and in truth, Christ himself interpreted the Psalm *ot* himself ; you have two witnesses to confirm it, Christ himself and the apostle. Matt. xxi. 16. When they cried hosanna to Christ, or "save now," and made him the Saviour of the world, the Pharisees were angry, our Saviour confuteth them by this very Psalm : ': Have ye not read," saith he, " out of the mouths of babes and sucklings thou hast perfected praise ?" He quoteth this very Psalmwhich speaks of himself -, and Paul, by his warrant, and perhaps from that hint, doth thus argue out of it, and convince the Jews by it.|*Thomas Goodwin.*

Verne 1.|" Hnw excellent it thy name in all the earth!" How illustrious is the name of Jesus throughout the world ! His incarnation, birth, humble arid obscure life, preaching, miracles, passion, death, resurrection, and ascension, arc celebrated through the whole world. His religion, the gifts and graces of his Spirit, his people|Christians, his gospel, and the preachers of it, are everywhere spoken of. No name is so universal, no power and influence so generally felt, as those of the Saviour of mankind. Amen.|*Adam Clarke.*

Verse I.|" *Above tlie heavens;"* not in the heavens, but " *abate the heatens ;""* even greater, beyond, and higher than they ; " angels, principalities, and powers, being made subject unto him." As Paul says, he hath " ascended up far above all heavens." And with this his glory above the heavens is connected, his sending forth his name upon earth through his Holy Spirit. As the apostle adds in this passage, " He hath ascended up far above all heavens ; and he gave some apostles." And thus here: "Thy name excellent in all the world ;" " Thy glory above the heavens."|*Isaac Williams.*

Verse 2.|" *Out of the mouth of lobes and sucklings hast thou ordained ttrcrigtli,'*1" etc. In a prophetical manner, speaking of that which was to be done by children m/wiy hundreds of years after, for the asserting of his infinite mercy in sending his Sn Jesus Christ into the world to save us from our sins. For so the Lord applieth their crying, " Hosannah to the Son of David " in the temple. And thus both Basil and other ancients, and some new writers also understand it. But Calvin will have it meant of God's wonderful providing for them, by turning their mothers' blood into milk, and giving them the faculty to suck, thus nourishing and preserving them, which sufficiently convinceth all gainsayers of God's wonderful providence towards the weakest and most shiftless of all creatures.|*John Afuyer,* 1853.

Verse 2.|Who are these " *babes and tucklings"?* 1. Man in general, who epringeth from so weak and poor a beginning as that of babes and sucklings, yet is at length advanced to such power as to grapple with, and overcome the enemy and the avenger. 2. David in particular, who being but a ruddy youth, God used him as an instrument to discomfit Goliath of Gath. 3. More especially our Lord Jesm Christ, who assuming our nature and all the sinless infirmities of it, and submitting to the weakness of an infant, and after dying is gone in the same nature to reign in heaven, till he hath brought all his enemies under his feet. Psalm ex. 1., and 1 Cor. xv. 27. Then was our human nature exalted above all other creatures, when the Son of God was made of a woman, carried in the womb. 4. The apostles, who to outward appearance were despicable, in a manner children and sucklings in comparison of the great ones of the world ; poor despised creatures, yet principal instruments of God's service and glory. Therefore 'tis notable, that when Christ glorifieth his Father for the wise and free dispensation of his saving grace (Matt. xi. 25), he saith, " I thank thee, O Father, Lord of heaven and earth, because thou hast hid these things from the wise and prudent, and hast revealed them unto babes," so called from the meanness of their condition. . . . And you shall see it was spoken when the disciples were sent abroad, and had power given them over unclean spirits. " In that hour Jesus rejoiced in spirit, and said, I thank thee. O Father, Lord of heaven and earth, that thou hast hid these things from the wise and prudent, and hast revealed them unto babes." This he acknowledged to be an act of infinite condescension in God. 5. Those children that cried *Hosanna* to Christ, make up part of the sense, for Christ defendeth their practice by this Scripture. ... 0. Not only the apostles, but all those that fight under Christ's banner, and are listed into his confederacy, may be called babes and sucklings ; first, because of their condition; secondly, their disposition. . . .

1. Because of their condition God in the government of the world is

pleased to subdue the enemies of his kingdom by weak: and despised instruments. -. Because of their disposition : they are most humble spirited. We are told (Matt, xviii. 3), "Except ye be converted, and become as little children," etc. As if he had said, you strive for pre-eminence and worldly greatness in my kingdom ; I tell you my kingdom is a kingdom of babes, and containeth none but the humble, and such as are little in their own eyes, and are contented to be small and despised in the eyes of others, and so do not seek after great matters in the world. A young child knoweth not what striving or state meaneth, and therefore by an emblem and visible representation of a child set in the midst of them, Christ would take them off from the expectation of a carnal kingdom. | *Thomas Manton,* 1620|1077.

Verfe 2.|" *That thou mightest still the enemy and the avenger.'*1" This very confusion and revenge upon Satan, who was the cause of man's fall, was aimed at by God at first ; therefore is the first promise and preaching of the gospel to Adam brought in rather in sentencing him than in speaking to Adam, that the seed of the woman should break the serpent's head, it being in God's aim as much to confound him as to save poor man. | *Thomas Ooodwin.*

Verse 2.|The work that is done in love loses half its tedium and difficulty. It is as with a stone, which in the air and on the dry ground we strain at but cannot stir. Flood the field where it lies, bury the block beneath the rising water ; and now, when its head is submerged, bend to the work. Put your strength to it. Ah ! it moves, rises from its bed, rolls on before your arm. So, when under the heavenly influences of grace the tide of love rises, and goes swelling over our duties and difficulties, a child can do a man's work, and a man can do a giant's. Let love be present in the heart, and " *out of the moutht ofbabef and sucklings* God ordaineth strength."|*Thomtu Outhrie, D.D.*

Verne 2.|" *Out of the mouth of babes and sucklings,"* etc. That poor martyr, Alice Driver, in the presence of many hundreds, did so silence Popish bishops, that she and all blessed God that the proudest of them could not resist the spirit in a silly woman ; so I say to thee, " *Out of the mouth of kibes and suct- lingt"* God will be honoured. Even thou, silly worm, shalt honour him, when it shall appear what God hath done for thee, what lusts he hath mortified, aud what graces he hath granted thee. The Lord can yet do greater things for thee if thou wilt trust him. He can carry thee upon eagles' wings, enable thee to bear and suffer strong affliction for him, to persevere to the end, to live by faith, and to finish thy course with joy. Oh 1 in that he hath made thee low in heart, thy other lowness shall be so much the more honour to thee. Do not all as much and more wonder at God's rare workmanship in the ant, the poorest bug that creeps, as in the biggest elephant ? That so many parts and limbs should be united in such a little space ; that so poor a creature should provide in the summer-time her winter food ? Who sees not as much of God in a bee as in a greater creature ? Alas ! in a great body we look for great abilities and wonder not. Therefore, to conclude, seeing God hath clothed thy uncomely ' parts with the more honour, bless God, and bear thy baseness more equally ; thy greatest glory is yet to come, that when the wise of the world have rejected the counsel of God, thou hast (with those poor publicans and soldiers), magnified the ministry of the gospel. Surely the Lord will also be admired in thee (1 Thess. i.), a poor silly creature, that even thou wert made wise to salvation and believest in that day. Be still poor in thine own eyes, and the Lord will make thy proudest scornful enemies to worship at thy feet, to confess God hath done much for thee, and wish thy portion when God shall visit them.|*Daniel Sogert,* 1643.

Verse 3.|" When I consider." Meditation fits for humiliation. When David had been contemplating the works of creation, their splendour, harmony, notion, influence, he lets the plumes of pride fall, and begins to have self- abasing thoughts. " *When I consider thy heavens, the work of thy fingers, themom and the stars which thou hast ordained, uhat it man that thou art mindful of him .'"|Thomas Walton.*

Verte 3.|" When I consider thy heavens," etc. David surveying the firmament, broke forth into this consideration : " *When I consider thy tiearen, tff work of thy fingers, t/te moon and the Stan, which thou hast* era/to/, *ichat i man..'"* etc. How cometh he to mention the moon and stars, and omit the sun ? the other being but his pensioners, shining with that exhibition of light which the bounty of the sun allots them. It is answered, this was David's night meditation, when the sun, departing to the other world, left the lesser lights only visible in heaven ; and as the sky is best beheld by day in the glory thereof, so too it is best surveyed by night in the variety of the same. Night was made for man to rest in. But when I cannot sleep, may I, with the psalmist, entertain my waking with good thoughts. Not to use them as opium, to invite my corrupt nature to slumber, but to bolt out bad thoughts, which otherwise would possess my soul. | *Thomas Fuller,* 1608|1061.

Verse 3.|" Thy heavens." The carnal mind sees God in nothing, not even in spiritual things, his word and ordinances. The spiritual mind sees him in everything, even in natural things, in looking on the heavens and the earth and all the creatures|" Thy *heavens;"* sees all in that notion, in their relation to God as his work, and in them his glory appearing ; stands in awe, fearing to abuse his creatures and his favours to his dishonour. " *The day is thine, and the night also is thine* ;" therefore ought not I to forget thee through the day, nor in the night.|*Robert Leighton, D.D.*

Verse 3.|" The stars." I cannot say that it is chiefly the contemplation of their infinitude, and the immeasurable space they occupy, that enraptures me in the stars. These conditions rather tend to confuse the mind ; and in this view of countless numbers and unlimited space there lies, moreover, much that belongs rathur to a temporary and human than to an eternally abiding consideration. Still less do I regard them absolutely with reference to the life after this. But the mere thought they are so far beyond and above everything terrestrial|the feeling, that before them everything earthly so utterly vanishes to nothing|that the single man is so infinitely insignificant in the comparison with these worlds strewn over all space|that his destinies, his enjoyments, and sacrifices, to which he attaches such a minute importance|how all these fade like nothing .before such immense objects ; then, that the constellations bind together all the races of man, and all the eras of the earth, that they have beheld all that has passed since the beginning of time, and will see all that passes until its end ; in thoughts like these I can always lose myself with a silent delight in the view of the starry firmament. It is, in very truth, a spectacle of the highest solemnity, when, in the stillness of night, in a heaven quite clear, the stars, like a choir of worlds, arise and descend, while existence, as it were, falls asunder into two separate parts ; the one, belonging to earth, grows dumb in the utter silence of night, and thereupon the other mounts upward in all its elevation, splendour, and majesty. And, when contemplated from this point of view, the starry heavens have truly a moral influence on the mind.|*Alexander Vo Humlmldt,* 1850.

Verse 3.|" *When I consider thy heavens,* " etc. Could we transport ourselves above the moon, could we reach the highest star above our heads, wo should instantly discover new skies, new stars, new suns, new systems, and perhaps more magnificently adorned. But even there, the vast dominions of our great Creator would not terminate ; we should then find, to our astonishment, that we had only arrived at the borders of the works of God. It is but little that we can know of his works, but that little should teach us to be humble, and to admire the divine power and goodness. How great must that Being be who produced these immense globes out of nothing, who regulates their courses, and whose mighty hand directs and supports them all 1 What is the clod of earth which we inhabit, with all the magnificent scenes it presents to us, in comparison of those innumerable worlds ? Were this earth annihilated, its absencewould no more be observed than that of a grain of sand from the sea shore. "What then are provinces and kingdoms -when compared -with those -worlds ? They are but atoms duncing in the air, which are discovered to us by the sunbeams. What then am I, when reckoned among the infinite number of God's creatures ? I am lost in mine own nothingness ! But little as I appear in this respect, I find myself great in others. There is great beauty in thisstairy firmament which God has chosen for his throne ! How admirable arc those celestial bodies ! I am dazzled with their splendour, and enchanted with their beauty ! But notwithstanding this, however beautiful, and however richly adorned, yet this sky is void of intelligence. It is a stranger to its own beauty, while I, who am mere clay, moulded by a divine hand, am endowed with sense and reason. I can contemplate the beauty of these shining worlds ; nay, more, I am already, to a certain degree, acquainted with their sublime Author ; and by faith I see some small rays of his divine glory. O may I be more and more acquainted with his works, and make the study of them my employ, till by a glorious change I rise to dwell with him above the starry regions. | *Chrutojilier Cfinttian Sturm's* " *Reflections,*" 1750|1780.

Verte 8.|" *Work of God's fingtrs.*" That is most elaborate and accurate : a metaphor from embroiderers, or from them that make tapestry.|*John Trapp.*

Verse 3.|" *When I consider thy heat-ens,* " etc. It is truly a most Christian exercise to extract a sentiment of piety from the works and the appearances of nature. It has the authority of the sacred writers upon its side, and even our Saviour himself gives it the weight and the solemnity of his example. " Behold the lilies of the field ; they toil not, neither do they spin, yet your heavenly Father careth for them." He expatiates on the beauty of a single flower, and draws from it the delightful argument of confidence in God. He gives us to see that taste may be combined with piety, and that the same heart may be occupied with all that is serious in the contemplations of religion, nnd be at the same time alive to the charms and the loveliness of nature. The psalmist takes a still loftier flight. He leaves the world, and lifts his imagination to that mighty expanse which spreads above it and around it. He wings his way through space, and wanders in thought over its immeasurable regions. Instead of a dark and unpeopled solitude, he sees it crowded with splendour, and filled with the energy of the divine presence. Creation rises in its immensity before him, and the world, with all which it inherits, shrinks into littleness at a contemplation so vast and so overpowering. He wonders that he is not overlooked amid the grandeur and the variety which are on every side of him ; and, passing upward from the majesty of nature to the majesty of nature's Architect, he exclaims, " What is man, that thou art mindful of him, or the son of man that thou shouldest deign to visit him ?" It is not for us to say whether inspiration revealed to the psalmist the wonders of the modern astronomy. But, even though the mind be a perfect stranger to the science of these enlightened times, the heavens present a great and an elevating spectacle, an immense concave reposing upon the circular boundary of the world, and the innumerable lights which are suspended from on high, moving with solemn regularity along its surface. It seems to have been at night that the piety of the psalmist was awakened by this contemplation ; when the moon and the stars were visible, and not when the sun had risen in his strength and thrown a splendour around him, which bore down nnd eclipsed all the lesser glories of the firmament.|*Thoma Cfuilnurt, D.D.,* 1817. *Verte* 3.|" *Thy heavens* ":|

Tliis prospect vast, what is it ?|woigh'd aright,
'Tis nature's system of divinity,
And every student of the nielli inspires.
'Tis elder Scripture, writ by God's own hand :
Scripture authcutic ! uncorrupt by num. *Edward J oung-*

Verte 3.|" *The itars.'* " When I gazed into these stars, have they not looked down on me as if with pity from their serene spaces, like eyes glistening with heavenly tears over the little lot of man !|*Thomas Carlyte.*

Yertet 3, 4.|" *When I consider thy heavens,*" etc. Draw spiritual inferencesfrom occasional objects. David did but wisely consider the heavens, and lie breaks out into self-abasement and humble admirations of God. Glean matter of insiruction to yourselves, and praise to your Maker from everything you see ; it will be u degree of restoration to a state of innocency, since this was Adam's task in paradise. Dwell not upon any created object only as a *virtuoso,* to gratify your rational curiosity, but as a Christian, call leligion to the feast, anil make a spiritual improvement. No creature can meet our eyes but affurds us lessons worthy of our thoughts, besides the general notices of the power anil wisdom of the Creator. Thus may the sheep read us a lesson of patience, the dove of innocence, the ant and bee raise blushes in us for our sluggishness, and

the stupid ox and dull ass correct and shame our ungrateful ignorance

He whose eyes are open cannot want an instructor, unless he wants a heart.| *Stephen Charnock.*

Verted.|" *What is man that than art mindful of him?*" etc. My readers must be careful to mark the design of the psalmist, which is to enhance, by this comparison, the infinite goodness of God ; for it is, indeed, a wonderful thing that the Creator of heaven, whose glory is so surpassingly great as to ravish us with the highest admiration, condescends so far as graciously to take upon him the care of the human race. That the psalmist makes this contrast may be inferred from the Hebrew word BnJX, enOsh, which we have rendered *man,* and which expresses the frailty of man rather than any strength or power

which he possesses Almost all interpreters render HpS, *pukad,* the last word of this verse, *to visit;* and I am unwilling to differ from them, since this sense suits the passage very well. But as it sometimes signifies *to remember,* and as we will often find in the Psalms the repetition of the same thought indifferent words, it may here be very properly translated *to remember;* as if David had said, "This is a marvellous thing, that God thinks upon men, and remembers them continually."|*John Calvin,* 1509|1564.

*Verse 4.|" What is man?'*1" But, O God, what a little lord hast thou made over this great world ! The least corn of sand is' not so small to the whole earth, as man is to the heaven. "When I see the heavens, the sun, the moon, and stars, O God, what is man ? Who would think thou shouldst make all these creatures for one, and that one well-near the least of all ? Yet none but he can see what thou hast done ; none but he can admire and adore thee in what he seeth : how had he need to do nothing but this, since he alone must do it 1 Certainly the price and value of things consist not in the quantity ; one diamond is worth more than many quarries of stone ; one loadstone hath more virtue than mountains of earth! It is lawful for us to praise thce in ourselves. All thy creation hath not more wonder in it than one of us : other creatures thou madest by a simple command ; Man, not without a divine consultation : others at once ; man thou didst form, then inspire : others in several shapes, like to none but themselves ; man, after thine own image : others with qualities fit for service ; man, for dominion. Man had his name from -thee they had their names from man. How should we be consecrated to thce above all others, since thou hast bestowed more cost on us than other!|*Joseph Hall, D.D., Bishop of Norwich,* 1574|1656.

Verse 4.|" What is man, that thou art mindful of him? or the son of man, that thou shouldst visit him?" And (Job vii. 17, 18) " What is man, that thou ehouldst magnify him ? and that thou shouldst set thy heart upon him ? and that thou shouldst visit him every morning?" Man, in the pride of his heart, secth no such great matter in it; but a humble soul is filled with astonishment. " Thus saith the high and lofty One that inhabiteth eternity, whose name is Holy ; I dwell in the high and holy place, with him also that is of a contrite and humble spirit, to revive the spirit of the humble, and to revive the heart of the contrite ones." Isaiah Ivii. 15. Oh, saith the humble soul, will the Lord have respect unto such a vile worm as I am ? Will the Lord acquaint himself with such a sinful wretch as I am ? Will the Lord open his arms, his bosom.bis heart to me ? Shall such a loathsome creature as I find favour in his eyes ? In Ezek. xvi. 1|5, we have a relation of the wonderful condescension of God to man, who is there resembled to a wretched infant cast out in the day of its birth, in its blood and filthiness, no eye pitying it ; such loathsome creatures are we before God ; and yet when he passed by, and saw us polluted in our blood, he said unto us, "Live." It is doubled because of the strength of its nature; it was "the time of love" (verse 8). This was love indeed, that God should take a filthy, wretched thing, and spread his skirts over it, and cover its nakedness and swear unto it, and enter into a covenant with it, and make it his ; that is, that he should espouse this loathsome thing to himself, that he would be a husband to it; this is love unfathomable, love inconceivable, self-principle love ; this is the love of God to man, for God is love. Oh, the depth of the riches of the bounty and goodness of God ! How is his love wonderful, and his grace past finding out ! How do you find and feel your hearts affected upon the report of these things ? Do you not see matter of admiration and cause of wonder ? Are you not as it were launched forth into an ocean of goodness, where you can see no shore, nor feel no bottom ? Ye may make a judgment of yourselves by the motions and affections that ye feel in yourselves at the mention of this. For thus Christ judged of the faith of the centurion that said unto him, "Lord, I am not worthy that thou shoiildst come under my roof. When Jesus heard this, he marvelled, and said to them thai followed him, I say unto you, I have not found so great fuith, no, not in Israel." Matthew viii. 8|10. If, then, you feel not your souls mightily affected with this condescension of God, say thus unto your souls, What aileth thee, O my soul, that thou art no more affected with the goodness of God ? Art thou dead, that thou canst not feel ? Or art thou blind, that thou canst not see thyself compassed about with astonishing goodness ? Behold the King of glory descending from the habitation of his majesty, and coming to visit thee ! Hearest not thou his voice, saying, " Open to me, my sister : behold, I stand at the door and knock. Lift up yourselves, O ye gates, and be ye lifted up, ye everlasting doors, that the King of glory may come in " ? Behold, O my soul, how he waits still while thou hast refused to open to him ! Oh, the wonder of his goodness ! Oh, the condescension of his love, to visit me, to sue unto me, to wait upon me, to be acquainted with me ! Thus work up your souls into an astonishment at the condescension of God.|*James Jancway,* 1674.

Versed.|*Man,* in Hebrew|infirm or miserable man|by which it is apparent that he speaks of man not according to the state of his creation, but as fallen into a state of sin, and misery, and mortality. *Art mindful of Mm, i.e.,* carest (or him, and conferrest such high favours upon him. *The son of man,* Heb., *the ton of Adam,* that great apostate from and rebel against God ; the sinful son of a sinful father|his son by likeness of disposition and manners, no less than by procreation ; all which tends to magnify the divine mercy. *That thou tkilett him*|not in anger, as that word is sometimes used, but with thy grace and mercy, as it if taken in Gen. xxi. 1 ; Ex. iv. 31 ; Psalm Ixv. 9 ; cvi. 4 ; cxliv. 3.

Verie 4.|" *What is* mare?" The Scripture gives many answers to this qnestion. Ask the prophet Isaiah, " *What i man?"* and he answers (xl. 6), man is " grass"|" All flesh is grass, and all the goodliness thereof is as the flower f the field." Ask David, " *What is man?"* He answers (Psalm Ixii. 9), man is "a &," not a liar only, or a deceiver, but "a *lie,"* and a deceit. All the answers the Holy Ghost gives concerning man, are to humble man : man is ready to flatter himself, and one man to flatter another, but God tells us plainly

'hat we are It is a wonder that God should vouchsafe a gracious

look upon such a creature as man ; it is wonderful, considering the distance between God and man, as man is a creature and God the creator. " *What is* ""m," that God should take notice of him ? Is he not a clod of earth, a piece of clay? But consider him as a sinful and an unclean creature, and we may Bonder to amazement: what is an unclean creature that God should magnifyhim ? Will the Lord indeed put value upon filthiness, and fix his approving eye upon an impure thing *1* One step further ; what is rebellious man, man an enemy to God, that God should magnify him I what admiration can answer this question ? Will God prefer his enemies, and magnify those who would cast him 'down ? Will a prince exalt a traitor, or give him honour who attempts to take away his life ? The sinful nature of man is an enemy to the nature of God, and would pull God out of heaven ; yet God even at that time is raising man to heaven : sin would lessen the great God, and yet God greatens sinful man.|*Joseph Caryl.*

Versed.|" *What i man?"* Oh, the grandeur and littleness, the excellence and the corruption, the majesty and meanness of man 1|*Pascal, 1623|1662.*

Versed.|" *Thou visitest* Aiwi." To visit is, first, to afflict, to chasten, yea, to punish ; the highest judgments in Scripture come under the notions of visitations. "Visiting the iniquity of the fathers upon the children" (Ex. xxxiv. 7), that is, punishing them. . . . And it is a common speech with us when a house hath the plague, which is one of the highest strokes of temporal affliction, we use to say, "Such a house is visited." Observe then, afflictions are visitations. . . . Secondly, to visit, in a good sense, signifies to show mercy, and to refresh, to deliver an I to bless ; " Naomi heard how that the Lord had visited his people in giving them bread." Ruth i. 6. " The Lord visited Sarah," etc. Gen. xxi. 1, 2. That greatest mercy and deliverance that ever the children of men had, is thus expressed, " The Lord hath visited nnd redeemed his people." Luke i. 68. Mercies are visitations ; when God comes in kindness and love to do us good, he viiiteth us. And these mercies are called visitations in two respects : 1. Because *O-jd comes near to us* when he doth us good ; mercy is a drawing near to a soul, a drawing near to a place. As when God sends a judgment, or afflicts, he is said to depart and go away from that place ; so when he doth us good, he comes near, and as it were applies himself in favour to our persons and habitations. 2. They are called a visitation because of *the freeness of them.* A visit is one of the freest things in the world ; there is no obligation but that of love to make a visit; because such a man is my friend and 1 love him, therefore I visit him. Hence, that greatest act of free grace in redeeming the world is called a visitation, because it was as freely done as ever any friend made a visit to see his friend, and with infinite more freedom. There was no obligation on man's side at all, miny unkinduesses and neglects there were ; God in love came to redeem man. Thirdly, to visit imports an act of care and inspection, of tutorage and direction. The pastor's office over the flock is expressed by this act (Zech. x. 8 ; Acts xv. 36) ; and the care we ought to have of the fatherless and widows is expressed by visiting them. " Pure religion." saith the apostle James, " is this, To visit the fatherless and widows in their affliction" (chap. i. 27) ; and in Matt. xxv. 34, Christ pronounceth the blessing on them who, when he was in prison, visited him, which was not a bare seeing, or asking ' how do you,' but it was care of Christ in his imprisonment, and helpfulness and provision for him in his afflicted members. That sense also agrees well with this place, Job vii. 17, 18, " *What ix man, that than shouldst fiM fiimf"*|*Joseph Caryl.*

Verne 4.|" *What* w *man, that thou art mindful of himf or the son of man, that thou visitest him ?"*

Lord, what is mnn that tlmn
So mindful art of him ? Or what's the son
Of man. that thon the hiL'hest heaven didst bow.
And to Ills aide didst ruime ?

Man's but n piece of clny
Thnt's animated by thy heavenly breath,
And when that breath thou tak'st away,
Hue's clay again by death.

He le not worthy of the least
Of all Thy mercies at the best.
Baser than clay is he,
For sin hath made him like the beasU that perish,
Though next the angels he wag in degree ;
Yet this beast thou dost cherish.

Hee is not worthy of the least,
Of all thy mercies, hee's a beast
Worse than a beast is man,
Who after thine own image made at first,
Became the divel's sonne by sin. And can
A thing be more accurst ?

Yet thou thy greatest mercy hast
On this accursed creature cast.
Thou didst thyself abase,
And put off all thy robes of majesty,
Taking his nature to give him thy grace.

To save his life didst dye.
He is not worthy of the least
Of all thy mercies; one's a feast.

Lo! mnn Is made now even
With the blest angels, yea, superiour farre,
Since Christ sat down at God's right hand in heaven,

And God and man one are.
Thus nil thy mercies man inherits,
Though not the least of them he merits.

Thomas Washbourne, D.D., 1654. *Verte* 4.l" *What is man* ."l
How poor, how rich, how abject, how august,
How complicate, how wonderful is man *i*
How passing wonder He who mudc him such !
Who centred in our make such strange extremes!
From different natures marvellously mix'd.
Connexion exquisite of distant worlds !
Distinguisb'd link in being's endless chain!

Midwiiy from nothing to the Deity !
A beam ethereal, sullied and absorb'd.
Though sullied and dishonour'd, still divine I
Dim miniature of greatness absolute !
An heir of glory ! a fruil child of dust!
Helpless, immortal! insect *injinite/*
A worm ! a god ! I tremble at myself,
And in myself am lost. *Edward Young,* 1681l1715.
Vtnet 4.l8l" *What is man,"* etc. :
Man is ev'ry thing,
    And more: he is a tree, yet bears no frnlt;
A beast, yet is, or should be more:
Reason and speech we onely bring.
Parrats may thank us, if they arc not mute,
They go upon the score.

Man is all symmetric.
    Full of proportions, one limbe to another,
Aud all to all the world besides :
Each part may call the farthest, brother.
For head with foot bath private umitie,
And both with moons and tides.

Nothing hath got so farre,
But man hath caught and kept it, as his prey.
His eyes dismount the highest starre :
He is in little all the sphere.
Herbs gladly cure our flush, because that they
Finde their acquaintance there.

For us the windos do blow ;
    The earth doth rest, heav'n move, and fountains flow.
Nothing we see, but means our good,
As our *delight,* or as onr *treasure:*
The whole is, cither onr cupboard of/ood,
Or cabinet of *pleasure.*

The starres have ns to bed ;
    Jfight draws the curtain, which the sun withdraws:
Mustek and light attend our head.
All things unto ourjloiA are kinde
In their *descent* and *being ;* to our *minde*
In their *aauerit* and *cause.*

Each thing Is full of dutle :
Waters united are our navigation ;
Distinguished, our habitation;
Below, our drink ; above, our meat:
Both are our clcanllnesse. Hath one such beantle
Then how arc all things neat 1

More servants wait on man,
Than he'l take notice of : in cv'ry path

He treads down that which dotli befriend him,
When sicknesse makes him pale and wan,
Oh, mightie love 1 Man is one world, and hath
Another to attend him.

George Herbert, 1598.

Verse 5.l" Thou hast made him a little lower than the angels." Perhaps it was not so much in nature as in position that man, as first formed, was inferior to the angels. At all Wents, we can be sure that nothing higher could be affirmed of the angels, than that they were made in the image of God. If, then, they bad originally superiority over man, it must have been in the degree of resemblance. The angel was made immortal, intellectual, holy, powerful, glorious, and in these properties lay their likeness to the Creator. But were not these properties given also to man ? . Was not man made immortal, intellectual,-holy, powerful, glorious ? And if the angel excelled the man, it was not, we may believe, in the possession of properties which had no counterpart in the man ; both bore God's image, and both therefore had lineaments of the attributes which centre in Deity. Whether or not these lineaments were more strongly marked in the angel than in the man, it were presumptuous to attempt to decide ; but it is sufficient for our present purpose that the same properties must have been common to both, since both were modelled after the same divine image ; and whatever originally the relative positions of the angel and the man, we cannot question that since the fall man has been fearfully inferior to the angels. The effect of transgression has been to debase all his powers, and so bring him down from his high rank in the scale of creation ; but, however degraded and sunken, he still retains the capacities of his original formation, and since these capacities could have differed in nothing but degree from the capacities of the angel, it must be clear that they may be so purged and enlarged as to produce,

if we may not say to restore, the equality Oh ! it may be, we again

say, that an erroneous estimate is formed, when we separate by an immense space the angel and the man, and bring down the human race to a low station in the scale of creation. If I search through the records of science, I may indeed find that, for the furtherance of magnificent purposes, God hath made man " a little lower than the angels ;" and I cannot close my eyes to the melan- 'choly fact, that as a consequence upon apostacy there has been a weakening and a rifling of those splendid endowments which Adam might have transmitted unimpaired to his children. And yet the Bible teems with notices, that so far from being by nature higher than men, angels even now possess not an importance which belongs to our race. It is a mysterious thing, and one to which we scarcely dare allude, that there has arisen a Redeemer of fallen men, but not of fallen angels. We would build no theory on so awful and inscrutable a truth ; but is it too much to say, that the interference on the behalf of man and the non-interference on the behalf of angels, gives ground for the persuasion, that men occupy at least not a lower place than angels in the love and the solicitude of their Maker? Besides, are not angels represented as "ministering spirits,sent forth to minister to the heirs of salvation!" And what is the idea conveyed by such a representation, if it be not that believers, being attended and waited on by angels, are as children of God marching forwards to a splendid throne, and so elevated amongst creatures, that those who have the wind in their wings, and are brilliant as a flame of fire, delight to do them honour ? And, moreover, does not the repentance of a single sinner minister gladness to a whole throng of angels ? And who shall say that this sending of a new wave of rapture throughout the hierarchy of heaven does not betoken such immense sympathy with men as goes far towards proving him the occupant of an immense space in the scale of existence ? We may add, also, that angels learn of men ; inasmuch as Paul declares to the Ephesians, that " now unto the principalities and powers in heavenly places is made known by the church, the manifold wisdom of God." And when we further remember, that in one of those august visions with which the Evangelist John was favoured, he beheld the representatives of the church placed immediately before the eternal throne, whilst angels, standing at a greater distance, thronged the outer circle, we seem to have accumulated proof that men are not to be considered as naturally inferior to angels|that however they may have cast themselves down from eminence, and sullied the lustre and sapped the strength of their first estate, they are still capable of the very loftiest elevation, and require nothing but the being restored to their forfeited position, and the obtaining room for the development of their powers, in order to their shining forth as the illustrious ones of the

creation, the breathing, burning images of the Godhead The Redeemer

is represented as submitting to be humbled|"made a little lower than the angels," for the sake or with a view to the glory that was to be the recompense of his sufferings. This is a very important representation|one that should be most attentively considered ; and from it may be drawn, we think, a strong and clear argument for the divinity of Christ.

We could never see how it could be humility in any creature, whatever tho dignity of his condition, to assume the office of a Mediator and to work out our reconciliation. We do not forget to how extreme degradation a Mediator must consent to be reduced, and through what suffering and ignominy he could alone schieve our redemption ; but neither do we forget the unmeasured exaltation which was to be the Mediator's reward, and which, if Scripture be true, was to make him far higher than the highest of principalities and powers ; and we know not where would have been the amazing humility, where the unparalleled condescension, had any mere creature consented to take the office on the prospect of such a recompense. A being who knew that he should be immeasurably elevated if he did a certain thing, can hardly be commended for the greatness of his humility in doing that thing. The nobleman who should become n slave, knowing that in consequence he should be made a king, does not seem to us to afford any pattern of condescension. He must be the king already, incapable of obtaining any accession to his greatness, ere his entering the state of slavery can furnish an example of humility. And, in like manner, we can never perceive that any being but a divine Being can justly be said to have given a model of

condescension in becoming our Redeemer If he could not lay aside

the perfections, he could lay aside the glories of Deity ; without ceasing to be God he could appear to be man ; and herein we believe was the humiliation- herein that self-emptying which Scripture identifies with our Lord's having been "made a little lower than the angels." In place of manifesting himself in the form of God, and thereby centering on himself the delighted and reverential regards of all unfallen orders of intelligences, he must conceal himself in the form of a servant, and no longer gathering that rich tribute of homage, which had flowed from every quarter of his unlimited empire, produced by his power, sustained by his providence, he had the same essential glory, the same real dignity, which he had ever had. These belonged necessarily to his nature, and could no more be parted with, even for a time, than could that nature itself. But every outward mark of majesty and of greatness might be laid aside ; and Deity,

in place of coming down -with such dazzling manifestations of supremacy as would have compelled the world he visited to fall prostrate and adore, might Bo veil his splendours, and so hide himself in an ignoble form, that when men saw him there should be no "beauty that they should desire him." And this was what Christ did, in consenting to be " made u little lower than the angels ;" and in doing this he emptied himself, or " made himself of no reputation." The very being who in the form of God had given its light and magnificence to

heaven, appeared upon earth in the form of a servant; and not merely si for

every creature is God's servant, and therefore the form of a servant would have been assumed, had he appeared as an angel or an archangel|but in the form of the lowest of these servants, being " made in the likeness of men"|of men the degraded, the apostate, the perishing.|*Henry Melvill, B.D., 1854.*

Verse 5, 6.|God magnifies man in the work of creation. The third verse shows us what it was that raised the psalmist to this admiration of the goodness of God to man : " *When, I consider thy heavens, the work of thy fingers, the mion and the stars, whieft thou hast ordained ; Lord, what is man t*" God in the work of creation made all these things serviceable and instrumental for the good of man. What is man, that he should have a sun, moon, and stars, planted in the firmament for him ? What creature is this ? When great preparations are m-xde in any place, much provisions laid in, and the house adorned with richest furnitures, we say, " *What is thi man that comes to such a house* ." When such a goodly fabric was raised up, the goodly house of the world adorned aud furnished, we have reason admiringly to say, What is this man that must be the tenant or inhabitant of this house ? There is yet a higher exaltation of man in the creation ; man was magnified with the stamp of God's image, one part whereof the psalmist describes in the sixth verse, " *Thou modest him to hate dominion over the works of thy hands; thou hast put all things under his feet,*" etc. Thus man was magnified in creation. What was man that he should have the rule of the world given him ? That he should be lord over the fish of the sea, and over the beasts of the field, and over the fowls of the air ? Again, man was magnified in creation, in that God set him in the next degree to the angels ; " *Thou, hast made him a little lower than the angels /*" there is the tit part of the answer to this question, man was magnified in being made so excellent a creature, and in having so many excellent creatures made for him. All which may be understood of man as created in God's image ; but since the transgression it is peculiar to Christ, as the apostle applies it (Heb. ii. (i), and if those who have their blood and dignity restored by the work of redemption, which is the next part of man's exaltation.l*Joseph Caryl.*

Verses 5|8.lAugustine having allegorised much about the wine-presses in the title of this Psalm, upon these words, " What is man, or the son of man," the one being called BHJN, from *misery,* the other DnK[?, the *Son of Adam,* or *man,* saith, that by the first is meant man in the state of sin and corruption ; by the other, man regenerated by grace, yet called the son of man because made more excellent by the change of his mind and life, from old corruption to newness, and from an old to a new man ; whereas he that is still carnal is miserable ; and then ascending from the body to the head, Christ, he extols his glory as being set over all things, even the angels, and heavens, and the whole ;world as is elsewhere showed that he is. Eph. i. 21. And then leaving the highest things he descended to *"sheep and oxen./*" whereby we may understand *sanctified men* and *preachers,* for to *sheep* are the *faithful* often compared, and *preachers* to *oxen.* Cor. ix. "Thou shalt not muzzle the mouth of the ox that treadeth out the corn." " *The beasfa of the field* " set forth the *voluptuous* that live at large, going in the broad way : *the fowls of the air,* the *lifted up ty pride:* " *the fishes of the sea,*" such as through a covetous desire of riches pierce into the lower parts of the earth, as the fishes dive to the bottom of the sea. And because men pass the seas again and again for riches, he addeth, " *that passeth through the way of the sea,*" and to that of diving to the bottom of the waters may be applied (1 Tim. vi. 9), "They that will berich, fall into many noisome lusts, that drown the soul in perdition." And hereby seem to be set forth the three things of the world of which it is said, they that love them, the love of the Father is not in them." " The lust of the heart " being sensuality ; "the lust of the eyes," covetousness ; to which is added, "the pride of life." Above all these Christ was set, because -without all sin ; neither could any of the' devil's three temptations, which may be referred hereunto, prevail with him. And all these, as well as "sheep and oxen,7' are in the church, for which it is said, that into the ark came all manner of beasts, both clean and unclean, and fowls ; and all manner of fishes, good and bad, came into the net, as it is in the parable. All which I have set down, as of which good use may be made by the discreet reader.l*John Mayer.*

Verge 6.l" *Thou hast put all things under his fat.*" Hermodius, a nobleman born, upbraided the valiant captain Iphicrates for that he was but a shoemaker's son. " My blood," saith Iphicrates, " taketh beginning at me ; and thy blood, at tb.ee now taketh her farewell;" intimating that he, not honouring his house with the glory of his virtues, as the house had honoured him with the title of nobility, was but as a wooden knife put into an empty sheath to fill up the place ; but for himself, be, by his valorous achievements was now beginning to be the raiser of his family. Thus, in the matter of spirituality, he is the best gentleman that is the best Christian. The men of Berea, who received the word with all readiness, were more noble than those of Thessalonica. The burgesses of God's city be not of base lineage, but truly noble ; they boast not of their generation, but their regeneration, which is far better ; for, by their second birth they are the sons of God, and the church is their mother, and Christ their elder brother, the Holy Ghost their tutor, angels their attendants, and all other creatures their subjects, the whole world their inn, and heaven their home.l*John Spencer's " Things New and Old."*

Verse 6. l*" Thou madent him to have dominion oner the works of thy hands,"* etc. For thy help against wandering thoughts in prayer .... labour to keep thy distance to the world, and that sovereignty which God hath given thee over it in its profits and pleasures, or whatever else may prove a snare to thee. While the father and master know their place, and keep their distance, so long children and servants will keep theirs by being dutiful and officious ; but when they forget this, the father grows fond of the one, and the master too familiar with the other, then they begin to lose their authority and the others to grow saucy and under no command ; bid them go, and it may be they will not stir ; set them a task, and they will bid you do it yourself. Truly, thus it fares with the Christian ; all the creatures aro his servants, and so long as he keeps his heart at a holy distance from them, and maintains his lordship over them, not laying them in his bosom, which God hath put *"under his feet,"* all is well; he marches to the duties of God's worship in a goodly order. He can be private with God, and these not be bold to crowd in to disturb him. l *William CfvrnaU.*

*Verses 7, 8.*lHe who rules over the material world, is Lord also of the intellectual or spiritual creation represented thereby. The souls of the faithful, lowly and harmless, are the sheep of his pasture ; those who, like oxen, are strong to labour in the church, and who, by expounding the Word of Life, tread out the corn for the nourishment of the people, own him for their kind and beneficent Master ; nay, tempers fierce and untractable as the beasts of the desert, are yet subject to his will; spirits of the angelic kind, that, like the birds of the air, traverse freely the superior region, move at his command ; and those evil ones whose habitation is in the deep abyss, even to the great leviathan himself, all are put under the feet of King Messiah.l *George Home, D.D.*

*Verse 8.*lEvery dish of fish and fowl that comes to our table, is an instance of this dominion man has over the works of God's hands, and it is a reason of our subjection to God our chief Lord, and to his dominion over us.

HINTS TO THE VILLAGE PREACHER.

*Verse i.*l*" O Lord, our Lord.'*1"lPersonal appropriation of the Lord as ours. The privilege of holding such a portion.

" *How excellent,"*'1 etc. The excellence of the name and nature of God in. all places, and under all circumstances.

Sermon or lecture upon the glory of God in creation and providence.

" *In all the earth."* The unive rsal revelation of God in nature and its excellency.

" *Thy glory above the heaven."* The incomprehensible and infinite glory of God.

" *Above the heavens."* The glory of God outsoaring the intellect of angels, and the splendour of heaven.

*Verse 2.*lInfant piety, its possibility, potency, "strength," and influence, " thut thou mightest still," etc.

The strength of the gospel not the result of eloquence or wisdom in the speaker.

Great results from small causes when the Lord ordains to work.

Great things which can be said find claimed by babes in grace.

The stilling of the powers of evil by the testimony of feeble believers.

The stilling of the Great Enemy by the conquests of grace.

Verse 4.|Man's insignificance. God's mindfulness of man. Divine visits. The question, "What is man?" Each of these themes may suffice for a discourse, or they may be handled in one sermon.

Verse 5. |Man's relation to the angels.

The position which Jesus assumed for our sakes.

Manhood's crown|the glory of our nature in the person of the Lord Jesus.

Verses 5. 6, 7, 8.|The universal providential dominion of our Lord Jesus.

Verse 6.|Man's rights and responsibilities towards the lower animals.

Verse 6.-|Man's dominion over the lower animals, and how he should exercise it.

Verse 6 (second clause).|The proper place for all worldly things, *"under his feet.'"*

Verse 9.|The wanderer in many climes enjoying the sweetness of his Lord's name in every condition.

PSALM IX.

Title -To the Chief Musician upon Muth-labben, a Psalm of David. *Vie meaning of this title is very doubtful. It may refer to the tune to which the Psalm was to be sung, & Wfileocks and others think; or it may refer to a musical instrument now unknown,* bid *common in those days; or it may have a reference to Ben, who is mentioned in 1 Chron.* xv. 18, *ax one of the Levitical singers, If either of these conjectures should be correct, the title of Muth-labben has no teaching for us, except it* is *meant to show us how careful David was that in the worship of God all things should be done according to due order. From a considerable company of learned witnesses we gather that the title will bear a meaning far more instructive, without being fancifully forced: U signifies a Psalm concerning the death of the San. The C7iaWe has, "concerning the death of the Cliampion icho went out between the camps," referring to Goliath of Oath, or some other Philistine, on account of icAo.se death many suppose ttis Psalm to have been written in after years by David. Believing that out of a thousand guesses this is at least an consistent with the sense of the Psalm an any other, ice prefer it ; and the more especially so because it enables us to refer it mystically to the victim/f Oa .Son of God over the champion of evil, even the enemy of souls (verse 6). We hace here before us most evidently a triumphal hymn; may it strengthen the faith of the militant believer and stimulate the courage of the timid saint, as he sees here* The Conqtjebor, *on whose vesture and thigh is the name written. King of kings and Lord of lords.*

Obdeb.|*Bonar remarks, " The position of the Psalms in their relation to each other is often remarkai/le. It is questioned whether the. present arrangement of them was the order in ttUcfc they were given forth to Israel, or whether some later compiler, perhaps Ezra, was inspired to attend to this matter, as well as to other points connected with the canon. Without attempting to decide this point, U is enough to remark that we liave proof that the order of the Psalms is as ancient as the completing of the canon, and if so, it seems obvious that the Holy Spirit wLihed this book to come down to us in its present order. We make these remarks, in order to invite attention to the fact, that as the eighth caught up the last line of the seventh, this nirdh Psalm opens with an apparent reference to the eighth:|*

" I will praise thec, O Lord, with my whole heart;
I will shew forth all thy marvellous works.

I will be glad and rejoice in thee. (Comp. Son? i. 4; Rev. xlx. 7.)
I will sing to Thy Name, O tliou Most High." Verses 1, 2.

As if ' The Name," so highly praised in the former Psalm, were still ringing in the ear of lu street singer of Israel. And in verse 10, 'he returns to it, celebrating their confidence who "know" that " name " as if Us fragrance slitt breathed in the atmosphere around.

Dmsiox.|*The strain so continually changes, that it is difficult to give an outline of it methodically arranged: we give the best ice can tnafce. From verses 1 to G is a song of jubilant thanksgiving ; from! to 12, there is a continued declaration of faith as to the future. Prayer doses the first great division of the Psalm in verses 13 and 14. The second portion f this triumphal ode. although much shorter, is parallel in all Us parts to the first portion, und is a sort of rehearsal of U. Observe the song for past judgments, verses 15, 16 ; At declaration of trust in future justice, 17, 18 ; and the closing prayer, 19, 20. Let n.v Mrcrte the conquests of the Redeemer as we read this Psalm, and U cannot but be a delightful fak if the Holy Ghost be wUh us.*

EXPOSITION.

I WILL praise *thee,* O Lord, with my whole heart; I will shew forth all thy marvellous works.

2 I will be glad and rejoice in thee : I will sing praise to thy name, O thou most High.

3 When mine enemies are turned back, they shall fall and perish at thy presence.

For thou hast maintained my right and my cause ; thou satest in the throne judging right.

5 Thou hast rebuked the heathen, thou hast destroyed the wicked, thou hast put out their name for ever and ever.

6 O thou enemy, destructions are come to a perpetual end : and thou hast destroyed cities ; their memorial is perished with them.

1. With a holy resolution the songster begins his hymn ; *I trill praine thee, 0 Lord.* It sometimes needs all our determination to face the foe, and bless the Lord in the teeth of his enemies ; vowing that whoever else may be silent *we* will bless his name ; here, however, the overthrow of the foe is viewed as complete, and the song flows with sacred fulness of delight. It is our duty to praise the Lord ; let us perform it as a privilege. Observe that David's praise is all given to the Lord. Praise is to be offered to God alone ; we may be grateful to the intermediate agent, but our thanks must have long wings and mount aloft to heaven. *With my whole heart.* Half heart is no heart. *I will xhow forth.* There is true praise in the thankful telling forth to others of our heavenly Father's dealings with us ; this is one of the themes upon which the godly should speak often to one another, and it will not be casting pearls before swine if we make even the ungodly hear of the loving-kindness of the Lord to us. *All thy*

martellou work. Gratitude for one mercy refreshes the memory is to thousands of others. One silver link in the chain draws up a long series of tender remembrances. Here is eternal work for us, for there can be no end to the showing forth of *all* his deeds of love. If we consider our own sinfulness and nothingness, we must feel that every work of preservation, forgiveness, conversion, deliverance, sanctiflcation, &c., which the Lord has wrought for us, or in us is a *marvellous* work. Even in heaven, divine loving-kindness will doubtless be as much a theme of surprise as of rapture.

2. Gladness and joy are the appropriate spirit in which to praise the goodness of the Lord. Birds extol the Creator in notes of overflowing joy, the cattle low forth his praise with tumult of happiness, and the fish leap up in his worship with excess of delight. Moloch may be worshipped with shrieks of pain, and Juggernaut may be honoured by dying groans and inhuman yells, but he whose name is Love is best pleased with the holy mirth, and sanctified gladness of his people. Daily rejoicing is an ornament to the Christian character, and a suitable robe for God's choristers to wear. God loveth a *cheerful* giver, whether it be the gold of his purse or the gold of his mouth which he presents upon his altar. *I will sing praite to thy name, 0 thou matt High.* Songs are the fitting expressions of inward thankfulness, and it were well if we indulged ourselves and honoured our Lord with more of them. Mr. B. P. Power has well said, " The sailors give a cheery cry as they weigh anchor, the ploughman whistles in the morning as he drives his team ; the milkmaid sings her rustic song as she sets about her early task ; when soldiers are leaving friends behind them, they do not march out to the tune of the ' Dead March in Saul,' but to the quick notes of some lively air. A praising spirit would do for us all that their songs and music do for them ; and if only we could determine to praise the Lord, we should surmount many a difficulty which our low spirits never would have been equal to, and we should do double the work which can be clone if the heart be languid in its beating, if we be crushed and trodden down in soul. As the evil spirit in Saul yielded in the olden time to the influence of the harp of the son of Jesse, so would the spirit of melancholy often take flight from us, if only we would take up the song of praise."

8. God's presence is evermore sufficient to work the defeat of our most furious foes, and their ruin is so complete when the Lord takes them in hand, that even flight cannot save them, they fall to rise no more when he pursues them. Wemust be careful, like David, to give all the glory to him whose presence gives the victory. If we have here the exultings of our conquering Captain, let us make the triumphs of the Redeemer the triumphs of the redeemed, and rejoice with him at the total discomfiture of all his foes.

4. One of our nobility has for his motto, "I will maintain it;" but the Christian has a better and more humble one, " Thou hast maintained it." " God and my right," are united by my faith : while God lives my right shall never be taken from me. If we seek to maintain the cause and honour of our Lord we may suffer reproach and misrepresentation, but it is a rich comfort to remember that he who sits in the throne knows our hearts, and will not leave us to the ignorant and ungenerous judgment of erring man.

5. God rebukes before he destroys, but when he once comes to blows with the wicked he ceases not until he has dashed them in pieces so small that their very name

is forgotten, and like a noisome snuff their remembrance is put out for ever and ever. How often the word " thon" occurs in this and the former verse, to show us that the grateful strain mounts up directly to the Lord as doth the smoke from the altar when the air is still. My soul send up all the music of all thy powers to him who has been and is thy sure deliverance.

6. Here the Psalmist exults over the fallen foe. He bends as it were, over his prostrate form, and insults his once vaunted strength. He plucks the boaster's song out of his mouth, and sings it for him in derision. After this fashion doth our fllorious Redeemer ask of death, " "Where is thy sting ?" and of the grave, "Where is thy victory!" The spoiler is spoiled, and he who made captive is led into captivity himself. Let the daughters of Jerusalem go forth to meet their King, and praise him with timbrel and harp.

7 But the LORD shall endure for ever : he hath prepared his throne for judgment.

8 And he shall judge the world in righteousness, he shall minister judgment to the people in uprightness.

9 The Lord also will be a refuge for the oppressed, a refuge in times of trouble.

10 And they that know thy name will put their trust in thee : for thou, Lord, hast not forsaken them that seek thee.

11 Sing praises to the Lord, which dwelleth in Zion : declare among the people his doings.

12 When he maketh inquisition for blood, he remembereth them : he forgetteth not the cry of the humble.

In the light of the past the future is not doubtful. Since the same Almighty God fills the throne of power, we can with unhesitating confidence, exult in our security for all time to come.

T. The enduring existence and unchanging dominion of our Jehovah, are the firm foun ".;uions of our joy. The tnemy and his destructions shall come to a perpetual end, but Qod and his throne shall *endure for ever.* The eternity of divine sovereignty yields unfailing consolation. By the throne being *prepared fa judgment,* are we not to understand the swiftness of divine justice. In heaven's court suitors are not worn out with long delays. Term-time lasts all the year round in the court of King's Bench above. Thousands may come at "ace to the throne of the Judge of all the earth, but neither plaintiff nor defendant shall have to complain that lie is not prepared to give their cause a fair

llWMjr.

8. Whatever earthly courts may do, heaven's throne ministers judgment in uprightness. Partiality and respect of persons are things unknown in the dealings of the Holy One of Israel. How the prospect of appearing before the impartial tribunal of the Great King should act as a check to us when tempted to sin, and as a comfort when we are slandered or oppressed.

9. He who gives no quarter to the wicked in the day of judgment, is the defence and refuge of his saints in the day of trouble. There are many forms of oppressioa ; both from man and from Satan oppression comes to us ; and for all its forms, a refuge is provided in the Lord Jehovah. There were cities of refuge under the law, God is our refuge-city under the gospel. As the ships when vexed with tempest make for

harbour, so do the oppressed hasten to the wing's of a just and gracious God. He is a high tower so impregnable, that the hosts of hell cannot carry it by storm, and from its lofty heights faith looks down -with. scorn upon her enemies.

10. Ignorance is worst when it amounts to ignorance of God, and knowledg-e is best when it exercises itself upon *tlie name* of God. This most excellent knowledge leads to the most excellent grace of faith. O, to learn more of the attributes and character of God. Unbelief, that hooting nightbird, cannot li *ve* in the light of divine knowledge, it flies before the sun of God's great and gracious name. If we read this verse literally, there is, no doubt, a glorious fulness of assurance in the names of God. We have recounted them in the " Hints for Preachers," and would direct the reader's attention to them. By knowing his name is also meant an experimental acquaintance with the attributes of God, which are everyone of them anchors to hold the soul from drifting in seasons of peril. The Lord may hide his face for a season from his people, but he never has utterly, finally, really, or angrily, *forsaken them that seek him.* Let the poor seekers draw comfort from this fact, and let the finders rejoice yet more exceedingly, for what must be the Lord's faithfulness to those who find if he is Bo gracious to those who seek.

" O hope of every contrite heart,
   O joy of all the muck,
To those who fall how kind thou art,
How good to those who seek.

" But what to those who find, ah, this
   Nor tongue nor pen can show
The love of Jesus what it is,
None but his loved ones know."

11. Being full of gratitude himself, our inspired author is eager to excite others to join the strain, and praise God in the same manner as he had himself vowed to do in the first and second verses. The heavenly spirit of praise is gloriously contagious, and he that hath it is never content unless he can excite all who surround him to unite in his sweet employ. Singing and preaching, as means of glorifying God, are here joined together, and it is remarkable that, connected with all revivals of gospel ministry, there has been a sudden outburst of the spirit of song. Luther's Psalms and Hymns were in all men's mouths, and in the modern revival under Wesley and Wliitefield, the strains of Charles Wesley, Cennick, Berridge, **Toplady**, Hart, Newton, and many others, were the outgrowth of restored piety. The singing of the birds of praise fitly accompanies the return of the gracious spring of divine visitation through the proclamation of the truth. Sing on brethren, and preach on, **and** these shall both be a token that the Lord still dwelleth in Zion. It will be well for us when coming up to Zion, to remember that the Lord dwells among his saints, and is to be had in peculiar reverence of all those that are about him.

12. When an inquest is held concerning the blood of the oppressed, the martyred saints will have the first remembrance ; he will avenge his own elect. Those saints who are living shall also be heard ; they shall be exonerated from blame, and kept

from destruction, even when the Lord's most terrible work is going on ; the man with the inkhorn by his side shall mark them all for safety, before the slaughtermen are permitted to sme the Lord's enemies. The humble cry of the poorest saints shall neither be drowned by the voice of thundering justice nor by the shrieks of the condemned.

13 Have mercy upon me, O Lord ; consider my trouble *which I suffer* of them that hate me, thou that liftest me up from the gates of death :

14 That I may shew forth all thy praise in the gates of the daughter of Zion : I will rejoice in thy salvation.

Memories of the past and confidences concerning the future conducted the man of God to the mercy seat to plead for the needs of the present. Between praising and praying he divided all his time. How could he have spent it more profitably ? His first prayer is one suitable for all persons and occasions, it breathes a humble spirit, indicates self-knowledge, appeals to the proper attributes, and to the fitting person. *Have mercy upon me, 0 Lord.* Just as Luther used to call some texts little bibles, so we may call this sentence a little prayer-book ; for it has in it the soul and marrow of prayer. It is multum in parvo, and like the angelic sword turns every way. The ladder looks to be short, but it reaches from earth to heaven.

What a noble title is here given to the Most High. *TJiou tlat liftest me up from the gate of death !* What a glorious lift ! In sickness, in sin, in despair, in temptation, we have been brought very low, nnd the gloomy portal bus seemed as if it would open to imprison us, but, underneath us were the everlasting arms, and, therefore, we have been uplifted even to the gates of

i must not *may ihow*

firth all thy praise.'1" Saints are not so selfish as to look only to self ; they desire mercy's diamond that they may let others see it flash and sparkle, and may admire Him who gives such priceless gems to his beloved. The contrast between the gates of death and the gates of the New Jerusalem is very striking ; let our gongs be excited to the highest and most rapturous pitch by the double consideration of whence we are taken, and to what we have been advanced, and let our prayers for mercy be made more energetic and agonizing by a sense of the grace which such a salvation implies. When David speaks of his stowing forth *all* God's praise, he means that, in his deliverance grace in all its "eights and depths would be magnified. Just as our hymn puts it:|

" O the length and breadth of love !

-I- -us, Saviour, can it be ?
All thy mercy's height I prove,
All the depth Is seen in me."

Here ends the first part of this instructive psalm, and in pausing awhile we feel bound to confess that our exposition has only flitted over its surface and has not digged into the depths. The verses are singularly full of teaching, and if the Holy Spirit shall bless the reader, he may go over this Psalm, as the writer hs done scores of times, and see on each occasion fresh beauties.

15 The heathen are sunk down in the pit *that* they made : in the net which they hid is their own foot taken.

16 The Lord is known *by* the judgment -*which* he executeth : the wicked is snared in the work of his own hands. Higgaion.

Selah.

In considering this terrible picture of the Lord's overwhelming judgments of Msm-cmies, we are called upon to ponder and meditate upon it with deep Wionsncss by the two untranslated words, Higgaion, Selah. Meditate, pause. Consider, and tune your instrument. Bethink yourselves and solemnly adjust Jmi hearts to the solemnity which is so well becoming the subject. Let us in a '"Bible spirit approach these verses, and notice, first, that the character of Godrequires the punishment of sin. *Jehovah is knotcn Jy the judgment which he eztcutfth;* his holiness and abhorrence of sin is thus displayed. A ruler who winked at evil would soon be known by all his subjects to be evil himself, and he, on the other hand, who is severely just in judgment reveals his own nature thereby. So long as our God is God, he will not, he cannot spare the guilty ; except through that one glorious way in which he is just, and yet the justifier ot him that believeth in Jesus. We must notice, secondly, that the manner of his judgment is singularly wise, and indisputably just. He makes the wicked become their own executioners. "The heathen are sunk down in the pit that they made," &c. Like cunning hunters they prepared a pitfall for the goilly and fell into it themselves : the foot of the victim escaped their crafty snares, but the toils surrounded themselves : the cruel snare was laboriously manufactured, and it proved its efficacy by snaring its own maker. Persecutors and oppressors are often ruined by their own malicious projects. " Drunkards kill themselves; prodigals beggar themselves;" the contentious are involved in ruinous costs ; the vicious are devoured with fierce diseases ; the envious eat their own hearts ; and blasphemers curse their own souls. Thus, men may read their sin in their punishment. They sowed the seed of sin, and the ripe fruit of damnation is the natural result.

17 The wicked shall be turned into hell, *and* all the nations that forget God.

18 For the needy shall not alway be forgotten : the expectation of the poor shall *not* perish for ever.

17. The justice which has punished the wicked, and preserved the righteous, remains the same, and-therefore in days to come, retribution will surely be meted out. How solemn is the seventeenth verse, especially in its warning to forgetters of God. The moral who are not devout, the honest who are not prayerful, the benevolent who arc not believing, the amiable who are not converted, these must all have their portion with the openly wicked in the hell which is prepared for the devil and his angels. There are whole nations of such ; the forgetters of God are far more numerous than the profane or profligate, and according to the very forceful expression of the Hebrew, the nethermost hell will be the place into which all of them shall be hurled headlong. Forgetfulness seems a small sin, but it brings eternal wrath upon the man who lives and dies in it.

18. Mercy is as ready to her work as ever justice can be. Needy souls fear that they are forgotten ; well, if it be so, let them rejoice that they *thall not alway* be so. Satan tells poor tremblers that their hope shall perish, but they have here the divine assurance that *their expectation shall not perish for ever.* " The Lord's people are a humbled people, afflicted, emptied, sensible of need, driven to a daily attendance

on God, daily begging of him, and living upon the hope of what is promised ;" such persons may have to wait, but they shall find that they do not wait in vain.

19 Arise, O LORD ; let not man prevail : let the heathen be judged in thy sight.

20 Put them in fear, O LORD : *that* the nations may know themselves *to be but* men. Selah.

19. Prayers are the believer's weapons of war. When the battle is too hard for us, we call in our great ally, who, as it were, lies in ambush until faith gives the signal by crying out, " Arise, O Lord." Although our cause be all but lost, it shall be soon won again if the Almighty doth but bestir himself. He will not Buffer man to prevail over God, but with swift judgments will confound their gloryings. In the very sight of God the wicked will be punished, and he who is now all tenderness will have no bowels of compassion for them, since they had no tears of repentance while their day of grace endured.

20. One would think that men would not grow so vain as to deny themselves to be bat men, but it appears to be a lesson which only a divine schoolmaster can teach to some proud spirits. Crowns leave their wearers *but men,* degrees of eminent learning make their owners not more than *men,* valour and conquest cannot elevate beyond the dead level of " *but men* ;" and all the wealth of Croesus, the wisdom of Solon, the power of Alexander, the eloquence of Demosthenes, if added together, would leave the possessor but a man. May we ever remember this, lest like those in the text, we should be *put in fear.*

Before leaving this Psalm, it will be very profitable if the student will peruse it again as the triumphal hymn of the Redeemer, as he devoutly brings the glory of his victories and lays it down at his Father's feet. Let us joy in hia joy, and our joy shall be full.

EXPLANATORY NOTES AND QUAINT SAYINGS.

WMe Psalm.|We are to consider this song of praise, as I conceive, to be the language of our great Advocate and Mediator, " in the midst of the church giving thanks unto God," and teaching us to anticipate by faith his great and final victory over all the adversaries of our peace temporal and spiritual, with especial reference to his assertion of his royal dignity on Zion, his holy mountain. The victory over the enemy, we find by the fourth verse, is again ascribed to the decision of divine justice, and the award" of a righteous judge, who has at length resumed his tribunal. This renders it certain, that the claim preferred to the throne of the Almighty, could proceed from the lips of none but our Melchizedec.|*John Fry, B.A.,* 1842.

Vent 1.|" I will praise thee, 0 Lord, with my whole heart." As a vessel by the scent thereof tells what liquor is in it, so should our mouths smell continually of that mercy wherewith our hearts have been refreshed : for we are called vessels of mercy.|*William Cowper,* 1612.

Vene 1.|" I tciU praite the Lord with my whole heart, I will shew forth all (Ay *mandloui works.'"* The words, " *With my inhale heart,'*1" serve at once to show the greatness of the deliverances wrought for the psalmist, and to distinguish him from the hypocrites|the coarser, who praise the Lord for his goodness merely with the lips ; and the more refined, who praise him with just half their heart, while they secretly ascribe the deliverance more to themselves than to him. " *All thy wonders,'*1" the marvellous tokens of thy grace. The psalmist shows by this term, that he recognized them in all their greatness. Where this is done, there the Lord is also praised with the whole heart. *Half-heartedness,* and the depreciation of divine grace, go hand in hand. The 3 is the 3 *instrum.* The heart is the instrument of praise, the mouth only its organ.|*E. W. IJengstenlerg.*

Ytrte 1 *(second elaute).*|When we have received any special good thing from the Lord, it is well, according as we have opportunities, to tell others of " When the woman who had lost one of her ten pieces of silver, found the musing portion of her money, she gathered her neighbours and her friends to- pether, saying, " Rejoice with me, for I have found the piece which I bad lost." We may do the same ; we may tell friends and relations that we have received nch and-such a blessing, and that we trace it directly to the hand of God. Why have we not already done this? Is there a lurking unbelief as to whether it really came from God ; or are we ashamed to own it before those who are perhapg accustomed to laugh at such things ? Who knows so much of the marvellous works of God as hia own people ; if they be silent, how can weexpect the world to see what he has done ? Let us not be ashamed to glorify God, by telling what we know and feel he has done ; let us watch our opportunity to bring out distinctly the fact of his acting ; let us feel delighted at having an opportunity, from our own experience, of telling what must turn to his praise ; and them that honour God, God will honour in turn ; if we be willing to talk of his deeds, he will give us enough to talk about.|*P. B. Power, in ' / Wills ' of the Psalmt.*

Verses 1, 2.|"*/ will confess unto thee, O Lord, with my whole heart,"* etc. Behold, with what a flood of the most sweet affections he says that he " *if ill confess,"* " *show forth," "rejoice,"* " *hi glad,"* and *"sing,"* being filled with ecstacy ! He does not simply say, " */ will confess,"* but, " *with my heart,"* and " *with my whole heart."* Nor does he propose to speak simply of " *works,"* but of the " *marvellous works"* of God, and of *"all"* those *"works."* Thus his spirit (like John in the womb) exults and rejoices in God his Saviour, who has done great things for him, and those marvellous things which follow. In which words are opened the subject of this Psalm : that is, that he therein sings the marvellous works of God. And these works are wonderful, because he converts, by those who are nothing, those who have all things, and, by the Almctii who live in hidden faith, and are dead to the world, he humbles those who Hourish in glory, and are looked upon in the world. Thus accomplishing such mighty things without force, without arms, without labour, by the cross only and blood. But how will his Buying, that he will show forth *"all"* his marvellous works, agree with that of Job ix. 10, " which doeth great things past finding out; yea, and wonders without number"? For, who can show forth all the marvellous works of God ? We may say, therefore, that these things are spoken in that excess of feeling in which he said (Psalm vi. 6), " I will water my couch with my tears." That is, he hath such an ardent desire to speak of the wonderful works of God, that, as far as his wishes are concerned, he *would* set the " *all*" forth, though he *could* not do it, for love has neither bounds nor end : and, as Paul saith (t Cor. xiii. 7), " Love beareth all things, be'lieveth all things, hopeth all things ;" hence it can do all things, and doea do all things, for God looketh at the heart and spirit.|*Martin Luther.*

Verse 3.|" Wlien mine enemies are turned back," etc. *Were turned baek,* repulsed, and put to flight. To render this in the present time, as our translators did, is certainly improper ; it destroys the coherence, and introduces obscurity. Ainsworth saw this, and rendered in the past, " When mine enemies turned backward." " *At thy presence."* That is, by thine anger. For as God's presence or fane denotes his favour to such as fear and serve him, so it denotes his anger towards the wicked. " The face of Jehovah is against them that do evil."| *B. Boothroyd,* 1824.

Verse 3.|" They shall fall and perish." | It refers to those thut either faint in a nnrch, or are wounded in a battle, or especially that in flight meet with galling haps in their way, and so are galled and lamed, rendered unable to go forward, and so fall, and become liable to all the chances of pursuits, and as iierci, are overtaken and perish in the fall.|*Henry Hammond, D.D.*

Verse H.|" Thou hast rebuked the heathen," etc.|Augustine applieth all this mystically, as is intimated (verse 1) that it should be applied, for, " I will speak," saith he, " of all thy wonderful works ;" and what so wonderful as the turning of the spiritual enemy backward, whether the devil, as when he said, " Get thee behind me, Satan ;" or the old man, which is turned backward when he is put off, and the new man put on ?|*John Mayer.*

Verse 8.|" He shall judge the world in righteoumts." In this judgment tears will not prevail, prayers will not be heard, promises will not be admitted, repentance will be too late ; and as for riches, honourable titles, sceptres, and diadems, these will profit much less ; and the inquisition shall be so curious anddiligent, that not one light thought nor one idle word (not repented of in the life past), shall be forgotten. For truth itself hath said, not in jest, but in earnest, " Of every idle word which men have spoken, they shall give an account in the day of judgment." Oh, how many which now sin with great delight, yea, even with greediness (as if we served a god of wood or of stone, which seeth nothing, or can do nothing), will be then astonished, ashamed, and silent ! Then shall the days of thy mirth be ended, and thou shalt be overwhelmed with everlasting darkness ; and instead of thy pleasures, thou shalt have everlasting torments.| *Thomas Tymme.*

Verse 8.|" He shall judge the world in righteousness.'" Even Paul, in his great address on Mars' Hill, a thousand years after, could find no better words in which to teach the Athenians the doctrine of the judgment-day than the Septua- gint rendering of this clause.| *William S'. Plumer.*

Verse 8.|The guilty conscience cannot abide this day. The silly sheep, when she is taken, will not bleat, but you may carry her and do what you will with her, and she will be subject ; but the swine, if she be once taken, she will roar and cry, and thinks she is never taken but to be slain. So of all things the guilty conscience cannot abide to hear of this day, for they know that when they hear of it, they hear of their own condemnation. I think if there were a general collection made through the whole world that there might be no judgment-day, then God would be so rich that the world would go a-begging and be a waste wilderness. Then the covetous judge would bring forth his bribes ; then the crafty lawyer would fetch out his bags ; the usurer would give his gain, and a double thereof. But all the money in the world will not serve for our sin, but the judge must answer his bribes, he that hath moufy must answer how he came by it, and just condemnation must come upon every eeul of them ; then shall the sinner be ever dying and never dead, like the salamander, that isever in the fire and never consumed.|*Henry Smith.*

Vtne fl.|It is reported of the Egyptians that, living in the fens, and being vexed with gnuts, they used to sleep in high towers, whereby, those creatures not being able to soar so high, they are delivered from the biting of them : so would it be with us when bitten with cares and fear, did we but run to God for refuge, and rest confident of his help.|*John Trapp.*

Tent 10.|" *They that know thy name will put their trust in thee.*" Faith is n intelligent grace ; though there can be knowledge without faith, yet there can be no faith without knowledge. One calls it quicksighted faith. Knowledge must carry the torch before faith. -2 Tim. i. 12. " For I know whom I have believed." As in Paul's conversion a light from heaven " shined round about him" (Acts ix. 8), so before 'faith be wrought, God shines in with a light upon the understanding. A blind faith is as bad as a dead faith : that eye may as well be said to be a good eye which is without sight, as that faith is good without knowledge. Devout ignorance damns ; which condemns the church of Rome, that think it a piece of their religion to be kept in ignorance ; these set up an altar to an unknown God. They say ignorance is the mother of devotion ; bnt sure where the sun is set in the understanding, it must needs be night in the affections. So necessary is knowledge to the being of faith, that the Scriptures do sometimes baptise faith with the name of knowledge. Isa. liii. 11. "By his knowledge shall my righteous servant justify many." Knowledge is put there for faith.|*Thomas Watson.*

Vme 10.|" *They that know thy name will put their trust in thee: for thou,* lord, *Itatt not forsaken them that seek thee.*'1" The mother of unbelief is ignorance of God,'his faithfulness, mercy, and power. *They that know thee, will tmit in thee.* This confirmed Paul, Abraham, Sarah, in the faith. " I know whom I have believed, and am persuaded that he is able to keep that which I have committed unto him against that day." 2 Tim. i. 12. " He is faithful that promised," and "able also to perform." Heb. x. 23, and xi. 11 ; Rom.iv. 81. The free promises of the Lord are all certain, his commandments right and good, the recompense of reward inestimably to be valued above thousands of gold and silver ; trust therefore in the Lord, O my soul, and follow hard after him. Thou hast his free promise, who never failed, who hath promised more than possibly thou couldst ask or think, who hath done more for thee than ever he promised, who is good and bountiful to the wicked and ungodly ; thou doest his work, who is able and assuredly will bear thee out. There is a crown of glory proposed unto thee above all conceit of merit ; stick fast unto his word, and suffer nothing to divide thee from it. Rest upon his promises though he seem to kill thee ; cleave unto his statutes though the flesh lust, the world allure, the devil tempt by flatteries or threatenings to the contrary.|*John Ball,* ,1632.

Verge 10.|" *They that 'know thy name will put their trust in thee.*1" They can do no otherwise who savingly know God's sweet attributes, and noble acts for his people. We never trust a man till we know him, and bad men are better known than trusted. Not so the Lord ; for where his name is ointment poured, forth, the virgins love him, fear him, rejoice in him, and repose upon him.| *John Trapp.*

Verse 12.|" *When he malceth inquisition for blood, he remembereth them.* 1' There i a time when God will make inquisition for innocent blood. The Hebrew word *doresh,* from *tlarash,* that is here rendered *inquisition,* signifies not barely to seek, to search, but to seek, search, and enquire with all diligence and care imaginable. Oh, there is a time a-coming when the Lord will make a very diligent and careful search and enquiry after all the innocent blood of his afflicted and persecuted people, which persecutors Rnd tyrants have spilt as water upon the ground ; and woe to persecutors when God shall make a more strict, critical, and careful enquiry after the blood of his people than ever was made in the inquisition of Spain, where all things are carried with the greatest diligence, subtlety, secrecy, and severity. O persecutors, there is a timo a-coming, when God will make a strict enquiry after the blood of Hooper, Bradford, Latimer, Taylor, Ridley, etc. There is a time a-coming, wherein God will enquire who silenced and suspended such- and-such ministers, and who stopped the mouths of such-and-such, and who imprisoned, confined, and banished such-and-such, who were once burning and shining lights, and who were willing to spend and be spent that sinners might be saved, and that Christ might be glorified. There is a time, when the Lord will make a very narrow enquiry into all the actions and practices of ecclesiastical courts, high commissions, committees, assizes, etc., and deal with persecutors as they have dealt with his people. | *Thomas Brookt.*

Verse 12.|" *When he malceth inquisition for blood, he remembereth them.* " There is *vox sanyuinis,* a voice of blood ; and " he that planted the ear, shall he not hear?" It covered the old world with waters. The earth is filled with cruelty ; it was *vox sanguinis* that cried, and the heavens heard the earth, and the windows of heaven opened to let fall judgment and vengeance upon it. *Edward Marbury,* 1649.

Verse 12.|" *When he maketh inquisition for blood,* " etc. Though God may seem to wink for a time at the cruelty of violent men, yet will call them at. last to a strict account for all the innocent blood they have shed, and for their unjust and unmerciful usage of meek and humble persons ; whose cry he never forgets (though he doth not presently answer it), but takes a fit time to be avenged of their oppressors.|*Symon Patrick, D.D.,* 1626|1707.

Verse 12.|" *He malceth inquisition for blood.* " He is so stirred at this sin, that he will up. search out the authors, contrivers, and commissioners of this scarlet sin, he will avenge for blood.| *William Greenhill.*

Verse 12.|"*He forgetteth not the cry of the humble.*'1" Prayer is a haven to the shipwrecked man, an anchor to them that are sinking in the waves, a staff to the limbs that totter, a mine of jewels to the poor, a healer of diseases, and a guardian of health. Prayer at once secures the continuance of our blessings,nd dissipates the clouds of our calamities. O blessed prayer ! thou art the unwearied conqueror of human woes, the firm foundation of" human happiness, the source of ever-enduring joy, the mother of philosophy. The man who can pray truly, thougli languishing in extremes! indigence, is richer than all beside, whilst the wretch who never bowed the knee, though proudly sitting as monarch of all nations, is of all men most destitute.|*Chrytoetom.*

Vtrte 14.|" *That I may thow forth all thy* prai," etc. To show forth *all* God's praise is to enter largely into the work. An occasional " *God, I thank* ttw," is no fit return for a perpetual stream of rich benefits.| *William S. Plumer.*

Verte 15.l" *The heathen are sunk dawn in (he pit that they made,'*11 etc. 'Whilst they are digging pits for others, there is a pit a-digging and a grave a-making for themselves. They have a measure to make up, and a treasure to fill, which at length will be broken open, which, methinks, should take off them which are set upon mischief from pleasing themselves in their plots. Alas ! they are but plotting their own ruin, and building a Babel which will fall upon tkeir own heads. If there were any commendation in plotting, then that great plotter of plotters, that great engineer, Satan, would go beyond us all, and take all the credit from us. But let us not envy Satan and his in their glory. They tad need of something to comfort them. Let them please themselves with their trade. The day is coming wherein the daughter of Sion shall laugh them to scorn. There will be a time wherein it shall be said, " Arise, Sion, and thresh." Micah iy. 18. And usually the delivery of God's children is joined with the destruction of his enemies ; Saul's death, and David's deliverance ; the Israelites' deliverance, and the Egyptians' drowning. The church and her opposites are like the scales of a balance ; when one goes up, the other goes down.*|Richard SifJut.*

Vertet 15|17. It will much increase the torment of the damned, in that their torments will be as large and strong us their understandings and affections, which will cause those violent passions to be still working. Were their loss never so great, and their sense of it never so passionate, yet if they could but lose the use of their memory, those passions would die, and that loss being forgotten, would little trouble them. But as they cannot lay by their life and being, though then they would account annihilation a singular mercy, so neither can they lay aside any part of their being. Understanding, conscience, affections, memory, must all live to torment them, which should have helped to their happiness. And as by these they should have fed upon the love of God, and drawa forth perpetually the joys of his presence, so by these must they now feed upon the wrath of God, and draw forth continually the dolours of his absence. Therefore, never think, that when I say the hardness of their hearts, and their blindness, dulness, and forgetfulness shall be removed, that therefore they are more holy and happy than before : no, but morally more vile, and hereby far more miserable. Oh, how many times did God by his messengers here call upon them, " Sinners, consider whither you are going. Do but make stand awhile, and think where your way will end, what is the offered glory that you so carelessly reject: will not this be bitterness in the end ?" And yet, these men would never be brought to consider. But in the latter days, saith the Lord, they shall perfectly consider it, when they are *ensnared in the teork of thrir ovn hands,* when God hath arrested them, and judgment is passed upon them, and vengeance is poured out upon them to the full, then they cannot choose but consider it, whether they will or no. Now they have no leisure to consider, nor any room in their memories for the things of another life. Ah ! but then they shall have leisure enough, they shall be where they shall have nothing else t'do but consider it: their memories shall have no other employment to hinder them; it shall even be engraven upon the tables of their hearts. God would hove the doctrine of their eternal state to have been written on the posts of their doors, on their houses, on their hands, and on their hearts : he wouldhave had them mind it and mention it, as they rise and lie down, and a ney walk abroad, that so it might have gone well with them at their latter end. And seeing they rejected this counsel of the Lord, therefore shall it be written always before them in the place of their thraldom, that which way soevci they look they may still behold it.|*Richard Baxter.*

*Verse 16.|" Tfte Lord if known by the judgment which he exeeuteth.'*1" Now if the Lord be known by the judgment which he executeth ; then, the judgment which he executeth must be known ; it must be an open judgment; and such are very many of the judgments of God, they are acted as upon a stage. And I may give you an account in three particulars why the Lord will sometimes do justice in the place of beholders, or in the open sight of others. First, that there may be witnesses enough of what he doth, and so a record of it be kept, at least in the minds and memories of faithful men for the generations to come. Secondly, the Lord doth it not only that he may have witnesses of his justice, but also that his justice and the proceedings of it, may have an effect and a fruit upon those who did not feel it, nor fall under it. This was the reason why the Lord threatened to punish Jerusalem in the sight of the nations. Ezek. v. 6,

7, 8, 14, 15 God would execute judgment in Jerusalem, a city placed

in the midst of the nations, that as the nations had taken notice of the extraordinary favours, benefits, deliverances, and salvations which God wrought for Jerusalem, so they might also take notice of his judgments and sore displeasure against them. Jerusalem was not seated in some nook, corner, or by-place of the world, but in the midst of the nations, that both the goodness and severity

of God towards them might be conspicuous God lets some sinners

suffer, or pimisheth them openly, both because he would have all others take notice that he dislikes what they have done, as also because he would not have others do the like, lest they be made like them, both in the matter and manner of their sufferings. 'Tis a favour as well as our duty, to be taught by other men's harms, and to be instructed by their strokes to prevent our own. . . . Thirdly, God strikes some wicked men in open view, or in the place of beholders for the comfort of his own people, and for their encouragement. Psalm lviii. 10, 11. " The righteous shall rejoice when he seeth the vengeance ;" not that he shall be glad of the vengeance, purely as it is a hurt or a suffering to the creature ; but the righteous shall be glad when he seeth the vengeance of God as it is a fulfilling of the threatening of God against the sin of man, and an evidence of his own holiness It is said (Exod. xiv. 30, 31), that God having overwhelmed the Egyptians in the Red Sea, the Israelites saw the Egyptians dead xipon the sea shore : God did not suffer the carcases of the Egyptians to sink to the bottom of the sea, but caused them to lie upon the shore, that the Israelites might see them ; and when Israel saw that dreadful stroke of the Lord upon the Egyptians, it is said, " The people feared the Lord, and believed the Lord, and his servant Moses." Thus they were confirmed in their faith by God's open judgments upon the Egyptians. They were smitten in the place of beholders, or in the open sight of others. | *Condensed from Joseph Caryl.*

Verse 16.|" The Lord is knmen by the judgment which he executeth ;" when he lays his hand upon sinners, saints tremble, consider his power, majesty, greatness, the nature of his judgments, and so judge themselves, and remove

out of the way whatever may provoke As fire begets a splendour

round about where it is, so do the judgments of God set out to the world his glory, justice, holiness.| *William G-reenhill.*

Verse 16.|" Snared in the work of his own hands." The wages that sin bargains with the sinner are life, pleasure, and profit; but the wages it pays him with are death, torment, and destruction. He that would understand the falsehood and deceit of sin, must compare its promises and its payment together. *Robert South, D.D.,* 1633|1716.

Verse 16.|" Higgaion, Selah," that is, as Ainsworth renders it, " Meditation, Selah :" showing this ought to be seriously considered of. The word " *Higgaion"*is again had (Psalm xcii. 3); being mentioned among other musical instruments, whereby we may gather it to be one of them ; for there is psaltery, nable, higgaion, and harp.|*John Mayer.*

Verse 16.|" The wicked is snared in the work of his own hand.'1'1 Not only do we read it in the word of God, but all history, all experience, records the same righteous justice of God, in snaring the wicked in the work of their own hands. Perhaps the most striking instance on record, next to Haman on his own gallows, is one connected with the horrors of the French Revolution, in which we are told that, " within nine months of the death of the queen Marie Antoinette by the guillotine, every one implicated in her untimely end, her accusers, the judges, the jury, the prosecutors, the witnesses, all, every one at least whose fate is known, perished by the same instrument as their innocent victim." " In the net which they had laid for her was their own foot taken|into the pit which they digged for her did they themselves fall."|*Barton Bouchier,* 1855.

*Yerte 17.|*The ungodly at death must undergo God's fury and indignation.

" *The tcicbed shjiU be turned into hell."*' I have read of a loadstone in Ethiopia which hath two corners, with one it draws the iron to it, with the other it puts the iron from it : so God hath two hands, of mercy and justice ; with the one he will draw the godly to heaven, with the other he will thrust the sinner to bell; and oh, how dreadful is that place ! It is called a fiery lake (Rev. xx. 15) ; a lake, to denote the plenty of torments in hell; a fiery lake, (o show the fierceness of them : fire is the most torturing element. Strabo in his geography mentions a lake in Galilee of such a pestiferous nature that it scaldeth off the skin of whatsoever is cast into it; but, alas ! that lake is cool compared with this fiery lake into which the damned are thrown. To demonstrate this fire terrible, there are two most pernicious qualities in it. 1. It is sulphureous, it is mixed with brimstone (Rev. xxi. 8), which is unsavoury and suffocating. 2. It is iacxtingiiishable ; though the wickrd shall be choked in the flames, yet net consumed (Rev. xx. 10); "And the devil was cast into the lake of fire and brimstone, where the beast and the false prophet are, and shall be tormented day and night forever and ever." Behold the deplorable condition of all ungodly ones in the other world, they shall have a life that always dies, and a death that always lives : may not this affright men out of their sins, and make them become godly? unless they are resolved to try how hot the hell-tire is. | *Thomas Watton.*

Verse 17.|" The vicked shall le turned into hell," etc. By " *the wicked*'1'1 here we must understand unregenerate persons, whoever they are that arc in a state of unregeneracy That person is here spoken of as a " *icickcd* " man that *"forgets* GW,*"* who does not think of him frequently, and with affection, with fear and delight, and those affections that are suitable to serious thoughts of God To forget God and to be a wicked person is all one. And these two things will abundantly evince the truth of this assertion : namely, that this forgetfulness of God excludes the prime and main essentials of religion, and also includes in it the highest anfl most heinous pieces of wickedness, and therefore must needs denominate the subject, a wicked person.

Forgetfulness of God excludes the principal and essential parts of

religion. It implies that a man doth neither esteem nor value the all-sufficiency and holiness of God, as his happiness and portion, as his strength and support ; nor doth he fear him, nor live in subjection to his laws and commands, as his rule; nor doth he aim at the glory of God as his end : therefore every one

ho thus forgets God, must certainly be a wicked person To

exclude God out of our thoughts and not to let him have a place there, not to mind, nor think upon God, is the greatest wickedness of the thoughts that Cm be. And, therefore, though you cannot say of such a one, he will be drunk, or he will swear, cozen, or oppress ; yet if you can say he will forget God, or that he lives all his days never minding nor thinking upon God, you say enough to speak him under -wrath, and to turn him into hell without remedy.l*John Saw,* 1630l1705.

Verne 17.l" The wicked shall be turned into hell." nVmS, *Liskolah | Tusad- long into /tell, down into hell.* The original is very emphatic. | *Adam Clarke.*

Verse 17. | All wickedness came originally with the wicked one from bell ; thither it will be again remitted, and they who hold on its side must accompany it on its return to that place of torment, there to be shut up for ever. The true state both of " nations," and the individuals of which they are composed, is to be estimated from one single circumstance ; namely, whether in their doings they remember, or " forget God." Remembrance of him is the well- spring of virtue ; forgetfulness of him, the fountain of vice. | *George Home, D.D.*

Verte 17.l

.Haz, their fit habitation, fraught with fire
Unquenchable, the house of woe aud paiu.

John Milton, 1G08l 1674.

Verse 17.l

Will without power, the element of *hell,*
Abortive all its acts returning still
Upon Itself; ...... Oh, anguish terrible !
Meet guerdon of self-love, its proper ill !
Malice would scowl upon the foe he fears;
And he witti lip of scorn would seek to kill ;
But neither sees the other, neither hears l
For darkness euch in his own dungeon bare,
Lust pines for dearth, and grief drinks its own tears l
Each in its solitude apart. Hate ware
Against himself, and feeds upon his chain.
Whose iron penetrates the soul it scars,
A dreadful solitude each mind insane,
Each its own place, its prison all alone,

And finds no sympathy to soften pain.
I. A. Heraud.

Verte 18.I" *For the needy shall not alway be forgotten,"* etc. This is a sweet promise for a thousand occasions, and when pleaded before the throne in his name who comprehends in himself every promise, and is indeed himself the great promise of the Bible, it would be found like all others, yea and amen.I *Robert Hawker, D.D.,* 1820.

Verse 18.I" *The expectation, of the poor shall not perish.'"* A heathen could say, when a bird, scared by a hawk, flew into his bosom, I will not betray thee unto thy enemy, seeing thou comest for sanctuary unto me. How much less will God yield up a soul unto its enemy, when it takes sanctuary in his name, saying, Lord, I am hunted with such a temptation, dogged with such a lust ; either thou must pardon it, or I am damned ; mortify it, or I shall be a slave to it ; take me into the bosom of thy love for Christ's sake ; castle me in the arms of thy everlasting strength ; it is in thy power to save me from, or give me up into the hands of my enemy ; I have no confidence in myself or any other : into thy hands I commit my caus? myself, and rely on thee. This dependence of a soul undoubtedly will awaken the almighty power of God for such a one's defence. He hath sworn the greatest oath that can come out of his blessed lips, even by himself, that such as thus fly for refuge to hope in him, shall have strong consolation. Heb. vi. 17. This indeed may give the saint the greater boldness of faith to expect kind entertainment when he repairs to God for refuge, because he cannot come before he is looked for ; God having set up his name and promises as a strong tower, both call? his people into these chambers and expects they should betake themselves thither. I *William Gurnall.*

Verse 18. I As sometimes God is said to hear us in not hearing us, so we may say he should sometimes deny us if he did not delay us. It is (suith Chrysostom) like money, which lying long in the bank, comes home at last with a duck in its mouth, with use upon use ; when money is out a great time, it makes a great return : we can stay thus upon men, and cannot we, shall not we, stay upon the Lord, and for the Lord, for a large return *1* God causeth us by delay

to make the more prayers ; and the more we pray, the longer we stay, the more comfort we shall have, and the more sure we are that we shall have it in the

latter end. Distinguish between denying and delaying In God

our Father are all dimensions of love, and that in an infinite degree ; infinitely infinite : what if he defer us ? so do we our children, albeit we mean no other but to give them their own asking, yet we love to see them wait, that so they may have from us the best things, when they are at the best, in the best time, and in the best manner : if a mother should forget her only boy, yet God hath an infinite memory, he nor can, nor will forget us ; the expectation of the *mailer* shall not *fail for ever,* that is, *never.*I*Richard Cupel.*

Vane 19.I" *Arise, O Lord,"* etc. What does this mean? Are we to consider the psalmist as praying for the destruction of his enemies, as pronouncing malediction, a curse upon them ? No ; these are not the words of one who is wishing that, mischief may happen to his enemies ; they are the words of a prophet, of one who is foretelling, in Scripture language, the evil that must befall them on account of their sins.I*Augustine.*

Vene 20.| *"Put them in fear, 0 Lord,"* etc. We should otherwise think ourselves gods. We are so inclined to sin that we need strong restraints, and o swelled with a natural pride against God, that we need thorns in the flesh to let out the corrupt matter. The constant hanging the rod over us makes us lick the dust, and acknowledge ourselves to be altogether at the Lord's mercy. Though God hath pardoned us, he will make us wear the halter about our necks to humble us.|*Stephen Charnock.*

Verte 20.|*" That the nations may know tJiemselves to be but men,"* The original word is BJlt, *enosh ;* and therefore it is a prayer that they may know themselves to be but miserable, frail, and dying men. The word is in the singular number, but it is used collectively.|*John Calvin.*

HINTS TO THE VILLAGE PREACHER.

Vene.|I. The only object of our praise|" thcc, O Lord." II. The abundant themes of praise|"all thy marvellous works." III. The proper nature of praise|" with my whole heart."|*B. Davies.*

Vene .|*" I trill show forth.'"* Endless employment and enjoyment.

Verte .|*" Thy marvellous works."* Creation, Providence, Redemption, are til marvellous, as exhibiting the attributes of God in such a degree as to excite the wonder of all God's universe. A very suggestive topic.

Verie 2.|Sacred song : its connection with holy gladness.

The duty, excellence, and grounds of holy cheerfulness.

Verte 4.|(1) The rights of the righteous are sure to be assailed, (2) but equally sure to be defended.

Vene 6.|I. The great enemy. II. The destructions he has caused. III. The means of his overthrow. IV. The rest which shall ensue.

Verse 7 *(Jiret clause).*|The eternity of God|the comfort of saints, the terror of sinners.

Verse 8.|The justice of God's moral government, especially in relation to the last great day.

Verse 9.|Needy people, needy times, all-sufficient provision.

Verse 10.|I. All-important knowledge|"know thy name." H. Blessed result|" will put their trust in thee." III. Sufficient reason|" for thou, Lord, bast not forsaken them that seek thec."|*T. W. Medhurtt.*

Knowledge, Faith, Experience, the connection of the three.

Verne 10.|The names of God inspire trust. JEHOVAH *Jireh, Tsidkenu, liophi, Shammah, Shalom, Nisti,* ELOHIM, SHADDAI, ADONAI, etc.

Verse 11.|I. Zion, what is it? II. Her glorious inhabitant, what doth he f III. The twofold occupation of her sons|"sing praises," " declare among- the people his doings." IV. Arguments from the first part of the subject to encourage us in the double duty.

Verse 12.|I. God on awful business. II. Remembers his people ; to spare, honour, bless, and avenge them. III. Fulfils their cries, in their own salvation, and overthrow of enemies. A consolatory sermon for times of war or pestilence.

Verse 13.|*" Have mercy upon me, 0 Lord."* The publican's prayer expounded, commended, presented, and fulfilled.

Verse 13. |*" T/tou that liftest me up from the gates of death."* Deep distresses, Great deliverances. Glorious exaltations.

Verse 14.|*" I will rejoice in thy salvation. "* Especially because it is *tk-ine,* O God, and therefore honours thee. In its freeness, fulness, suitability, certainty, everlastingness. Who can rejoice in this ? Reasons why they should always do so.

Verse 15.|*Lex talionis.* Memorable instances.

Verse 16.|Awful knowledge ; a tremendous alternative as compared with verse 10.

Verse 17.|A warning to forgetters of God.

Verse 18.|Delays in deliverance. I. Unbelief's estimate of them|" forgotten," "perish." II. God's promise|" not always." III. Faith's duty| wait.

Verse 19. *" Let not man prevail."* A powerful plea. Cases when employed in Scripture. The reason of its power. Times for its use.

Verse 20.|A needful lesson, and how it is taught.

PSALM X.

Since this Psalm has no title of Us own, it is supposed by some to be a fragment of Psalm ii. H prefer, however, since it is complete in itself, to consider U as a separate composition. We Have had instances already of Psalms which seem meant to form a pair (Ps. i. and U., Ps. iii. and iv.,) and this, with the ninth, is another specimen of the double Psalm.

The prevailing theme seems to be the oppression and persecution of the wicked, we will, therefore,/or our own guidance, entitle it, The Cby or The Oppressed.

Division.| *The first verse, in an exclamation of surprise, explains the intent of the Psalm, viz., to invoke the interposition of God for the deliverance of his poor and persecuted people, from* t-erse 2 *to* 11, *the character of the oppressor is described in powerful language. In terse* 12, *the cry of the first verse bursts forth again, but with a clearer* utterance. *In the not place (vfrses* 13-15), *God's eye is clearly beheld as regarding all the cruel deeds of the* iticttd; *and as a consequence of divine omniscience, the ultimate judgment of the oppressed isftiyously anticipated (verses* 16-18). *To the Church of God during times of persecution, and to individual saints who are smarting under the hand of the proud sinner, this Psalm fvrnisties suitable language both for prayer and praise.*

EXPOSITION.

WHY standest thou afar off, O LORD ? -*why* hidest thou *thyself* in times of trouble ?

To the tearful eye of the sufferer the Lord seemed to *stand* still, as if he calmly looked on, and did not sympathize -with his afflicted one. Nay, more, the Lord appeared to be *afar off,* no longer "a very present help in trouble," but an inaccessible mountain, into which no man would be able to climb. The presence of God is the joy of his people, but any suspicion of his absence is distracting beyond measure. Let us, then, ever remember that the Lord is nigh us. The refiner is never far from the mouth of the furnace when his gold is in the fire, nd the Son of God is always walking in the midst of the flames when his holy children are cast into them. Yet he that knows the frailty of man will little wonder that when we are sharply exercised, we find it hard to bear the apparent neglect of the Lord when he forbears to work our deliverance.

" Why hitlest thou thyself in times of trouble ?" It is not the trouble, but the hiding of our Father's face, which cuts us to the quick. When trial and desertion come together, we are in as perilous a plight as Paul, when his ship fell into a place where two seas met

(Acts xxvii. 41). It is but little wonder if we are like the vessel which ran aground, and the fore-part stuck fast, and remained uumoveable, while the hinder part was broken by the violence of the waves. When our sun is eclipsed, it is dark indeed. If we need an answer to the question, " Why hidest thou thyself ?" it is to be found in the fact that there is " needs-be," not only for trial, but for heaviness of heart under trial (1 Pet. i. 6); but how could this be the case, if the Lord should shine upon us while he is afflicting us ? Should the parent comfort his child while he is correcting him, where would be the use of the chastening ? A smiling face and a rod are not fit companions. God bares the back that the blow may be felt; for it is only *ftlt* affliction which can become *blest* affliction. If we were carried in the arms of God over every stream, where would be the trial, and where the experience, which trouble is meant to teach us ?

2 The wicked in *his* pride doth persecute the poor : let them be taken in the devices that they have imagined.

3 For the wicked boasteth of his heart's desire, and blesseth the covetous, *whom* the LORD abhorreth.

4 The wicked, through the pride of his countenance, will not seek *after God:* God *is* not in all his thoughts.

$ His ways are always grievous ; thy judgments *are* far above out of his sight : *as for* all his enemies, he puffeth at them.

6 He hath said in his heart, I shall not be moved : for / *s/ia/l* never *be* in adversity.

7 His mouth is full of cursing and deceit and fraud : under his tongue *is* mischief and vanity.

8 He sitteth in the lurking places of the villages : in the secret places doth he murder the innocent : his eyes are privily set against the poor.

9 He lieth in wait secretly as a lion in his den : he lieth in vait to catch the poor : he doth catch the poor, when he draweth him into his net.

10 He croucheth, *and* humbleth himself, that the poor may fall by his strong ones.

11 He hath said in his heart, God hath forgotten : he hideth his face ; he will never see *it.*

2. The second verse contains the formal indictment against the wicked : " *The wicked in hit pride doth persecute the poor.*'1" The accusation divides itself into two distinct charges,|pride and tyranny ; the one the root and cause of the other. The second sentence is the humble petition of the oppressed : " *Let them be taken in the devices that they hate imagined."* " The prayer is reasonable, just, and natural. Been our enemies themselves being judges, it is but right that men should be done by as they wished to do to others. We only weigh you in your own scales, and measure your corn with your own bushel. Tumble shall be thy day, O persecuting Babylon ! when thou shalt be made to drink of the wine- cup which thou thyself hast filled to the brim with the blood of saints. There are none who will dispute the justice of God, when he shall hang every Haman on his own gallows, and cast all the enemies of his Daniels into their own den of lions.

3. The indictment being read, and the petition presented, the evidence is now heard upon the first count. The evidence is very full and conclusive upon the matter of *pride,* and no jury could hesitate to give a verdict against the prisoner at the bur. Let us,

however, hear the witnesses one by one. The first testifies that he is a boaster. " *For the wicked loasteth of his heart's desire.'*" He is a very silly boaster, for he glories in a mere desire : a very brazen-faced boaster, for that desire is villainy ; and a most abandoned sinner, to boast of that which ia his shame. Bragging sinners are the worst and most contemptible of men, especially when their filthy desires, ltoo filthy to be carried into act,lbecome the theme of their boastings. When Mr. Hate-Good and Mr. Heady are joined in partnership, they drive a brisk trade in the devil's wares. This one proof is enough to condemn the prisoner at the bar. Take him away, jailor ! But stay, another witness desires to be sworn and heard. This time, the impudence of the proud rebel is even more apparent; for he " *Heseth the covetous, whom the Lord abhorreth.'*" This is insolence, which is pride unmasked. He is haughty enough to differ from the Judge of all the earth, and bless the men whom God hath cursed. So did the sinful generation in the days of Malachi, who called the proud happy, and set up those ttmt worked wickedness (Mai. iii. 15). These base pretenders would dispute with their Maker ; they wouldl

" Snatch from his hand the balance and the rod,
Rejudge his justice, be the god of God."

How often have we heard the wicked man speaking in terms of honour of the covetous, the grinder of the poor, and the sharp dealer ! Our old proverb hath it,l
" I wot well how the world wags;
He is moBt lovud that hath most bags."

Pride meets covetousness, and compliments it as wise, thrifty, and prudent. We say it with sorrow, there are many professors of religion who esteem a rich man, and flatter him, even though they know that he has fattened himself upon the flesh and blood of the poor. The only sinners who are received as respectable are covetous men. If a man is a fornicator, or a drunkard, we put him out of the church ; but who ever read of church discipline against that idolutrous wretch,lthe covetous man ? Let us tremble, lest we be found to be partakers of this atrocious sin of pride, " blessing the covetous, whom Jehovah abnorreth."

4. The proud boastings and lewd blessings of the wicked have been received in evidence against him, and now his own face confirms the accusation, and his empty closet cries aloud against him. " *The wicked, through the pride of hit countenance, will not seek after Clod.*" Proud hearts breed proud looks and stiff knees. It is an admirable arrangement that the heart is often written on the countenance, just as the motion of the wheels of a clock find their record on its face. A brazen face and a broken heart never go together. We are not quite sure that the Athenians were wise when they ordained that men should be tried in the dark lest their countenances should weigh with the judges ; for there is much more to be learned from the motions of the muscles of the face than from the words of the lips. Honesty shines in the face, but villainy peeps out at the eyes.

See the effect of pride ; it kept the man from seeking God. It is hard to pray with a stiff neck and an unbending knee. " *God is not in all his thoughts:*" he thought much, but he had no thoughts for God. Amid heaps of chaff there was not a grain of wheat.

The only place where God is not is in the thoughts of the wicked. This is a damning accusation ; for where the God of heaven is not, the Lord of hell is reiguing and raging ; and if God be not in our thoughts, our thoughts will bring us to perdition.

5. " *His ways are always grievous.*" To himself they are hard. Men go a rough road when they go to hell. God has hedged-up the way of sin : O what folly to leap these hedges and fall among the thorns ! To others, also, his ways cause much sorrow and vexation ; but what cares he ? He sits like the idol god upon his monstrous car, utterly regardless of the crowds who are crushed as he lolls along. " *Thy judgments are far above out of his sight:*" he looks high, but not high enough. As God is forgotten, so are his judgments. He is not able to comprehend the things of God ; a swine may sooner look through a telescope at the stars than this man study the Word of God to understand the righteousness of the Lord. " *As for all his enemies, he puffeth at them.*" He defies and domineers ; and when men resist his injurious behaviour, he sneers at them, and threatens to annihilate them with a puff. In most languages there is u word of contempt borrowed from the action of puffing with the lips, and in English we should express the idea by saying, " He cries, ' Pooh ! Pooh ! ' *at* his enemies." Ah! there is one enemy who will not thus be puffed at. Death will puff at the candle of his life and blow it out, and the wicked boaster will find it grim fork to brag in the tomb.

6. The testimony of the sixth verse concludes the evidence against the prisoner upon the first charge of pride, and certainly it is conclusive in the highest degree. The present witness has been prying into the secret chambers of the heart, and has come to tell us what he has heard. " *fie hath said in his heart, I tafl not oe moved: for I shall never le in adversity.*" O impertinence run to swd ! The man thinks himself immutable, and omnipotent too, for *he, he* is never to be in adversity. He counts himself a privileged man. He sits alnnp, ad shall see no sorrow. His nest is in the stars, and he dreams not of a hand that shall pluck him thence. But let us remember that this man's house is built upon the sand, upon a foundation no more substantial than the rolling waves ofthe sea. He that is too secure is never safe. Boastings are not buttresses, and self-confidence is a sorry bulwark. This is the ruin of fools, that when they succeed they become too big, and swell with self-conceit, as if their summer would last for ever, and their flowers bloom on eternally. Be humble, 0 man ! for thou art mortal, and thy lot is mutable.

The second crime is now to be proved. The fact that the man is proud and arrogant may go a long way to prove that he is vindictive and cruel. Hainan's pride was the father of a cruel design to murder all the Jews. Nebuchadnezzar builds an idol ; in pride he commands all men to bow before it ; and then cruelty stands ready to heat the furnace seven times hotter for those who will not yield to his imperious will. Every proud thought is twin brother to a cruel thought. He who exalts himself will despise others, and one step further will make him a tyrant.

7. Let us now hear the witnesses in court. Let the wretch speak for himself, for out of his own mouth he will be condemned. " *His mouth ii full of cursing and deceit and fraud.*" There is not only a little evil there, but his mouth is full of it. A three-headed serpent hath stowed away its coils and venom within the den of his black mouth. There is *carting* which he spits against both God and men, *denit* with which he entraps the unwary, and *fraud* by which, even in his common dealings, he robs his neighbours.

Beware of such a man : have no sort of dealing with him : none but the silliest of geese would go to the fox's sermon, and none but the most foolish will put themselves into the society of knaves. But we must proceed. Let us look under this man's tongue as well as in his mouth; *"under his tongue is mischief and vanity."* Deep in his throat are the unborn words which shall come forth as mischief and iniquity.

8. Despite the bragging of this base wretch, it seems that he is as cowardly as he is cruel. " *He sitteth in the lurking places of the villages : in the secret placet doth he murder the innocent: his eyes are privily set against the poor."* He acts the part of the highwayman, who springs upon the unsuspecting traveller in some desolate part of the road. There are always bad men lying in wait for the saints. This is a land of robbers and thieves ; let us travel well armed, for every lish conceals an enemy. Everywhere there are traps laid for us, and foes thirsting for our blood. There are enemies at our table as well as across the sea. We arc never safe, save when the Lord is with us.

9. The picture becomes blacker, for here is the cunning of the lion, and of the huntsman, as well as the stealthiness of the robber. Surely there are some men who come up to the very letter of this description. With watching, perversion, slander, whispering, and false swearing, they ruin the character of the righteous, and murder the innocent ; or, with legal quibbles, mortgages, bonds, writs, and the like, they catch the poor, and draw them into a net. Chrysostom was peculiarly severe upon this last phase of cruelty, but assuredly not more so than was richly merited. Take care, brethren, for there are other traps besides these. Hungry lions are crouching in every den, and fowlers spread their nets in every field.

Quarles well pictures our danger in those memorable lines,|

" The close pursuers' busy hands do plant
Snares in thy substance ; snares attend thy wants ;
Snares In thy credit; snares in thy disgrace ;
Snares in thy high estate ; snares in thy base;
Snares tuck thy bed ; and ennrea surround thy hoard ;
Snares watch thy thoughts ; and snares attack thy word;

Snares In thy quiet; snares in thy commotion;
Snares in thy diet; snares in thy devotion;
Snares lurk in thy resolves; smires in thy doubt ;
Snares lie within thy heart, and snares without;
Snares are above thy head, and snares beneath ;
Snares in thy sickness ; smircs are in thy death."

O Lord 1 keep thy servants, and defend us from all our enemies !

10. " *He croucheth and humbleth himself, that the poor may fall by his strong ones."* Seeming humility is often armour-bearer to malice. The lion crouchesthat he may leap with the greater force, and bring down his strong limbs upon bis prey. When a wolf was old, and had tasted human blood, the old Saxon cried, " Ware, wolf !" and we may cry, " Ware fox 1" They who crouch to our feet are longing to make us fall. Be very careful of fawners ; for friendship and flattery aie deadly enemies.

11. As upon the former count, so upon this one ; a witness is forthcoming, who has been listening at the keyhole of the heart. Speak up, friend, a.nd let us hear your story. " *He hath Mid in his heart, God hath forgotten: he hideth his fate; he mil never tee it.*" This cruel man comforts himself with the idea that God is blind, or, at least, forgetful : a foiiJ and foolish fancy, indeed. Men doubt Omniscience when they persecute the saints. If we had a sense of God's presence with us, it would be impossible for us to ill-treat his children. In fact, there can scarcely be a greater preservation from sin than the constant thought of " thou, God, seest me."

Thus has the trial proceeded. The case has been fully stated ; and now it is hut little wonder that the oppressed petitioner lifts up the cry for judgment, which we find in the following verse : I

12 Arise, O LORD ; O God, lift up thine hand : forget not the humble.

With what bold language will faith address its God ! and yet what unbelief is mingled with our strongest confidence. Fearlessly the Lord is stirred up to rise and lift up his hand, yet timidly is he begged not to forget the humble ; aa if Jehovah could ever be forgetful of his saints. This verse is the incessant cry of the Church, and she will never refrain therefrom until her Lord shall come in his glory to avenge her of all her adversaries.

13 Wherefore doth the wicked contemn God ? he hath said in his heart, Thou wilt not require *it.*

14 Thou hast seen *it* / for thou beholdest mischief and spite, to requite *it* with thy hand : the poor committeth himself unto thee ; thou art the helper of the fatherless.

15 Break thou the arm of the wicked and the evil *man :* seek out his wickedness /zV/thou find none.

In these verses the description of the wicked is condensed, and the evil of his character traced to its source, viz., atheistical ideas with regard to the government of the world. We may at once perceive that this is intended to be another urgent plea with the Lord to show his power, and reveal his justice. When the 'wicked call God's righteousness in question, we may well beg him to teach them terrible things in righteousness. In verse 13, the hope of the infidel and his heart-wishes are laid bare. He despises the Lord, because he will not believe that sin will meet with punishment : " *he hath said in his heart, Thou wilt not require it.*" If there were no hell for other men, there ought to be one for those who question the justice of it. This vile suggestion receives its answer in yeree 14. " *Thou hast seen it; for thou Mtoldent mischief and spite, to requite with thy hand.*" God is all-eye to see, and all-hand to punish his enemies. From Divine oversight there is no hiding, and from Divine justice there is no fleeing. Wanton mischief shall meet with woeful misery, and those who harbour pitc shall inherit sorrow. Verily there is a God which judgeth in the earth, or is this the only instance of the presence of God in the world ; for while he chastises the oppressor, he befriends the oppressed. " *The poor committeth him- "y wito thee.*" They give themselves up entirely into the Lord's hands. Resigning their judgment to his enlightenment, and their wills to his supremacy, they rest assured that he will order all things for the best. Nor does he deceive ᵀᴹir hope. He preserves them in times of need, and causes them to rejoice in ha goodness. " *Thou art the helper of the fatherless.*" God is the parent of all orphans. When the earthly father sleeps beneath the sod, a heavenly Fathersmiles from above. By some means or other, orphan children are fed, and well they may when they have such a Father.

15. In this verse we hear again the burden of the psalmist's prayer : " *BreaJc thou the arm of the wicked and the etil man.*1' l Let the sinner lose his power to sin ; stop the tyrant, arrest the oppressor, weaken the loins of the mighty, and dash in pieces the terrible. They aeny thy justice : let them feel it to the full. Indeed, they shall feel it; for God shall hunt the sinner for ever : so long as there is a grain of sin in him it shall be sought out and punished. It is not a little worthy of note, that very few great persecutors have ever died in their beds : the curse has manifestly pursued them, and their fearful sufferings have made them own *that* divine justice at which they could at one time launch defiance. God permits tyrants to arise as thorn-hedges to protect his church from the intrusion of hypocrites, and that he may teach his backsliding children by them, as Gideon did the men of Succoth with the briers of the wilderness ; but he soon cuts up these Herods, like the thorns, and casts them into the fire. Thales, the Milesian, one of the wise men of Greece, being asked what he thought to be the greatest rarity in the world, replied, " To see a tyrant live to be an old man." See how the Lord breaks, not only the arm, but the neck of proud oppressors ! To the men who had neither justice nor mercy for the saints, there shall be rendered justice to the full, but not a grain of mercy.

16 The Lord *is* King for ever and ever: the heathen are perished out of his land.

17 Lord, thou hast heard the desire of the humble : thou wilt prepare their heart, thou wilt cause thine ear to hear :

18 To judge the fatherless and the oppressed, that the man of the earth may no more oppress.

The Psalm ends with a song of thanksgiving to the great and everlasting King, because he has granted the desire of his humble and oppressed people, has defended the fatherless, and punished the heathen who trampled upon his poor and afflicted children. Let us learn that we are sure to speed well, if we carry our complaint to the King of kings. Rights will be vindicated, and wrongs redressed, at his throne. His government neglects not the interests of the needy, nor docs it tolerate oppression in the mighty. Great God, we leave ourselves in thine hand ; to thee we commit thy church afresh. Arise, O God, and let the man of the earthlthe creature of a daylbe broken before the majesty of thy power. Come, Lord Jesus, and glorify thy people. Amen and Amen.

EXPLANATORY NOTES AND QUAINT SAYINGS.

*Whole Psalm.*lThere is not, in my judgment, a Psalm which describes the mind, the manners, the works, the words, the feelings, and the fate of the ungodly with so much propriety, fulness, and light, as this Psalm. So that, if in any respect there has not been enough said heretofore, or if there shall be anything wanting in the Psalms that shall follow, we may here find a perfect image and representation of iniquity. This Psalm, therefore, is a type, form, and description of that man, who, though he may be in the sight of himself and of men more excellent than Peter himself, is detestable in the eyes of God ; and this it was that moved Augustine, and those who followed him, to understand the Psalm of Antichuist. But as the Psalm is without a title, let us embrace the most general and common understanding of it (as I said), and let us look at the picture of ungodliness which it sets before us. Not that we would deny the propriety of the acceptation in which others receive it, nay, we will, in our

general acceptation of the Psalm, include also its reference to Antichrist. A.nd, indeed, it will not be at all absurd if we join this Psalm with the preceding, in its order thus. That David, in the preceding, spoke of the ungodly converted, and prayed for those who were to be converted. But that here he is speaking of the ungodly that are still left so, and in power prevailing over the weak Almcth, concerning whom he has no hope, or is in a great uncertainty of mind, whether they ever will be converted or not.|*Martin Luther.*

Vene 1.|" *Why hidett thou thyself in times of trouble t"* The answer to this is not far to seek, for if the Lord did not hide himself it would not be a time of trouble at all. As well ask why the sun does not shine at night, when for certain there could be no night if he did. It is essential to our thorough chastisement that the Father should withdraw his srnile : there is a needs be not only for manifold temptations, but that we be in heaviness through them. The design of the rod is only answered by making us smart. If there be no pain, there will be no profit. If there be no hiding of God, there will be no bitterness, and consequently no purging efficacy in his chastisements.| *C. If. 8.*

Vene 1 *(last clause).*|" *Times of trouble"* should be times of confidence ; fixedness of heart on God would prevent fears of heart. Psalm cxii. 7. " He shall not be afraid of evil tidings : his heiirt is fixed." How? " Trusting in the Lord. His heart is established, he shall not be afraid." Otherwise without it we shall be as light as a weather-cock, moved with every blast of evil tidings, onr hopes will swim or sink according to the news we hear. Providence would seem to sleep unless faith and prayer awaken it. The disciples had but little faith in their Master's accounts, yet that little faith awakened him in a storm, and he relieved them. Unbelief doth only discourage God from showing his power in taking our parts.|*Stephen CharnocTc.*

Vene 2.|" *The wicked in his pride doth persecute the poor.""* The Oppressor's Ea. I seek but what is my own by law ; it was his own free act and deed| the execution lies for goods and body ; and goods or body I will have, or else my money. "What if his beggarly children pine, or his proud wife perish ? they perish at their own charge, not mine ; and what is that to me *1* I must be paid, or he lie by it until I have my utmost farthing, or his bones. The law is just and good; and, being ruled by that, how can my fair proceedings be unjust f What is thirty in the hundred to a man of trade ? Are we born to thrum caps or pick straws ? and sell our livelihood for a few tears, and a whining face ? I thank God they move me not so much as a howling dog at midnight. I'll give no day if heaven itself would be security. I must have present money, or his bones. . . . Fifteen shillings in the pound composition ! I'll hang first. Come, tell me not of a good conscience : a good conscience is no parcel of my trade ; it hath made more bankrupts than all the loose wives in the universal city. My conscience is no fool : it tells me my own is my own, and that a well crammed bag is no deceitful friend, but will stick close to me when all my friends forsake nie. If to gain a good estate out of nothing, and to regain a desperate debt which is as good as nothing, be the fruits and sign of a bad conscience, God help the good. Come, tell me not of griping and oppression. The world is nard, and he that hopes to thrive must gripe as hard. What I give I give, and hat I lend I lend. If the way to heaven be to turn beggar upon earth, let them take it that like it. I know not what you call oppression, the law is my direction ; but of the two, it is more profitable to oppress than to be oppressed, "debtors would be honest and discharge, our hands were bound ; but when their failing offends my bags, they touch the apple of my eye, and I must right them.*Francis Quarles.*

Verte 2.*That famous persecutor, Domitian, like others of the Roman wnperors, assumed divine honours, and heated the furnace seven times hotter gainst Christians because they refused to worship his image. In like manner, hen the popes of Rome became decorated with the blasphemous titles of*Hasten of the World,* and *Universal Fathers,* they let loose their blood-hounds upon the faithful. Pride is the egg of persecution.*C. H. 8.*

Verse 2.*" Pride,'*1" is a vice which cleavcth so fast unto the hearts of men, that if we were to strip ourselves of all faults one by one, we should undoubtedly find it the very last and hardest to put off.*Richard Hooker,* 1554*1600.

Verse 3*" The wicked boaateth,'"* etc. He braggeth of his evil life, whereof he maketh open profession ; or he boasteth that lie will accomplish his wicked designs ; or glorieth that he hath already accomplished them. Or it may be understood that he commendeth others who are according to the desires of his own soul; that is, he rcspecteth or honoureth none but such as are like him, and them only he esteemeth. Psalm xxxvi. 4, and xlix. 18 ; Rom. i. 32.*John Diodati,* 1648.

Verse 8.*" The wicked. . . . Wesseth the covetous.'*1'1 Like will to like, as the common proverb is. Such as altogether neglect the Lord's commandments not only commit divers gross sins, but commend those who in sinning are like themselves. For in their affections they allow them, in their speeches they flatter and extol them, and in their deeds they join with them and maintain them.* Peter Muffet,* 1594.

Verne 3.*" The covetous."* Covetousness is the desire of possessing that which we have not, and attaining unto great riches and worldly possessions. And whether this be not the character of trade and merchandise and traffic of every kind, the great source of those evils of over-trading which are everywhere complained of, I refer to the judgment of the men around me, who are engaged in the commerce and business of life. Compared with the regular and quiet diligence of our fathers, and their contentment with small but sure returns, the wild and wide-spread speculation for great gains, the rash and hasty adventures which are daily made, and the desperate gamester-like risks which are run, do reveal full surely that a spirit of Covetousness hath been poured out upon men within the last thirty or forty years. And the providence of God corresponding thereto, by wonderful and unexpected revolutions, by numerous inventions for manufacturing the productions of the earth, in order to lead men into temptation, hath impressed upon the whole face of human affairs, a stamp of earnest world- liness not known to our fathers : insomuch that our youth do enter life no longer with the ambition of providing things honest in the sight of men, keeping their credit, bringing up their fstmily, and realising a competency, if the Lord prosper them, but with the ambition of making a fortune, retiring to their ease, and enjoying the luxuries of the present life. Against which crying sin of covetous- ness, dearly beloved brethren, I do most earnestly call upon you to wage a good warfare. This place is its seat, its stronghold, even this metropolitan city of Christian Britain ; and ye who are called by the grace of God out of the great thoroughfare of Mammon, are so elected for the express purpose of testifying against this and all other the backslidings of the church planted here ; and especially against this, aa being in my opinion, one of the most evident and the most common of them all. For who hath not been snared in the snare of Covetousness ?|*Edward Irving, 1828.*

'Verse 3.|" The covetous, whom the Lord abhorreth.'1" Christ knew what he epake when he said, " No man can serve two masters." Matt. vi. 24. Meaning God and the world, because each would have all. As the angel and the devil strove for the body of Moses (Jude 9), not who should have a part, but who should have the whole, so they strive still for our souls, who shall have alL Therefore, the apostle saith, "The love of this world is enmity to God (James iv. 4). signifying such emulation between these two, that God cannot abide the world should have a part, and the world cannot abide that God should have a part. Therefore, the love of the world must needs be enmity to God, and therefore the lovers of the world must ueeds be enemies to God, and so no covetous man is God's servant, but God's enemy. For this cause covetousneas is called idolatry (Eph. v. 5), which is the most contrary sin to God, because astreason sets up another king in the king's place, so idolatry sets up another god in God's place.|*Henry Smith.*

Firw 4.|" *The wicked, through the pride of hit countenance, will not seek after God.*" He is judged a proud man (without a jury sitting on him), who when condemned will not submit, will not stoop so low as to accept of a pardon. I must indeed correct myself, men are willing to be justified, but they would have their duties to purchase their peace and the favour of God. Thousands will die and be damned rather than they will have a pardon upon the sole account of Christ's merits and obedience. Oh, the cursed pride of the heart ! When will men cease to be wiser than God ? To limit God ? When will men be contented with God's way of saving them by the blood of the everlasting covenant ? How dare men thus to prescribe to the infinitely wise God ? Is it not enough for thee that thy destruction is of thyself ? But must thy salvation be of thyself too ? Is it not enough that thou hast wounded thyself, but wilt thou die for ever, rather than be beholden to a plaister of free grace ? Wilt be damned unless thou mayest be thine own Saviour ? God is willing (" God so loved the world that he gave his only Son"), art thou so proud as that thou wilt not be beholden to God ? Thou wilt deserve, or have nothing. What shall I say f Poor thou art, and yet proud ; thou hast nothing but wretchedness and misery, and yet thou art talking of a purchase. This is a provocation. " God resisteth the proud," especially the spiritually proud. He that is proud of his clothes and parentage, is not so contemptible in God's eyes as he that is proud of his abilities, and so scorns to submit to God's methods for his salvation by Christ, and by his righteousness alone. | *Lewis Stuckley.*

Itm 4.|" *The wicked, through the pride of hit countenance, mil not seek after God.*" The pride of the wicked is the principal reason why they will not seek after the knowledge of God. This knowledge it prevents them from seeking in various ways. In the first place, it renders God a disagreeable object of contemplation to the wicked, and a knowledge of him as undesirable. Pride consists in an unduly exalted opinion of one's self. It is, therefore, impatient of a rival, hates a superior, and cannot endure a master. In proportion as it prevails in the heart, it makes us wish to see nothing above us, to acknowledge no law but our own wills, to follow no rule but our own inclinations. Thus it led Satan to rebel against his Creator, and our first parents to desire to be as gods. Since such are the effects of pride, it is evident that nothing can be more painful to a proud heart than the thoughts of such a being as God ; one who is infinitely powerful, just, and holy ; who can neither be resisted, deceived, nor deluded ; who disposes, according to his own sovereign pleasure, of all crettures and events ; and who, in an especial manner, hates pride, and is determined to abase and punish it. Such a being pride can contemplate only with feelings of dread, aversion, and abhorrence. It must look upon him as its natural enemy, the great enemy, whom it has to fear. But the knowledge of God directly tends to bring this infinite, irresistible, irreconcilable enemy full lo the view of the proud man. It teaches him that he has a superior, a master, from whose authority he cannot escape, whose power he cannot resist, snd whose will he must obey, or be crushed before him, and be rendered miserable forever. It shows him what he hates to see, that, in despite of his opposition, God's counsel shall stand, that he will do all his pleasure, and that in all things wherein men deal proudly, God is above them. These truths torture the pioud inhumbled hearts of the wicked, and hence they hate that knowledge of God which teaches these truths, and will not seek it. On the contrary, they wish to remain ignorant of such a being, and to banish all thoughts of him from their nunds. With this view, they neglect, pervert, or explain away those passages ol revelation which describe God's true character, and endeavour to believe tuilheis altogether such a one as themselves.

How foolish, how absurd, how niinous, how blindly destructive of its own ot)ject, does pride appear ! By attempting to soar, it only plunges itself in themire ; and while endeavouring to erect for itself a throne, it undermines the ground on which it stands, and digs its own grave. It plunged Satan from heaven into hell ; it banished our first parents from paradise ; and it will, in a similar manner, ruin all who indulge in it. It keeps us in ignorance of God, shuts us out from his favour, prevents us from resembling him, deprives us in this world of all the honour and happiness which communion with him would confer ; and in the next, unless previously hated, repented of, and renounced, will bar for ever against us the door of heaven, and close upon us the gates of hell. O then, my friends, beware, above all things, beware of pride ! Beware, lest you indulge it imperceptibly, for it is perhaps, of all sins, the most secret, subtle, and insinuating.|*Edward Payson, D.D.,* 1783|1827.

Verne 4.|David speaks in Psalm x. of great and potent oppressors and politicians, who see none on earth greater than themselves, none higher than they, and think therefore that they may *impune* prey upon the smaller, as beasts use to do ; and in the fourth verse this is made the root and ground of all, that God is not in all his thoughts. " *The wicked, through the pride of his countenance, will not iteek after God: Ood is not in all hit thoughts."* The words are diversely read, and all make for this sense. Some read it, " No God in all his crafty presumptuous purposes ;" others," All his thoughts are, there is no God." Themean- ing whereof is not only that among the swarm and crowd of thoughts that fill his mind, the thought of God is seldom to be found, and comes not in among the rest, which yet is enough for the purpose in hand ; but further, that in all his projects and plots, and consultations of his heart (the first reading of the words intends), whereby he contrives and lays the plot, form, and draught of all his actions, he never takes God or his will into consideration or consultation, to square and frame all accordingly, but proceeds and goes on in all, and carries on all as if there were no God to be consulted with. He takes not him along with him, no more than if he were no God ; the thoughts of him and his will sway him not. As you use to say, when a combination of men leave out some one they should advise with, that such a one is not of their counsel, is not in the plot ; so nor is God in their purposes and advisings, they do all without him. But this is not all the meaning, but farther, all their thought is, that there is no God. This is there made the bottom, the foundation, the groundwork and reason of all their wicked plots and injurious projects, and deceitful carriages and proceedings, that seeing there is no God or power above them to take notice of it, to regard or requite them, therefore they may be bold to go on.|*Thomas Goodwin.*

Versi 4.|" *Of his countenance.* " Which pride he carrieth engraven in his very countenance and forehead, and makes it known in all his carriages and gestures. " *Will not seek*" namely, he contemneth all divine and human laws, he feareth not, respecteth not God's judgments ; he careth for nothing, so he may fulfil his desires ; enquires after, nor examines nothing ; all things are indifferent to him.|*John Diodati.*

Verse 4.|" *All his thoughts are,* there is *no God;*" thus some read the passage. 8eneca says, there are no atheists, though there would be some ; if any say there is no God, they lie ; though they say it in the day time, yet in the night when they are alone they deny it; howsoever some desperately harden themselves, yet if God doth but show himself terrible to them, they confess him. Many of the heathens and others, have denied that there is a God, yet when they were in distress, they did fall down and confess him, as Diagoras, that grand atheist, when he was troubled with the strangullion, acknowledged a deity which he had denied. These kind of atheists I leave to the tender mercies of God, of which I doubt it whether there be any for them.| *Richard Stack.*

Verse 4.|-' *God is not in all his thoughts.* " It is the black work of an ungodly man or an atheist, that God is not in all his thoughts. What comfort can be had in the being of God without thinking of him with reverence and delight f A God forgotten is as good as no God to us.|*Stephen Charnock.*

Vtrse 4.| Trifles possess us, but " *God is not in attour thoughts,* " seldom the sole object of them. We have durable thoughts of transitory things, and flitting thoughts of a durable and eternal good. The covenant of grace engageth the whole heart to God, and bars anything else from engrossing it; but what strangers are God and the souls of most men ! Though we have the knowledge of him by creation, yet he is for the most part an unknown God in the relations wherein he stands to us, because a God undelighted in. Hence it is, as one obsjrves, that because we observe not the ways of God's wisdom, conceive not of him in his vast perfections, nor are stricken with an admiration of his goodness, that we have fewer good sacred poems than of any other kind. The wits of men hang the wing when they come to exercise their reasons and fancies about God. Parts and strength are given us, as well as corn and wine to the Israelites, for the service of God, but those are consecrated to some cursed Baal, Hosea ii. 8. . Like Venus in the poet, we forsake heaven to follow some Adonis. *Stephen Charnaek.*

Verses 4, 5.|The world hath a spiritual fascination and witchcraft, by which, where it hath once prevailed, men are enchanted to an utter forgetfulness of themselves and God, and being drunk with pleasures, they are easily engaged to a madness and height of folly. Some, like foolish children, are made to keep a great stir in the world for very trifles, for a vain show ; they think themselves great, honourable, excellent, and for this make a great bustle, when the world hath not added one cubic to their stature of real worth. Others are by this Circe transformed into savage creatures, and act the pait of lions and tigers. Others, like swine, wallow in the lusts of uncleanness. Others are unmanned, putting off all natural affections, care not who they ride over, so they may rule over or be made great. Others are taken with ridiculous frenzies, so that a man that stands in the cool shade of a sedate composure would judge them out of their wits. It would make a man admire to read of the frisks of Cains Caligula, Xerxes, Alexander, and many others, who because they were above many men, thought themselves above human nature. They forgot they were born and must die, and did such things as would have made them, but that their greatness overawed it, a laughing-stock and common scorn to children. Neither must we think that these were but some few or rare instances of worldly intoxication, when the Scripture notes it as a general distemper of all that bow down to worship this idol. They live " without God in the world,1' saith the apostle, that is, they so carry it as if there were no God to take notice of them to check them for their madness. " *God wnot in all his thoughts.*" Verse 4. " *The yudy- mt of Ood are far above out of his sight;*" he puffs at his enemies (ver. 5), andsaith in his heart, he " *ihall never le moved.*" Verse 6. The whole Psalm describes the -worldling as a man that hath lost all his understanding, and is acting the part of a frantic bedlam. What then can be a more fit engine for the deril to work with than the pleasures of the world ?|*Richard Oilpin.*

Yerte 5.|" *Grievous,*" or troublesome ; that is, all his endeavours and actions aim at nothing but at hurting others. " *Are far above,*" for he is altogether carnal, he hath not any disposition nor correspondence with the justice of thy law, which is altogether spiritual ; and therefore cannot lively represent unto himself thy judgments, and the issue of the wicked according to the said law. Rom. vii. 14 ; 1 Cor. ii. 14. " *He puffeth ;*" he doth most arrogantly despise them, and is confident he can overthrow them with a puff.|*John JJiodati.*

VerieS.|" *Thy judgments are far aboteout of hit sight.*" Because God does not immediately visit every sin with punishment, ungodly men do not see that in due time he judges all the earth. Human tribunals must of necessity, by promptness and publicity, commend themselves to the common judgment, but the Lord's modes of dealing with sin are sujblimer and apparently more tardy, hence the bat's eyes of godless men cannot see them, and the grovelling wits of men Rffluot comprehend them. If God sat in the gate of every village and held his court there, even fools might discern his righteousness, but they are not capable of perceiving that for a matter to be settled in the highest court, even in heaven

6

SECTION 6

---

itself, is a far more solemn matter. Let believers take heed lest they fall in a degree into the same error, and begin to criticise the actions of The Great Supreme, when they are too elevated for human reason to comprehend them.l *0. II. 8.*

*Verne 5.l" The judgment of God are far above out of his tight.'*1" Out of his Bight, as an eagle at her highest towering so lessens herself to view, that he sees not the talons, nor fears the grip. Thus man presumes till he hath sinned, and then despairs as fast afterwards. At first, " Tush, doth God see it ?" At lust, "Alas! will God forgive it?" But if a man will not know his sins, his sins will know him ; the eyes which presumption shuts, commonly despair opens. *Thomas Adam.*

*Verse 5.l" As for all his enemies, he puffeth at them.'*1" David describeth a *proud man, puffing at his enemies:* he is puffed up and swelled with high conceits of himself, as if he had some great matter in him, and he puffs at others as if he could do some great matter against them, forgetting that himself is but, as to his being in this world, a puff of wind which passeth away.l*Joseph Caryl.*

Verse 5. l" As for all his enemies, he puffeth at them ;" literally, " *He whittle at them."* He is given over to the dominion of gloomy indifference, and he cares as little for others as for himself. Whosoever may be imagined by him to be an enemy he cares not. Contempt and ridicule are his only weapons ; and he hiis forgotten how to use others of a more sacred character. His mental habits are marked by scorn ; and he. treats with contempt the judgments, opinions, and practices of the wisest of men.|*John Morison.*

Verse 6.|" He hath said in his heart, I shall not be moved: for I shall neter le in adversity." Carnal security opens the door for all impiety to enter into the soul. Pompey, when he had in vain assaulted a city, and could not take it by force, devised this stratagem in way of agreement; he told them he would leave the siege and make peace with them, upon condition that they would let in u few weak, sick, and wounded soldiers among them to be cured. They let in the soldiers, and when the city was secure, the soldiers let in Pompey's army. A carnal settled security will let in a whole army of lusts into the soul.| *Thomas Brooks.*

Verse 6.|" He hath said in his heart, I shall not be moved: for I shall nntr be in aihersity." To consider religion always on the comfortable side ; to congratulate one's self for having obtained the end before we have made use of the means ; to stretch the hands to receive the crown of righteousness before they have been employed to fight the battle ; to be content with a false peace, and to use no efforts to obtain the graces to which true consolation is annexed : this is a dreadful calm, like that which some voyagers describe, and which is a very singular forerunner of a very terrible event. All on a sudden, in the wide ocean, the sea becomes calm, the surface of the water clear as a crystal, smooth as glass|the air serene ; the unskilled passenger becomes tranquil and happy, but the old mariner trembles. In an instant the waves froth, the winds murmur, the heavens kindle, a thousand gulfs open, a frightful light inflames the air, and every wave threatens sudden death. This is an image of many men's assurance of salvation.|*James Saurin,* 1677|1730.

Verse 7.|" Under his tongue is 'mischief and vanity." The striking allusion of this expression is to certain venomous reptiles, which are said to carry bags of poison under their teeth, and, with great subtlety to inflict the most deadly injuries upon those who come within their reach. How affectingly does this represent the sad havoc which minds tainted with infidelity inflict on the community ! By their perversions of trutH, and by their immoral sentiments and practices, they are as injurious to the mind as the deadliest poison can be to the body.|*John Morison.*

*Verse 1.|*Cursing men are cursed men.|*John Trapp.*

*Vines 7, 9.|*In Anne Askew's account of her examination by Bishop Bonner, we have an instance of the cruel craft of persecutors : " On the morrow after, my lord of London sent for me at one of the clock, his hour being appointed at three. And as I came before him, he said he was very sorry of my trouble, and desired to know my opinion in such matters as were laid against me. He required me nlso boldly in any wise to utter the secrets of my heart ; bidding me not to fear in any point, for whatsoever I did say within his house, no man should hurt me for it. I answered, For so much as your lordship hath appointed three of the clock, and my friends shall not come till that hour, I desire you to paidon me of giving answer till they come.'" Upon this Bale remarks: "In this preventing of the hour may the diligent peiceive the greediness of this Babylon bishop, or bloodthirsty wolf, concerning his prey. 'Swift are their feet,' saith David, 'in the effusion of innocent blood, which have fraud in their tongues, venom in their lips, and most cruel vengeance in their months.' David much marvelleth in the spirit that, taking upon them the spiritual governance of the people, they can fall into such frenzy or forget fulness of themselves, as to believe it lawful thus to oppress the faithful, and to devour them with as little compassion as he that greedily devoureth a piece of biead. If such have read anything of God, they have little minded their true duty therein. 'More swift,' saith Jeremy, 'are our cruel persecutors than the eagles of the air. They follow upon us over the mountains, and lay privy wait for us in the wilderness.' He that will know the crafty hawking of bishops to hring in their prey, let him learn it here. Judas, I think, had never the tenth prtof their cunning workmanship.' "*John Bale, D.D., Bishop of Omory, 1495*| *1503, in " Examination of Anne Askew." Parker Society's Publication.*

Yerte 8.|" *He titteth in the lurking places of the villages,'*1" etc. The Arab robber lurks like a wolf among these sand-heaps, and often springs out suddenly upon the solitary traveller, robs him in a trice, and then plunges again into the wilderness of sand-hills and reedy downs, where pursuit is fruitless. Our friends are careful not to allow us to straggle about, or lag behind, and jet it seems absurd to fear a surprise here|Kaifa before, Acre in the rear, and travellers in sight on both sides. Robberies, however, do often occur, just where e now are. Strange country ! and it has always been so. There are a hundred allusions to just such things in the history, the Psalms, tind the prophets of Israel. A whole class of imagery is based upon them. Tims, in Psalmx. 8|10, "He sits in the lurking places of the villages: in the seciet places doth he murder the innocent : he lieth in wait secretly as a lion in his den: he lieth in wait to catch the poor: he doth catch the poor, when he draweth him into his net ; he croucbcth and humbleth himself, that the poor My fall by his strong ones." And a thousand rascals, the living originals of 'to picture, are this day crouching and lying in wait all over the country to catch poor helpless travellers. You observe that all these people we meet or Pss we armed ; nor would they venture to go from Acre to Kaifa without their musket, although the cannon of the castles seem to command every foot of the y. Strange, most strange land ! but it tallies wonderfully with its ancient story.-ir. *M. Thomson., D.D., in " The Land and the Book,"* 1859.

Vene 8.|My companions asked me if I knew the danger I had escaped. "&," I replied ; " What danger?" They then told me that, just after they started, they saw a wild Arab skulking after me, crouching to the ground, with 'musket in his hand ; and that, as soon as he had reached within what appeared to them musket-shot of me, he raised his gun ; but, looking wildly around him, 88 a man will do who is about to perpetrate some desperate act, he caught 'Bin of them and disappeared. Jeremiah knew something of the ways of these Arabs when he wrote, (chap. iii. 2) " In the ways hast thou sat for them, as the Arabian in the wilderness ;" and the simile is used in Psalm x. 9, 10, for the Arabs wait and watch for their prey with the greatest eagerness and perse- prance. *-John Gadsby, in "My Wanderings,"* 1860.

Verm 8.|" *lie sitteth in the lurking places of the villages: in the tecret plaee doth he murder the innocent: his eyes are privily set against the poor."* All this strength of metaphor and imagery is intended to mark the assiduity, the cunning-, the low artifice, to which the enemies of truth and righteousness will often resort in order to accomplish their corrupt and vicious designs. The extirpation of true religion is their great object; and there is nothing to which they will not stoop in order to effect that object. The great powers which have oppressed the church of Christ, in different ages, have answered to this description. Both heathen and papistical authorities have thus condescended to infamy. They have sat, as it were, in ambush for the poor of Christ's flock ; they have adopted every stratagem that infernal skill could invent ; they have associated themselves with princes in their palaces, and with beggars on their dunghill; they have resorted to the village, and they have mingled in the gay and populous city ; and all for the vain purpose of attempting to blot out a " name which shall endure for ever, and which shall be continued as long as the sun."|*John Jforison.*

Verse 9.|" *He doth catch the poor."* The poor man is the beast they hunt, who must rise early, rest late, eat the bread of sorrow, sit with many a hungry meal, perhaps his children crying for food, while all the fruit of his pains is served into Nimrod's table. Complain of this while you will, yet, as the orator said of Verres, *pecuniosus nescit damnari.* Indeed, a money-man may not be damnified, but he may be damned. For this is a crying sin, and the wakened cars of the Lord will hear it, neither shall his provoked hands forbear it. *Si tacuerint pavperes lognentur lapides.* If the poor should hold their peace, the very stones would speak. The fines, rackings, enclosures, oppressions, vexations, will cry to God for vengeance. " The stone will cry out of the wall, and the beam out of the timber shall answer it." Hab. ii. 11. You see the beasts they hunt. Kot foxes, not wolves, nor boars, bulls, nor tigers. It is a certain observation, no beast hunts 3ts own kind to devour it. Now, if these should prosecute wolves, foxes, &c., they should then hunt their own kind ; for they are these themselves, or rather worse than these, because here *homo homini lupus.* But though they are men they hunt, and by nature of the same kind, they are not so by quality, for they are lambs they persecute. In them there is blood, and flesh, and fleece to be had ; nnd therefore on these do they gorge themselves. In them there is weak armour of defence against their cruelties ; therefore over these they may domineer. I will speak it boldly : there is not a mighty Nimrod in this land that dares hunt his equal ; but over his inferior lamb he insults like a young Nero. Let him be graced by high ones, and he must not be saluted under twelve score off. In the country he proves a termagant ; his very scowl is a prodigy, and breeds an earthquake. He would be a Caesar, and tax all. It is well if he prove not a cannibal ! Only Macro salutes Sejanus so long as he is in Tiberius's favour ; cast him from that pinnacle, and the dog is ready to devour him. | *Thomas Adams.*

Vtrne 9.|" *He draweth him into his net."* " They hunt with a net." Micah vii. 2. They have their politic gins to catch men ; gaudy wares and dark shops (and would you have them love the light that live by darkness, as many shopkeepers ?) draw and tole customers in, where the crafty leeches can soon feel their pulses : if they must buy they shall pay for their necessity. And though they plead, We compel none to buy our ware, *caveat cmptor ;* yet with fine voluble phrases, damnable protestations, they will cast a mist of error before an eye of simple truth, and with cunning devices hunt them in. So some among us "have feathered their nests, not by open violence, but politic circumvention. They have sought the golden fleece, not by Jason's merit, but by Medea's pubtletv, by Medea's sorcery. If I should intend to discover these hunters' plots, nnd to deal punctually with them, I should afford you more matter than you would afford me time. But I limit myself, and answer all their plans with Augustine. Their tricks may hold *in jitre fori.* but not *in jure poll*|in the common-pleas of earth, not before the king's bench in heaven.|*Thomas Adams.*

Vene 9.|Oppression turns princes into roaring lions, and judges into ravening wolves. It is an unnatural sin, against the light of nature. No creatures do oppress them of their own kind. Look upon the birds of prey, as upon eagles, vultures, hawks, and you shall never find them preying upon their own kind. Look upon the beasts of the forest, as upon the lion, the tiger, the wolf, the bear, and you shall ever find- them favourable to their own kind ; and yet men unnaturally prey upon one another, like the fish in the sea, the great swallowing up the small.|*Thomas Brooks.*

Vene 10.|" *JTe croucheth, and hunibhth himself,"* etc. There is nothing too mean or servile for them, in the attempt to achieve their smister ends. You shall see his holiness the Pope washing the pilgrims' feet, if such a stratagem be necessary to act on the minds of the deluded multitude ; or you shall see him sitting on a throne of purple, if he wishes to awe and control the kings of the earth.|*John Morison.*

"Verse 10.|If you take a wolf in a lambskin, hang him up ; for he is the worst of the generation.| *Thomas Adams.*

Verge 11.|" *He hath said in his heart, Ood hath forgotten.""* Is it not a, senseless thing to be careless of sins committed long ago ? The old sins forgotten by men, stick fast in an infinite understanding. Time cannot raze out that which hath been known from eternity. Why should they be forgotten many years after they were acted, since they were foreknown in an eternity before they were committed, or the criminal capable to practise them ? Amalek must pay their arrears of their ancient unkindness to Israel in the time of Saul, though the generation that committed them were rotten in their graves. 1 Sam. iv. 2. Old sins are written in a book, which lies always before God ; and not only our own sins, but the sins of our fathers, to be requited upon their posterity. "Behold it is written." Isa. Ixv. 6. 'Viat a vanity is it then to be legardless of the sins of an age that went before us ; because they ure in some measure out of our knowledge, are they therefore blotted out of God's remembrance? Sins are bound up with him, as men do bonds, till they resolve to sue forthedebt. " The iniquity of Ephraim is bound up." Hosea xiii. 12. As his foreknowledge extends to all acts that shall be done, so his remembrance extends to all acts that have been done. We may ns well say, God foreknows nothing that shall be done to the end of the world, as that he forgets anything that hath been done from the beginning of the world.|*Stephen Charnock.*

Verte 11.|" *He hath snid in hu heart, God hath forgotten : lie hideth his face; fovill never see it."* Many say in their hearts, "God seeth them not," while ith their tongues they confess he is an all-seeing God. The heart hath a tongue in it as well as the head, and these two tongues seldom spenk the same language. While the head-tongue saith, " We cannot hide ourselves from the sight of God," the heart-tongue of wicked men will say, " God will hide himself from us, he will not see." But if their heart speak not thus, then as the prophet saith (Isa. xxix. 15), " They dig deep to hide their counsel from the Lord ;" surely they have a hope to hide their counsels, else they would not dig deep to hide them. Their digging is not proper, but tropical ; as men dig deep to hide what they would not have in the earth, so they by their wits, plots, and devices, do their best to hide their counsels from God, nnd they say, " Who seeth, who knoweth ? We, surely, are not seen either by God or man."|*Joseph* Caryl.

Vene 11.|The Scripture everywhere places sin upon this root. " *Ood hath forgotten: he hideth his face; he will never nee it.* " He hath turned his back upon the world. This was the ground of the oppression of the poor by the 'icked, which he mentions, verses 9, 10. There is no sin but receives both its Wrth and nourishment from this bitter root. Let the notion of providence be once thrown out, or the belief of it faint, how will ambition, covetousness, neglect of Ood, distrust, impatience, and all other bitter gourds, grow up in a night!It *is* from this topic all iniquity will draw arguments to encourage itself ; fot nothing so much discountenances those rising corruptions, and puts them out of heart, as an actuated belief that God takes care of human affairs.|*Stephen Charndfk.*

Verte 11.|" *He hath laid in hit heart,* " etc. "Because sentence against an evil work is not executed speedily, therefore the heart of the sons of men is fully set in them to do evil." Eccl. viii. 11. God forbears punishing, therefore men forbear repenting. He doth not smite upon their back by correction, therefore they do not smite upon their thigh by humiliation. Jer. .i. 19. The sinner thinks thus : " God hath spared me all this while, he hath eked out patience into longsuffering ; surely he will not punish." " *He hath taid in Ait heart, God hath forgotten.* " God sometimes in infinite patience adjourns his judgments and puts off the sessions a while longer , he is not willing to punish. 2 Peter iii. 9. The bee naturally gives honey, but stings only when it is angered. The Lord would have men make their peace with him. Isa. xxvii. 5. God is not like a hasty creditor that requires the debt, and will give no time for the payment ; he is not only gracious, but " waits to be gracious'1 (Isa. xxx. 18) ; but God by his patience would bribe sinners to repentance ; but alas ! how is this patience abused. God's longsuffering hardens : because God stops the vials of his wrath, sinners stop the conduit of tears. | *Thomas Watton.*

Vere 11.|" *He hath laid in hii heart, Ood hath forgotten : he hideth hit face / he will never see* t$." Because the Lord continues to spare them, therefore they go on to provoke him. As he adds to their lives, so they add to their lusts. What is this, but as if a man should break all his bones because there is a surgeon who is able to set them again ? . . . . Because justice seems to *wink,* men suppose her *blind;* because she delays punishment, they imagine she denies to punish them ; because she does not always reprove them for their sins, they suppose he always approves of their sins. But let such know, that the silent arrow can destroy as well as the roaring-cannon. Though the patience of God be *lasting,* yet it is not *everlasting.*| William Seeker.

Verset 11, 12, 13.|The atheist denies God's ordering of sublunary matters. " Tush, doth the Lord see, or is there knowledge in the Host High ?" making him a maimed Deity, without an eye of providence, or an arm of powpr, and at most restraining him only to matters above the clouds. But he that dares to confine the King to heaven, will soon after endeavour to depose him, and fall at last flatly to deny him.|*Thomas Fuller.*

Verse 13.|" *He hath taid in. his heart, Thou wilt not require* if." As when the desperate pirate, ransacking and rifling a bottom, was told by the master, that though no law could touch him for the present, he should answer it at the day of judgment,

replied, " If I may stay so long ere I come to it, I will take thee and thy vessel too."
A conceit wherewith too many land-thieves and oppressors flatter themselves in their
hearts, though they dare not utter it with their lips. *Tluimas Adams.*

Verses 13, 14.|What, do you think that God doth not remember our sins which we
do not regard ? for while we sin the score runs on, and the Judge scttcth down all in
the table of remembrance, and his scroll reacheth up to heaven. Item, for lending to
usury ; item, for racking of rents ; item, for starching thy ruffs ; item, for curling thy
hair ; item, for painting thy face ; item, for selling of benefices ; item, for starving of
souls ; item, for playing at cards ; item, for sleeping in the church ; item, for profaning
the Sabbath-day, with a number more hath God to cull to account, for every one must
answer for himself. The fornicator, for taking of filthy pleasure ; the careless prelate,
for murthering so many thousand souls ; the landlord, for getting money from his poor
tenants by racking of his rents ; see the rest, all they shall come like very sheep when
the trumpet shall souiid, and the heaven and earth shall come to judgment against
them ; when the heavens shall vanish like a scroll, and the earth shall consume like
fire, and all the creatures standing against them ; the rocks shall cleaveasunder, and
the mountains shake, and the foundation of the earth shall tremble, and they shall say
to the mountains, Cover us, fall upon us, and hide us from the presence of his anger
and wrath whom we have not cared to offend. But they shall not be covered and hid
; but then shall they go the back way, to the soak.es and serpents, to be tormented of
devils for ever.|*Henry Smith.*

Verge 14.|" *Thou hast seen it; for thou beholdest mischief and spite, to requite it
with thy hands,* " etc. This should be a terror to the wicked, to think that whatsoever
they do, they do it in the ../;//'* of him 1 hut shall *judge* them, and call them to a strict
account for every thought conceived against hia majesty ; and therefore, it should
make them afraid to sin ; because that when they burn with lust, and toil with hatred,
when they scorn the just and wrong the innocent, they do all this, not only *in conspectu
Dei,* within the compass of God's sight, but also in *sinu dimnitatis,* in the bosom of
that Deity, who, though he suffered them for a time to run on, like " a wild ass used to
the wilderness," yet he will find them out at the last, and then cut them off and destroy
them. And as this is terror unto the wicked, so it may be a comfort unto the godly to
think that he who should hear their prayers and send them help, is so near unto them
; and it should move them to rely still upon him, because we are sure of his presence
wherever we are.|*O. Williams,* 1636.

Verse 14.|" *The poor committeth himself unto thee.* " The awkwardness of our hearts
to suffer comes much from distrust. An unbelieving soul treads upon the promise as
a man upou ice ; at first going upon it he is full of fears and tumultuous thoughts lest
it should crack. Now, daily resignation of thy heart, as it will give thee an occasionof
conversing more with the thoughts of God's power, faithfulness, and other of his
attributes (for want of familiarity with which, jealousies arise in our hearts when put
to any great plunge), so also it will furnish thee with many experiences of the reality
both of his attributes and promises ; which, though they need not any testimony from
sense, to gain them credit with us, yet so much are we made of sense, so childish and
weak is our faith, that we find our hearts much helped by those experiences we have
had, to rely on him for the future. Look, therefore, carefully to this ; every morning

leave thyself and ways in God's hand, as the phrase is. Psalm x. 14. And at night look again how well God hath looked to his trust, and sleep not till thou hast affected thy heart with his faithfulness, and laid a stronger charge on thy heart to trust itself again in God's keeping in the night. And when any breach is made, and seeming loss befalls thee in any enjoyment, which thou hast by faith insured of thy God, observe how God fills up that breach, and makes up that loss to thee ; and rest not till thou hast fully vindicated the good name of God to thy own heart. Be sure thou lettest no discontent or dissatisfaction lie upon thy spirit at God's dealings ; but chide thy heart for it, us David did his. Psalm xlii. And thus doing, with God's blessing, thou shall keep thy faith in breath for a longer race, when called to run it.I *W. Ournall.*

Verse 14.I" *Thou art the helper of the fatherless.'"* God doth exercise a more special providence over men, as clothed with miserable circumstances ; and therefore among his other titles this is one, to be a " *helper of the fatherless."* It is the argument the church used to express her return to God ; Hosea xiv. 3, "For in thee the fatherless find mercy." Now what greater comfort is there than this, that there is one presides in the world who is so wise he cannot be mistaken, so faithful he cannot deceive, so pitiful he cannot neglect his people, and so powerful that he can make stones even to be turned into bread if he

please! God doth not govern the world only by his will as an

absolute monarch, but by his wisdom and goodness as a tender father. It is not his greatest pleasure to show his sovereign power, or his inconceivable wisdom, but his immense goodness, to which he makes the other attributes subservient.I*Stephen Charnock.*

Veru 14.I" *Thou hast seen it,"* etc. If God did not see our ways, we might sin and go unpunished ; but forasmuch as he seeth them with purer eyes thanto behold iniquity and approve it, he is engaged both in justice and honour to punish all that iniquity of our ways which he seeth or beholdeth. David makes this the very design of God's superintendency over the ways of men : " *Thou hat seen it; for thou beholdest mischief and spite, to requite it with thy hand : the poor committeth himself unto thee ; t/unt art the helper of the fatherle&g.* " Thus the psalmist represents the Lord as having taken a view or survey of the ways of men. " *Thou hast teen.'*1" What huth God seen? Even all that wickedness and oppression of the poor spoken of in the former part of the Psalm, as also the blasphemy of the wicked against himself (verse 13), " *Wherefore doth the wicked contemn Oodf ha hath said in hit heart, Thouicilt not require it."* What saith the psalmist concerning God, to this vain, confident man ? " *Thou,'*1" saith he, " *beholdest mischief and spite;"* but to what purpose f the next words tell us thatI" *to requite it with thy hand."* As thou hast seen what mischief they have done spitefully, so in due time thou wilt requite it righteously. The Lord is not a bare spectator, he is both a rewarder and an avenger. Therefore, from the ground of this truth, that the Lord seeth all our ways, and counteth all our steps, we, as the prophet exhorts (Isaiah iii. 10, II), may " say to the righteous, that it shall be well with him : for they shall eat the fruit of their doings." We may also say, " Woe unto the wicked ! it shall be ill with him : for the reward of his hands shall be given him." Only idols which have eyes and sec not, have hands and strike not.I*Joseph Caryl.*

Verse 14.|" *Thou hast seen it; for thou beholdest mischief and spite, to requite it with thy hand: the poor committeth himself unto thee ; thou art the helper of the fatherless.*'1" Let the poor know that their God doth take care of them, to visit their sins with rods who spoil them, seeing they have forgotten that we are members one of another, and have invaded the goods of their brethren ; God will arm them against themselves, and beat them with their own staves ; either their own compassing and over-reaching wits shall consume their store, or their unthrifty posterity shall put wings upon their riches to make them fly ; or God shall not give them the blessing to take use of their wealth, but they shall leave to such as shall be merciful to the poor. Therefore let them follow the wise man's counsel (Eccles. x. 20), " Curse not the rich, no, not in thy bedchamber ;" let no railing and unchristian bitterness wrong a good cause ; let it be comfort enough to them that God is both their supporter and avenger. Is it not sufficient to lay all the storms of discontent against, their oppressors, that God sees their affliction, and cometh down to deliver and avenge them ?| *Edward Marbury.*

Verse 14.|" *Thou hast seen it; for thou oeholdtst mischief and spite, to requite it with thy hand,"* etc. God considers all your works and ways, and will not you consider the works, the ways of God ? Of this be sure, whether you consider the ways of God, his word-ways, or work-ways, of this be sure, God will consider your ways, certainly he will ; those ways of yours which in themselves are not worth the considering or looking upon, your sinful ways, though they are so vile, so abominable, that if yourselves did but look upon them and consider them, you would be utterly ashamed of them ; yea, though they are an abomination to God while he beholds them, yet he will behold and consider them. The Lord who is of purer eyes than to behold any the least iniquity, to approve it, will yet behold the greatest of your iniquities, and your impurest ways to consider them. " *Thou,"* saith David, " *beholdest mischief and spite, to requite it:"* God beholdeth the foulest, dirtiest ways of men, their ways of oppression and unrighteousness, their ways of intemperance and lasciviousness, their ways of wrath and maliciousness, at once to detest, detect, and requite them. If God thus considereth the ways of men, even those filthy and crooked ways of men, should not men consider the holy, just, and righteous ways of God ?|*Joseph Caryl.*

Verses 14|18.|" *God delights to help ttt-e poor."* He loves to take part with the best, though the weakest side. Contrary to the course of most, who when a controversy arises use to stand in a kind of indifferency or neutrality, till they*see* which part is strongest, not which is justest. Now if there be any consideration (besides the cause) that draws or engages God, it is the weakness of the ride. He joins with many, because they are weak, not with any, because they are strong ; therefore he is called *the helper of the friendless, and with, him the fatherless,* (the orphans) *find mercy.* By fatherless we are not to understand such only whose parents are dead, but any one that is in distress ; as Christ promiseth his disciples ; " *I will not leave you orphans,"* that is, helpless, and (as we translate) *comfortless;* though ye are as children without a father, yet I will be a father to you. Men are often like those clouds which dissolve into the sea ; they send presents to the rich, and assist the strong ; but God sends his rain upon the dry land, and lends his strength to those who are weak. . . . The prophet makes this report to God of himself (Isaiah xxv. 4) : " *Thou hast Iten a strength to the poor, a strength to the needy in his distress, a refuge from the storm,"* etc.|*Joseph Caryl.*

Verse 16.|" *The Lord, is King for ever and ever: the heathen are perished oat of his land.*" Such confidence and faith must appear to the world strange and unaccountable. It is like what his fellow citizens may be supposed to have felt (if the story be true) toward that man of whom it is recorded, that his powers of vision were so extraordinary, that he could distinctly see the fleet of the Carthaginians entering the harbour of Carthage, while he stood himself at LilybcBum, in Sicily. A man seeing across an ocean, and able to tell of objects so far off ! he could feast his vision on what others saw not. Even thus does faith now stand at its Lilybosum, and see the long tossed fleet entering safely the desired haven, enjoying the bliss of that still distant day, as if it was already come.|*Andrew A. Bonar.*

Verte 17.|There is a humbling act of faith put forth in prayer. Others style it praying in humility ; give me leave to style it praying in faith. In faith which sets the soul in the presence of that mighty God, and by the sight of him, which faith gives us, it is that we see our own vileness, sinfulness, and abhor ourselves, and profess ourselves unworthy of any, much less of those mercies we are to seek for. Thus the sight of God had wrought in the prophet (Isaiah vi. 5), " Then said I, Woe is me ! for I am undone ; because I am a man of unclean lips : for mine eyes have seen the King, the Lord of hosts." And holy Job speaks thus (Job xlii. 5, 6), " Now mine eye seeth thee : wherefore I abhor myself, and repent in dust and ashes." This is as great a requisite to prayer as any other act; I may say of it alone, as the apostle (James i. 7), that without it we shall receive nothing at the hands of God ! God loves to fill empty vessels, he looks to broken hearts. In the Psalms how often do we read that God hears the prayers of the humble ; which always involves and includes faith in it. Psalm ix. 12, " He forgetteth not the cry of the humble," nd Psalm x. 17, " *Lord, thou hast heard the desire of the humble: thou wilt prepare their heart, thou wilt cause thine ear to hear.*" To be deeply humbled is to have the heart prepared and fitted for God to hear the prayer ; and therefore you find the psalmist pleading *sub forma pauper is,* often repeating, " I am poor and needy." And this prevents our thinking much if God do not grant the particular thing we do desire. Thus also Christ himself in his great distress (Psalm xxii.), doth treat God (verse 2), " O my God, I cry in the day-time, but thou nearest not; and in the night season am not silent. Our fathers trusted in thee. They cried unto thee, and were delivered. But I am a worm, and no man ; reproached of men, and despised of the people ; (verse 6)" and he was " heard " in the end " in what he feared." And these deep humbliogs of ourselves, being joined with vehement implorations upon the mercy of God to obtain, is reckoned into the account of praying by faith, both by God and Christ. Matt, viii.|*Thomas Goodwin.*

Verte 17.|" *Lord, thou hast heard the desire of the humble.*" A spiritual prayer is a *humble* prayer. Prayer is the asking of an alms, which requireshumility. " The publican, standing afar off, -would not lift np *so* much as his eyes unto heaven, but smote upon his breast, saying, God be merciful to me a sinner." Luke xviii. 13. God's incomprehensible glory may even amaze us and strike a holy consternation into us when we approach nigh unto him : " O my God, I am ashamed and blush to lift up my face to thee." Ezra ix. 6. It is comely to see a poor nothing lie prostrate at the feet of its Maker. " Behold now, I have taken upon me to speak unto the Lord, which am but dust and ashes." Gen. xviii. 27. The lower the heart descends, the higher the prayer ascends. | *Thomas Watson.*

Verse 17.|" *Lord, thou hast heard the desire of the humMe,*" etc. How- pleasant is it, that these benefits, which are of so great a value both on their own account, and that of the divine benignity from whence they come, should be delivered into our hands, marked, as it were, with this grateful inscription, *that they have been obtained by prayer !|Robert Leighton.*

Verge 17.|" *The desire of the humble.*" Prayer is the offering up of our desires to God in the name of Christ, for such things as arc agreeable to his will. It is an offering of our *desires.* Desires are the soul and life of prayer ; words are but the body ; now as the body without the soul is dead, so are prayers unless they are animated with our desires : " *Lord, thou hast heard tfte desire of the hurri/ile.*" God heareth not words, but *desires.| Thomas Watson.*

*Verne 17.|*God's choice acquaintances are humble men.|*Robert Leighton.*

*Verne 17.|*He that sits nearest the dust, sits nearest heaven.|*Andrew Orai/, of Glasgow,* 1616.

*Verse 17.|*There is a kind of omnipotency in prayer, as having an interest and prevalency with God's omuipotency. It hath loosed iron chains (Acts xvi. 25, 26) ; it hath opened iron gates (Acts xii. 5|10) ; it hath unlocked the windows of heaven (1 Kings xviii. 41) ; it hath broken the burs of death (John xi. 40, 43). Satan hath three titles given in the Scriptures, setting forth his malignity against the church of God : a dragon, to note his mafice ; a serpent, to note his subtlety ; and a lion, to note his strength. But none of all these can stand before prayer. The greatest malice of Haman sinks under the prayer of Esther ; the deepest policy, the counsel of Ahithophel, withers before the prayer of David ; the largest army, a host of a thousand Ethiopians, run nway like cowards before the prayer of Asa.|*Edward Reynolds,* 1599|1676.

Verse 18.|" *To judge the fatherless and the oppressed,*" etc. The tears of the poor fall down upon their cheeks, *et ascendunt ad cadvm,* and go up to heaven and cry for vengeance before God, the judge of widows, the father of widows and orphans. Poor people be oppressed even by laws. Woe worth to them that mike evil laws against the poor, what shall be to them that hinder and mar good laws ? What will ye do in the day of great vengeance when God shall visit you ? he saith he will hear the tears of the poor women, when he goeth on visitation. For their sake he will hurt the judge, be he never so high, he will for widows' sakes change realms, bring them into temptation, pluck the judges' skins over their heads. Cambyses was a great emperor, such another as our master is, he had many lord deputies, lord presidents, and lieutenants under him. It is a great while ago since I read the history. It chanced he had under him in one of his dominions a briber, a gift-taker, a gratificr of rich men ; he followed gifts as fast as he that followed the pudding : a handmaker in his office, to make his son a great man, as the old saying is, " Happy is the child whose father goeth to the devil." The cry of the poor widow came to the emperor's ear, and caused him to slay the judge quick, and laid his skin in his chair of judgment, that all judges that should give judgment afterward, should sit in the same skin. Surely it was a goodly sign, a goodly monument, the sign of the judge's skin. I pray God we may once see the sign of the skin in England. Ye will say, peradventure, that this is cruelly and uncharitably spoken. Np, no ; I do it charitably, for a love I bear to my country. God aith, ' I will visit." God hath two visitations ; the first is when he revealethhis word by preachers ; and where the first is accepted, the second cometh not. The second visitation is vengeance. He went to visitation when he brought the judge's skin over his ears. If this word be despised, he cometh with the second visitation with vengeance.*Hugh Latimer,* 1480|1555.

Verse 18.|" *Man of the earth,"* etc. In the eighth Psalm (which is a circular Psalm, ending as it did begin, " O Lord our God, how excellent is thy name in all the world !" That whithersoever we turn our eyes, upwards or downwards, we may see ourselves beset with his glory round about), how doth the prophet base and discountenance the nature and whole race of man ; as may appear by liis disdainful and derogatory interrogation, " What is man that thou art mindful of him ; and the Son of Man, that thou regardest him ?" In the ninth Psalm, " Rise, Lord ; let not man have the upper hand ; let the nations be judged in thy sight. Put them in fear, O Lord, that the heathen may know themselves to be but men." Further, in the tenth Psalm, " Thou judgest the fatherless and the poor, that the man of the earth do no more violence."

The Psalms, as they go in order, so, methinks they grow in strength, and each hath a weightier force to throw down our presumption. 1. We are "men," and the " sons of men," to show our descent and propagation. 2. " Men in our own knowledge," to show that conscience and experience of infirmity doth convict us. 3. "Men of the earth," to show our original matter whereof we are framed. In the twenty-second Psalm, he addeth more disgrace ; for cither in his own name, regarding the misery and contempt wherein he was held, or in the person of Christ, whose figure he was, as if it were a robbery for him to take upon him the nature of man, he falleth to a lower style, *at ego turn vermit et runt* n'ry but I am a worm, and no man. For as corruption is the father of all flesh, so are the worms his brethren and sisters, according to the old verse|

" First man, next worms, then stench and loathsomeness,
Thus man to no man alters by changes."

Abraham, the father of the faithful (Genesis xviii.), sifteth himself into the coarsest man that can be, and resolveth his nature into the elements whereof it first rose : " Behold I have begun to speak to my Lord, being dust and ashes." And if any of the children of Abraham, who succeed him in the faith, or any of the children of Adam, who succeed him in the flesh, thinketh otherwise, let him know that there is a threefold cord twisted by the finger of God, that shall tie him to his first original, though he contend till his heart break. " O earth, earth, earth, hear the word of the Lord " $Jer. xxii.) ; that is, earth by creation, earth by continuance, earth by resolution. Thou earnest earth, thou remainest earth, and to earth thou must return.*John King.*

Verse 18.|" *The man of the earth."* Man dwelling in the earth, and made of earth.*Thomas Wilcoclct.*

HINTS TO THE VILLAGE PREACHER.

Tone 1.|The answer to these questions furnishes a noble topic for nn experimental sermon. Let me suggest that the question is not to be answered in the same manner in all cases. Past sin, trials of graces, strengthening of faith, discovery of depravity, instruction, etc., etc., are varied reasons for the hiding of our Father's face.

Verne 2.|Religious persecution in all its phases based on pride.

Verge 3.|God's hatred of covetousness : show its justice.

VT04.|Pride the barrier in the way of conversion.

Verse ±(*lastclause*).|*ThoughtsinwhichGodisnot, weighedandcondemned.*

Verse 5.|" Thy judgments are far above out of his sight.1' Moral inability of men to appreciate the *clmructur and acts of God.*

Vene tt.|The vain confidence of sinners.

Verse 8.|Dangers of godly men, or the snares in the way of believers.

Verse 9.|The ferocity, craftiness, strength, and activity of Satan.

Verse 9 (list clause).|The Satanic fisherman, his art, diligence, success, etc.

Verne 10.|Designing humility unmasked.

Verse 11.|Divine omniscience and the astounding presumption of sinners.

Verse 12.|" Arise, 0 Lord." A prayer needful, allowable, seasonable, etc.

Verse 13 (Jirst clause).|An astounding fact, and a reasonable enquiry.

Verse 13.|Future retribution : doubts concerning it. I. By whom indulged : " *the wicked." II. Where fostered : " in his heart." III. For what purpose: quieting* *of'conscience, etc. IV. With what practical tendency : " contemn God." He who* *disbelieves hell distrusts heaven.*

Verses 13, 14.|Divine government in the world. I. Who doubt it? and why ? II. *Who believe it ? and what does this faith cause them to do ?*

Verse 14 (last clause).|A plea for orphans.

Verse 16.|The Eternal Kingship of Jehovah.

Verse 17 (first clause).|I. The Christian's character|" humbh." II. An attribute of *the Christian's whole life|" desire:" he desires more holiness, communion, knowl-* *edge, grace, and usefulness ; and then he desires glory. III. The Christian's great* *blessedness|"Lord, thou hast heard the desire of the humble."*

Verse 17 (whole verse).|I. Consider the nature of gracious desires. IL Their origin. *III. Their result. The three sentences readily suggest these divisions, and the subject* *may be very profitable.*

PSALM XL

SrsrecT.|Charles Simeon gives an excellent summary of this Psalm in the /(Mowing *antencts:|" The Psalms are a rich repository of experimental knowledge. David, at the* *di/ereni periods of his life, was placed in almost every situation in which a believer,* *vfather rich or poor, can be placed; in these heavenly compositions he delineates* *all the workings of the heart. He introduces, too, the sentiments and conduct of the* *various persons who Kfrt accessory either to his troubles or his joys ; and thus sets* *before us a compendium of aU that is passing in the hearts of men throughout the* *world. When he penned this Psalm he vas wader persecution from Said, who sought* *his life, and hunted him ' as a partridge upon tlit mountains.' His timid friends were* *ofarmed for his safety, and recommended him to flee Jo tome mountain where he had* *a hiding-place, and thus to conceal himself from the rage of Sad. Bui David, being* *strong in faith, spurned the idea of resorting to any such prusiuani- Wks expedients,* *and determined confidently to repose his trust in God."*

To assist us to remember this sltort, but sweet Psalm, we will give it the name of " *The Soso Of The Stedfast."*

Ditbios.\from 1 to 3, David describes the temptation with which he was assailed, and from 4 to 7, the arguments by which his courage was sustained.

EXPOSITION.

IN the LORD put I my trust : how say ye to my soul, Flee as a 1 bird to your mountain ?

2 For, lo, the wicked bend their bow, they make ready their arrow upon the string, that they may privily shoot at the upright in heart.

3 If the foundations be destroyed, what can the righteous do ?

These verses contain an account of a temptation to distrust God, with which David was, upon some unmentioned occasion, greatly exercised. It may be, that in the days when he was in Saul's court, he was advised to flee at a time 'hen this flight would have been charged against him as a breach of duty to the king, or a proof of personal cowardice. His case was like that of Nehimiah, 'hen his enemies, under the garb of friendship, hoped to entrap him by advising him to escape for his life. Had he done so, they could then have found aground of accusation. Nehemiah bravely replied, "Shall such a man I flee?" and David, in a like spirit, refuses to retreat, exclaiming, " In the Lord put I my trust: how tay ye to my soul, Flee as a ford to yovr mountain.'" TVhen Satan cannot overthrow us by presumption, how craftily will he seek to ruin us by distrust ! He will employ our dearest friends to argue us out of our confidence, and he will use such plausible logic, that unless we once for all assert our immovable trust in Jehovah, he will make us like the timid bird which flies to the mountain whenever danger presents itself. How forcibly the case is put I The bow is bent, the arrow is fitted to the string: " Flee, flee, thou defenceless bird, thy safety lies in flight ; begone, for thine enemies will send their shafts into thy heart ; haste, haste, for soon wilt thou be destroyed !" David seems to have felt the force of the advice, for it came home to his sovl; to jet he would not yield, but would rather dare the danger than exhibit a distrust in the Lord his God. Doubtless, the perils which encompassed David ere great and imminent ; it was quite true that his enemies were ready to shoot Ji% at him ; it was equally correct that the very foundations of law and justice were destroyed under Saul's unrighteous government: but what were 11 these things to the man whose trust was in God alone ? He could brave the rs, could escape the enemies, and defy the injustice which surrounded His answer to the question, " What can the righteous do ?" would bethe counter-question, "What cannot they do?" When prayer engages God on our side, and when faith secures the fulfilment of the promise, what cause can there be for flight, however cruel and mighty our enemies ? With a sling and a stone, David had smitten a giant before whom the w hole hosts of Israel were trembling, sind the Lord, who delivered him from the uncircumcised Philistine, could surely deliver him from King Saul and his myrmidons. There is no such word as " impossibility1' in the language of faith ; that martial grace knows how to fight and conquer, but she knows not how to flee.

4 The LORD a in his holy temple, the Lord's throne is in heaven : his eyes behold, his eyelids try, the children of men.

5 The Lord trieth the righteous : but the wicked and him that loveth violence his soul hateth.

6 Upon the wicked he shall rain snares, fire and brimstone, and an horrible tempest : this shall be the portion of their cup.

7 For the righteous Lord loveth righteousness ; his countenance doth behold the upright.

David here declares the great source of his unflinching courage. He borrows his light from heaven\from the great central orb of deity. The God of the believer is never far from him ; he is not merely the God of the mountain fastnesses, but of the dangerous valleys and battle plains.

"Jehovah is in hit holy temple.'1" The heavens are above our heads in all regions of the earth, and so is the Lord ever near to us in every state and condition. This is a very strong reason why we should not adopt the vile suggestions of distrust. There is one who pleads his precious blood in our behalf in the temple above, and there is one upon the throne who is never deaf to the intercession of his Son. Why, then, should we fear ? What plots can men devise which Jesus will not discover ? Satan has doubtless desired to have us, that he m ly sift us as wheat, but Jesus is in the temple praying for us, and how can our faith fail? What attempts can the wicked make which Jehovah shall not bshold ? And since he U in his holy temple, delighting in the sacrifice of his Son, will he not defeat every device, and send us a sure deliverance?

" JehnnK't throne it in 1'ie heavens ;" he reigns supreme. Nothing can be done in heaven, or earth, or hell, which he doth not ordain and over-rule. He is the world's great Emperor. Wherefore, then, should we flee ? If we trust this King of kings, is not this enough ? Cannot he deliver us without our cowardly retreat ? Yes, blessed ba tho Lord our God, we can salute him as Jehovah-nissi ; in his name we set up our banners, and, instead of flight, we once more raise the shout of war.

" ITn eyes behold." The eternal Watcher never slumbers; his eyes never know a sleep.   *" His eyelids try the children of men ;"* he narrowly inspects their actions, words, and thoughts. As men, when intently and narrowly inspecting somo very minute object, almost close their eyelids to exclude every oilier object, so will the Lord look all men through and through. God sees each man as much and as perfectly as if there were no other creature in the .universe. He sees us always ; he never removes his eye from us ; he sees us entirely, reading the recesses of the soul ns readily as the glancings of the eye. I not this a sufficient ground of confidence, and an abundant answer to the solicitations of despondency ? My danger is not hi 1 from him ; he knows my extremity, and I may rest assured that he will not suffer me to perish while I rely alone on him. Wherefore, then, should I take wings of the timid bird, and fl-e from the dangers which beset me ?

" T/te Lord trieth the righteon:" he doth not hate them, but only tries them. They are precious to him. and therefore he refines them with afflictions. None of tho Lord's children may hope to escape from trial, nor, indeed, in our right minds, would any of us desire to do so, for trial is the channel of many blessings.

" "Tls my happiness below

Not to live without the crone;
But the Savidur's power to know,
Sanctifying every loss.

Trials make the promise sweet;
Trials give new life to prayer ;
Trials bring me to his feet

Lay me low, and keep me there.
Did I meet no trials here
No chastisement by the way
Might I not, with reason, fear

I should prove a cast-away '
Bastards may escape the rod,
Sunk in earthly vain delight;
But the true-born child of God

Must not\would not, if ho might. "\William Cowper.

Is not this a very cogent reason why we should not distrustfully endeavour to shun a trial ?\for in so doing we are seeking to avoid a blessing.

" But the wicked and Mm that loneth violence his soul hateth:" why, then, shall I flee from these wicked men ? If God hateth them, I will not fear them. Haman was very great in the palace until he lost favour, but when the king abhorred him, how bold were the meanest attendants to suggest the gallows for the man at whom they had often trembled ! Look at the black mark upon the faces of our persecutors, and we shall not run away from them. If God is in the quarrel as well as ourselves, it would be foolish to question the result, or avoid the conflict. Sodom and Gomorrah perished by a fiery hail, and by a brimstone ihower from heaven ; so shall all the ungodly. They may gather together like Gog and Magog to battle, but the Lord will rain upon them " nn overflowing rain, and great hailstones, fire, and brimstone :" Ezek. xxxviii. 22. Some expositors think that in the term " horrible tempest," there is in the Hebrew an allusion to that burning, suffocating wind, which blows across the Arabian deserts, and is known by the name of Simoom. " A burning storm," Lowth call? it, while another great commentator reads it " wrathwind ;" in either version the Unguage is full of terrors. What a tempest will that be which shall overwhelm the despisers of God l Oh! what a shower will that be which shall pour out itself for ever upon the defenceless heads of impenitent sinners in hell ! Repent, ye rebels, or this fiery deluge shall soon surround you. Hell's horrors shall be your inheritance, your entailed estate, " the portion of your cup." The dregs of that cup you shall wring out, and drink for ever. A drop of hell is terrible, but what must a full cup of torment be ? Think of it\a cup of misery, but not a drop of mercy. O people of God, how foolish is it to fear the faces of men who shall soon be faggots in the fire of hell ! Think of their end, their fearful end, and all fear of them must be changed into contempt of their threatenings, and pity for their miserable estate.

The delightful contrast of the last verse is well worthy of our observation, Mil it affords another overwhelming reason why we should be stedfast, un- tnoTible, not carried away with fear, or led to adopt carnal expedients in order to avoid trial. " For the righteous Lord loveth righteousness.'" It is not only his office to defend it, but his *nature to love it. He would deny himself if he did not defend the just. It is essential to the very being of God that he should be just; fear not, then, the end of all your trials, but " be just, and fear not." God approves, and, if men oppose, what matters it? "Hit countenance doth Mold the uprights'1 We need never be out of countenance, for God countenances He observes, he approves, he delights in the upright. He sees his own image in them, an image of his own fashioning, and therefore with complacency he regards them. Shall we dare to put forth our hand unto iniquity in order to escape affliction ? Let us have done with by-ways and short turnings, andlet us keep to that fair path of right along which Jehovah's smile shall light us. Are wu tempted to put our light under a bushel, to conceal our religion from our neighbours ? Is it suggested to us that there are ways of avoiding1 the cross, and shunning the reproach of Christ ? Let us not hearken to the voice of the charmer, but seek an increase of faith, that we may wrestle with principalities and powers, and follow the Lord, fully going without the camp, bearing his reproach. Mammon, the flesh, the devil, will all whisper in our ear, " Flee as a bird to your mountain ;" but let us come forth and defy them all. " Resist the devil, and he will flee from you." There is no room or reason for retreat. Advance ! Let the vanguard push on! To the front! all ye powers and passions of our soul. On ! on ! in God's name, on 1 for " the Lord of hosts is with us ; the Qod of Jacob is our refuge."*

EXPLANATORY NOTES AND QUAINT SAYINGS.

Whole Psalm.\The most probable account of the occasion of this Psalm is that given by Amyraldus. He thinks it was composed by David while he was in the court of Saul, at a time when the hostility of the king was beginning to show itself, and before it had broken out into open persecution. David's friends, or those professing to be so, advised him to flee to his native mountains for a time, and remain in retirement, till the king should show himself more favourable. David docs not at that time accept the counsel, though afterwards he seems to have followed it. This Psalm applies itself to the establishment of the church against the calumnies of the world and the compromising counsel of man, in that confidence which is to be placed in God the Judge of all.\ W. Wilson, D.D., in loc., 1860.

Whole Psalm.\If one may offer to make a modest conjecture, it is not improbable this Psalm might be composed on the sad murder of the priests by Saul (1 Sam. xxii. 19), when after the slaughter of Abimelech, the high priest, Doeg, the Edomite, by command from Saul, " slew in one day fourscore and five persons which wore a linen ephod." I am not so carnal as to build the spiritual church of the Jews on the material walls of the priests' city at Nob (which then by Doeg was smitten with the edge of the sword), but this is most true, that " knowledge must preserve the people ;" and (Mai. ii. 7), " The priests' lips shall preserve knowledge ;" and then it is easy to conclude, what an earthquake this massacre might make in the foundations of religion.\Thomat Fuller.

Whole Psalm.\Notice how remarkably the whole Psalm corresponds with the deliverance of Lot from Sodom. This verse, with the angel's exhortation, " Escape to the mountains, lest thou be consumed," and Lot's reply, " I cannot escape to the mountains, lest some evil take me and I die." Genesis six. 17\19. And again, " The Lord's seat is in heaven, and vpon the ungodly he shall rait snares, fire, brimstone, storm and

tempest," with " Then the Lord rained upon Sodom and Gomorrah brimstone and fire
out of heaven :" and again, " flit

countenance mil behold the thing that is just,' 1 ' 1 with " Delivered just Lot

for that righteous man vexed his righteous soul with their ungodly deeds." 2 Peter
ii. 7, 8.\Casriodorus (a.d., 560) in John Mason Neale's " Commentary on the Ptalms,
from Pi'imithe and Medueaal Writers," 1860.

Whole Psalm.\The combatants at the Lake Thrasymene are said to have been so
engrossed with the conflict, that neither party perceived the convulsions of nature that
shook the ground\

" An earthquake reeled unheeding!)- away.
None felt stern nature rocking nt his feet."

From a nobler cause, it is thus with the soldiers of the Lamb. They believe,

and, therefore, make no haste ; nay, they can scarcely be said to feel earth's
convulsions as other men, because their eager hope presses forward to the issue at
the advent of the Lord.\Andrew A. Sonar.

Verse 1.\" / triut in the Lord: June do ye ay to my soul, Sieeree on to your mountain
like a birdf" (others, " O thou bird.") Saul and his adherents mocked and jeered David
with such taunting speeches, as conceiving that he knew no other shift or refuge, but
so betaking himself unto wandering and lurking on the mountains ; hopping, as it
were, from one place to another like & silly bird ; but they thought to ensnare and
take him well enough for all that, not considering God who was David's comfort, rest
and refuge.\Theodore Baat't " Translation of the Dutch Annotations, as ordered by the
Synod of Dort, in 1818." London, 1057.

Yene 1.\" With Jehovah I have taken shelter ; how say ye to my soul. Flee, tfarrows,
to your Milt" " Tour hill," that hill from which you say your help cometh : a sneer.
Repair to that boasted hill, which may indeed give you the help which it gives the
sparrow : a shelter against the inclemencies of a stormy sky, no defence against our
power.\Samuel Hoi-sley, in loe.

Verte 1.\" In the Lord put I my trust: how say ye to my soul, Flee as a bird to your
mountain I" The holy confidence of the saints in the hour of great trial is beautifully
illustrated by the following ballad which Anne Askew, who was burned at SinithtU ! i
in 1546, made and sang when she was in Newgate :\

Like Ib the armed knight,
Appointed to the Held,
With this world will I fight,
And Christ shall be my shield.

Faith is thnt weapon strong,
Which will not fall at need:
My foes, therefore, among,
Therewith will I proceed.

As it Is had in strength
And force of Christe's way,
It will prevail at length,
Though all the devils say nay.

Faith in the fathers old
Obtained righteousness ;
Wbich make me very bold
To fear no world's distress.

I now rejoice in heart,
And hope bids me do so;
For Christ will take my part,
And ease me of my woe.

Thou say'st Lord, whoso knock,
To them wilt thou attend :
Undo therefore the lock,
And thy strong power send.

More encmie now I have
Than hairs upon my head :
Let them not me deprave,
But fight thou in my stead.

On thec my care I cast,
For all their cruel spite:
I set not by their haste;
For thou art my delight.

I am not she that list
My anchor to let fall
For every drizzling mist,
My ship substantial.

Not oft use I to write,
In prose, nor yet In rhyme;
Yet will I shew one sight
That I saw in my time.

I saw a royal throne,
Where justice should have sit,
But In her stead was one
Of moody, cruel wit.

Absorbed was righteousness,
As of the raging flood :
Satan, in his excess,
Sucked up the guiltless blood.

Then thought I, Jesus Lord,
When thou shall judge us all,
Hard it is to record
On these men what will fail.

Tet, Lord, I thee desire.
For that they do to me.
Let them not taste the hire
Of their iniquity.

*Venel.\" How say ye to my soul, Flee as a bird to your mountain t" We inay observe,
that David is much pleased with the metaphor in frequently com- Pring himself to
a bird, and that of several sorts : first, to an eagle (Psalm ciii. 5), " My youth is
renewed like the eagle's ;" sometimes to an owl (Psalm cii. 6), "I am like an owl
in the desert ;" sometimes to a pelican, in the same Terse, "Like a pelican in the
wilderness;" sometimes to a sparrow (Psalm . "i), " I watch, and am as a sparrow
;" sometimes to a partridge, " As when one doth hunt a partridge." I cannot say that
he doth compare himself to a dove, bat he would compare himself (Psalm lv. 6), " O
that I had the wings of adove, for then I would flee away, and be at rest." Some will
say, How is it possible that birds of so different a feather should all so fly together
as to meet in the character of David ? To whom we answer, That no two men can
more differ one from another, that the same servant of God at several times differeth
from himself. David in prosperity, when commanding, was like an eagle; in adversity,
when contemned, like an owl; in devotion, when retired, like a pelican; in solitariness,
when having no company, like a sparrow; in persecution, wheu fearing too much
company (of Savf), like a partridge. This general metaphor of a bird, which David so
often used on himself, his enemies in the first verse of this Psalm used on him, though
not particularising the kind thereof : " Flee as a, bird to your mountain;'1" that is,
speedily betake thyself to thy God, in whom thou hopcst for succour and security.*

*Seeing this counsel was both good in itself, and good at this time, why doth David
seem so angry and displeased thereat ? Those his words, " Why say you to my soul.
Flee as a bird to your mountain ." import some passion, at leastwise, a disgust of the
advice. It is answered, David was not offended with the counsel, but with the manner
of the propounding thereof. His enemies did it ironically in a gibing, jeering way, as if
his flying thither were to no purpose, and he unlikely to find there the safety he sought
for. However, David was not hereby put out of conceit with the counsel, beginning
this Psalm with this his firm resolution, " In the Lord put I my trust: how say ye then
to my sovl," etc. Learn we from hence, when men give us good counsel in a jeering
way, let us take the counsel, and practise it; and leave them the jeer to be punished
for it. Indeed, corporal cordials may be envenomed by being wrapped up in poisoned*

papers ; not so good spiritual advice where the good matter receives no infection from the ill manner of the delivery thereof. Thus, when the chief priests mocked our Saviour (Matt, xxvii. 43), " He trusted in God, let him deliver him now if he will have him." Christ trusted in God never a whit the less for the fleere and flout which their profaneness was pleased to bestow upon him. Otherwise, if men's mocks should make us to undervalue good counsel, we might in this age be mocked out of our God, and Christ, and Scripture, and heaven ; the apostle Jude, verse 18, having foretold that in the last times there should be mockers, walking after their own lusts.\Thomas Fuller.

Verse 1.\It is as great an offence to make a new, as to deny the true God. " In t/te Lord put I my trust /" how then " say ye -unto my soul " (ye seducers of souls), ' thtit she should fly unto the mountains as a bird;" to seek unnecessary and foreign helps, as if the Lord alone were not sufficient? " The Lord is my rock, and my fortress, and he that delivereth me, my God, and my strength ; in him will I trust : my shield, the horn of my salvation, and my refuge. I will call upon the Lord, who is worthy to be praised, so shall I be safe from mine enemies." "Whom have I in heaven but thee," amongst those thousands of angels and saints, what Michael or Gabriel, what Moses or Samuel, what Peter, what Paul? " and there is none in earth that I desire in comparison of thee." John King, 1608.

Verse 1.\In temptations of inward trouble and terror, it is not convenient to dispute the matter with Satan. David in Psalm xlii. 11, seems to correct himself for his mistake ; his soul was cast down within him, and for the cure of that temptation, he had prepared himself by arguments for a dispute ; but perceiving himself in a wrong course, he calls off his soul from disquiet to an immediate application to God and the promises, " Trust still in God, for I shall yet praise him ;" but here he is more aforehand with his work ; for while his enemies were acted by Satan to discourage him, he rejects the temptation at first, before it settled upon his thoughts, and chaseth it away as a thing that he would not give ear to. " In the Lord put I my trust: how say ye to my soul, Flee as a bird to your mountain ?" And there are weighty reasons that should dissuade us from entering the lists with Satan in temptation of inward trouble.\Richard Gilpin.

Verse 1.\The shadow will not cool except in it. What good to have the

shadow though of a mighty rock, when we sit in the open sun ? To have almighty power engaged for us, and we to throw ourselves out of it, by bold sallies in the mouth of temptation ! The saints' falls have been when they have run out of their trench and stronghold ; for, like the conies, they are a weak people in themselves, and their strength lies in the rock of God's almightiness, which is their habitation.\William (Jurnall.

I'erse 1.\The saints of old would not accept deliverances on base terms. They scorned to fly away for the enjoyment of rest except it were with the wings of a dove, covered with silver innocence. As willing were many of the martyrs to die as to dine. The tormentors were tired in torturing Blandina. " We are ashamed, O Emperor ! The Christians laugh at your cruelty, and grow the more resolute," said one of Julian's nobles. This the heathen counted obstinacy ; but they knew not the power of the Spirit, nor the secret armour of proof which saints wear about their hearts.\John Trapp.

Verted |" *For, lo, the wicked lend their few,"* etc. *This verse presents an unequal combat betwixt armed power, advantaged with polity, on the one side ; and naked innocence on the other. First, armed power: " They lend their boics, and mate ready their arrows,"" being all the artillery of that age ; secondly, advantaged urith policy : " that they may primly shoot,'l" to surprise them with an ambush unawares, probably pretending amity and friendship unto them ; thirdly, naked innocence: if innocence may be termed naked, which is its own armour ; "at the upright in heart.'l"|Thomas Fuller.*

Verse 2.|" *For, lo, the ungodly lend their low, and make ready their arrows vithin the quiver: that they may privily shoot at them which are true of heart.'l'l The plottings of he chief priests and Pharisees that they might take Jesus by subtlety and kill him. They bent their bow, when they hired Judas Iscariot for the betrayal of his Master ; they made ready their arrows within the quiver when they sought " false witnesses against Jesus to put him to death." Matt, xivi. 59. " Them which are true of heart.'l'l Not alone the Lord himself, the only true and righteous, but his apostles, and the long line of those who should faithfully cleave to him from that lime to this. And as wi(h the Master, so with the servants : witness the calumnies and the revilings that from the time of Joseph's accusation by his mistress till the present day, have been the lot of God's people. |Mithael Aygunn, 1416, in J. M. Neale's Commentary.*

Verse 2.|" *That they may secretly shoot at them which are upright in heart." They bear not their bows and arrows as scarecrows in a garden of cucumbers, to fray, but to shoot, not at stakes, but men ; their arrows are jactila mortifera (Psalm vii.), deadly arrows, and lest they should fail to hit, they take advantage of the dark, of privacy and secrecy ; they shoot privily. Now this is the covenant of hell itself. For what created power in the earth is able to dissolve that work which cruelty and subtlety, like Simeon and Levi, brothers in evil, are combined and confederate to bring to pass ? Where subtlety is ingenious, insidious to invent, cruelty barbarous to execute, subtlety giveth counsel, cruelty giveth the stroke. Subtlety ordereth the time, the place, the means, sccommodateth, concinnateth circumstances ; cruelty undertaketh the act : subtlety hideth the knife, cruelty cutteth the throat : subtlety with a cunning head Uyeth the ambush, plotteth the train, the stratagem ; and cruelty with as savage heart, sticketh not at the dreadfullcst, direfullest objects, ready to wade up to the ankles, the neck, in a whole red sea of human, yea, country blood : how fearful is their plight that are thus assaulted !|John King.*

Verge 3.|"*If the foundations be destroyed, what can the r iyhteous do ?" But now we are met with a giant objection, which with Goliath must be removed, or else it will obstruct our present proceedings. Is it possible that the foundation of religion should be destroyed ? Can God be in so long a sleep, yea, so long a lethargy, ai patiently to permit the ruins thereof? If he looks on, and yet doth not see these foundations when destroyed, where then is his omnitciency fIf he seeth it, and cannot help it, where then is his omnipotency f If lie seeth it, can help it, and will not, where then is his goodness and mercy f Martha said to Jesus (John xi. 21), " Lord, if thou hadst been here, my brother had not died." But many will say, Were God effectually present in the world with his aforesaid attributes, surely the foundation had not died, had not been destroyed. We answer negatively, that it is impossible that the foundations of religion should ever be totally and finally destroyed, either in relation to the church in general, or in reference to every true and lively member thereof. For the first, we have an express promise of Christ. Matt. xvi. 18. " The gates of hell shall not prevail against it." Fundamenta tamen stant incancussa Sionis. And as for every particular Christian (2 Tim. ii. 19), " Nevertheless, the foundation of God standeth sure, having this seal, the Lord knoweth them that are his." However, though for the reasons aforementioned in the objections (the inconsistency thereof with the attributes of God's omnipotency, omnisciency, and goodness), the foundations can never totally and finally, yet may they partially be destroyed, quoad gradum, in a fourfold degree, as followeth. First, in the desires and utmost endeavours of wicked men,*

(1. Hoc telle, They bring their 2. Hoc agere,
(3. Totum posse.

If they destroy not the foundations, it is no thanks to them, seeing all the world will bear them witness they have done their best (that is, their worst), what, their might and malice could perform. Secondly, in their own vainglorious imaginations : they may not only vainly boast, but also verily believe that they have destroyed the foundations. Applicable to this purpose, is that high rant of the Roman emperor (Luke ii. 1) : " And it came to pass in those days, that there went out a decree from Csesar Augustus, that all the world should be taxed." All the world ! whereas he had, though much, not all in Europe, little in Asia, less in Africa, none in America, which was so far from being conquered, it was not so much as known to the Romans. But hyperbole is not a figure,' but the ordinary language of pride ; because indeed Augustus had very much he pro-

claitneth himself to have all the world Thirdly, the foundations may lie

destroyed as to all outward visible illustrious apparition. The church in persecution is like unto a ship in a tempest; down go all their masts, yea, sometimes for the more speed they are forced to cut them down : not a piece of canvas to play with the winds, no sails to be seen ; they lie close knotted to the very keel, that the tempest may have the less power upon them, though when the storm is over, they can hoist up their sails as high, and spread their canvas as broad as ever before. So the church in the time of persecution feared, but especially felt, loseth all gayness and gallantry which may attract and allure the eyes of beholders, and contenteth itself with its own secrecy. In a word, on the work-days of affliction she weareth her worst clothes, whilst her best are laid up in her wardrobe, in sure and certain hope that God will give her a holy and happy day, when with joy she shall wear her best garments. Lastly, they may be destroyed in the jealous apprehension of the best saints and servants of God, especially in their melancholy fits. I will instance in no puny, but in a star of the first magnitude and greatest eminency, even Elijah himself complaining (1 Kings xix. 10) : " And I, even I only, am left; and they seek my life, to take it away."\Thomas Fuller.

Verse 3.\" If." It is the only word of comfort in the text, that what is said is not positive, out suppositive; not thetical, but hypothetical. And yet this comfort which is but a spark (at which we would willingly kindle our"hopes), is quickly sadded with a double consideration. First, impossible suppositions produce impossible consequences, " As is the mother, so is the daughter." Therefore, surely God's Holy Spirit would not suppose such a thing but what was feasible and possible, but what either had, did, or *might come to pass. Secondly, the Hebrew word is not the conditional im, si, si forte, but clii, quia, quoniam.because, and (although here it be favourably rendered (/"), seemeth to import, more therein, that the sad case had already happened in David's days. I see, therefore, that this if, our only hope in the text, is likely to prove with Job's friends, but a miserable comforter. Well, it is good to know the worst of things, that we may provide ourselves accordingly ; and therefore let us behold this duleful case, not as doubtful, but as done ; not as feared, but felt; not as suspected, but at this time really come to pass.\Thomas Fuller.*

Verse 3.\"If the foundations," etc. My text is an answer to a tacit objection which some may raise ; namely, that the righteous are wanting to them- atlves, and by their own easiness and inactivity (not daring and doing so much as they might and ought), betray themselves to that bad condition. In whose defence David shows, that if God in his wise will and pleasure seeth it fitting, for reasons best known to himself, to suffer religion to be reduced to terms of extremity, it is not placed in the power of the best man alive to remedy and redress the same. "If the foundations be destroyed, what can the righteous do " My text is hung about with mourning, as for a funeral sermon, and contains : First, a sad case supposed, " If the foundations be destroyed." Secondly, a sad question propounded, " What can the righteous dot" Thirdly, a sad answer implied, namely, that they can do just nothing, as to the point of re-establishing the destroyed foundation.\Thomas Fuller.

VmeS.\" If the foundations If. destroyed," etc. The civil foundation of a nation or people, is their laws and constitutions. The order and power that's among them, that's the foundation of a people ; and when once this foundation is destroyed, " What can the righteous dot" What can the best, the wisest in the world, do in such a case ? What can any man do, if there be not a foundation of government left among men ? There is no help nor answer in such a case but that which follows in the fourth verse of the Psalm, " The Lord is in tit holy temple, the ford's throne is in heaven: his eyes behold, his eyelids try, the rhiillren of men;" as if he had said, in the midst of these confusions, when is it is said (Psalm Ixxxii. 5), " All the foundations of the earth are out of course ;" yet God keeps his course still, he is where he was and as he was, without variableness or shadow of turning.\Joseph Caryl.

Vene 3.\" The righteous." The righteous indefinitely,, equivalent to the righteous universally ; not only the righteous as a single arrow, but in the whole sheat; not only the righteous in their personal, but in their diffusive capacity, "ere they all collected into one body, were all the righteous living in the same age wherein the foundations are destroyed, summoned up and modelled into one corporation, all their joint endeavours would prove ineffectual to the re-establishing of the fallen foundations, as not being man's work, but only God's work to perform.\Thomas VuVer.

Vene 3.\" The foundations." Positions, the things formerly fixed, placed, and settled. It is not said, if the roof be ruinous, or if the side walls be shattered, but if the foundations.

Yene 3.\" Foundations be destroyed." In the plural. Here I will not warrant my skill in architecture, but conceive this may pass for an undoubted troth: it is possible that a building settled on several entire foundations (suppose them pillars) close one to another, if one of them fall, yet the structure may still stand, or rather hang (at *the least for a short time) by virtue of the wmpluatite, which it receiveth from such foundations which still stand secure. But in case there be a total rout, and an utter ruin of all the foundations, none can fancy to themselves a possibility of that building's subsistence.\Thomas Fuller.*

VerieS.\" What Can the righteous t" The can of the righteous is a limited "n, confined to the rule of God's word ; they can do nothing but what they can awfully do. 2 Cor. xiii. 8. " For we can do nothing against the truth, out for the truth :" Tllud possumut, quod jure possumus. Wicked men can do anything; their conscience, which is so wide that it is none at all, will bear them out to act anything how unlawful soever, to stab, poison, massacre, by anymeans, at any time, in any place, whosoever standeth betwixt them and the effecting their desires. Not Bo the righteous ; they have a rule whereby to walk, which they will not, they must not, they dare not, cross. If therefore a righteous man were assured, that by the breach of one of God's commandments he might restore decayed religion, and re-settle it ttatu quo print, his hands, head, and heart are tied up, he can do nothing, because their damnation it just who say (Rom. iii. 8), " Let us do nil that good may come thereof.'1 "

Verse 3.\" Do." It is not said, What can they think? It is a great blessing which God hath allowed injured people, that though otherwise oppressed and straitened, they may freely enlarge themselves in their thoughts.\Thomat Puller.

Verse 3.\Sinning times have ever been the saints' praying times : this sent Ezra with a heavy heart to confess the sin of his people, and to bewail their abominations before the Lord. Ezra ix. And Jeremiah tells the wicked of his degenerate age, that ' his soul should weep in secret places for their pride." Jer. xiii. 17. Indeed, sometimes sin comes to such a height, that this is almost all the godly can do, to get into a corner, and bewail the general pollutions of the age. " If the foundations be destroyed, what can the righteous do ?" Such dismal days of national confusion our eyes have seen, when foundations of government were destroyed, and all hurled into military confusion. "When it is thus with a people, " What can the righteous do?" Yes, this they mny, and should do, "fast and pray." There is yet a God in heaven to be sought to, when a people's deliverance is thrown beyond the help of human policy or power. Now ia the fit time to make their appeal to God, as the words following hint: " The Lord is in hit holy temple, the Lord's throne is in heaven y" in which words God is presented sitting in heaven as a temple, for their encourage ment, I conceive, in such a desperate state of affairs, to direct their prayers thither for deliverance. And certainly this hath been the engine that hath been instrumental, above any, to restore this poor nation again, and set it upon the foundation of that lawful government from which it had so dangerously deoarted.\ William OurnaU.

Verse 4.\The infinite understanding of God doth exactly know the sins of men ; he knows so as to consider. He doth not only know them, but intently behold them : " His eyelids try the children of men," a metaphor taken from men, that contract the eyelids when they would wistly and accurately behold a thing : it is not a transient and careless look.\Stephen Charnock.

Verse4.\"Hit eyes be?iold," etc. God searcheth not as man searcheth, by enquiring into that which before was hid from him ; his searching is no moic but his beholding ; he seeth the heart, he beholdeth the reins ; God's very sight is searching. Heb.

iv. 18. " All things are naked, and opened unto his eyes," Terpainfttva, dissected or anatomised. He hath at once as exact a view of the most hidden things, the very entrails of the soul, as if they had been with never so great curiosity anatomised before him.\Richard Alleine, 1611\1681.

Vei'se 4.\" Sis eyes behold," etc. Consider that God not only sees into all you do, but he sees it to that very end that he may examine and search into it. He doth not only behold you with a common and indifferent look, but with a searching, watchful, and inquisitive eye : he pries into the reasons, the motives, the ends of all your actions. " The Lord's throne is in heaven: his eyes behold, his eyelids try, the children of men." Rev. i. 14, where Christ is described, it is said, his eyes are as aflame of fire: you know the property of fire is to search and make trial of those things which are exposed unto it, and to separate the dross from the pure metal : so. God's eye is like fire, to try and examine the actions of men : he knows and discerns how much your very purest duties have in them of mixture, and base ends of formality, hypocrisy, distractedness, and deadness : he sees through all your specious pretences, that which you cast as a mist before the eyes of men when yet thou art but a juggler in religion : all your tricks and sleights of outward profession, all those things that you use tocozen and delude men withal, cannot possibly impose upon him : he is a God that can look through all those fig-leaves of outward profession, and discern the nakedness of your duties through them.\Ezekiel Hopkins, D.D.

Vene 4.\" Hit eyes behold," etc. Take God into thy counsel. Heaven overlooks bell. God at any time can tell thee what plots are hatching there ngainst thee.\ William Qurnall.

Verne 4.\" Hi eyes behold, his eyelids try, the children of men.' 11 When an offender, or one accused for any offence, is brought before a judge, and stands at the bar to be arraigned, the judge looks upon him, eyes him, sets his eye upon him, and he bids the offender look up in his face : " Look upon me," saiththe judge, " and speak up :" guiltiness usually clouds the forehead and clothes the brow ; the weight of guilt holds down the head ! the evil doer hath an HI loot, or dares not look up ; how glad is he if the judge looks off him. We have such an expression here, speaking of the Lord, the great Judge of heaven and e&rtb.: " Hit eyelids try the children of men," as a judge tries a guilty person with his eye, and reads the characters of his wickedness printed in his face. Hence we have a common speech iu our language, such a one looks suspiciously, ot, he hath a guilty look. At that great gaol-delivery described in Rev. vi. 16, All the prisoners cry out to be hid from the face of him that sat upon the throne. They could not look upon Christ, and they could not endure Christ should look on them ; the eyelids of Christ try the children of men Wickedness cannot endure to be under the observation of any eye, much less of the eye of justice. Hence the actors of it say, " Who seeth usf" It is very hard not to show the guilt of the heart in the face, and it is as hard to have it seen there.\ Jiaeph Caryl.

Vent 5.\" The Lord trieth the righteous.' 1 " Except our sins, there is not such plenty of anything in all the world as there is of troubles which come from sin, as one heavy messenger came to Job after another. Since we are not in paradise, but in the wilderness, we must look for one trouble after another. As a bear came to David after a lion, and a giant after a bear, and a king after a giant, and Philistines after a *king, so, when believers have fought with poverty, they shall fight with envy ; when they have fought with envy, they shall fight with infamy ; when they have fought with infamy, they shall fight with sickness ; they shall be like a labourer who is never out of work.\Henry Smith.*

Verse 5.\" The Lord trieth the righteous."\Times of affliction ind perse- cation will distinguish the precious from the vile, it will difference the counterfeit professor from the true. Persecution is a Christian's touchstone, it is a lapU lydius that will try what metal men are made of, whether they be silver or tin, gold or dross, wheat or chaff, shadow or substance, carnal or spiritual, sincere or hypocritical. Nothing speaks out more soundness and uprightness than a pursuing after holiness, even then when holiness is most afflicted, pursued, and persecuted in the world : to stand fast in fiery trials argues much integrity within.\Thomas Brooks.

Verse 5.\Note the singular opposition of the two sentences. God hates the wicked, and therefore in contrast he loves the righteous ; but it is here said that he tries them : therefore it follows that to trv and to love are with God the same thing.\ C. H. 8.

Verse 6.\' Upon the wicked he shall rain snares.'1 'I Snares to hold them ; then if they be not delivered, follow fire and brimstone, and they cannot escape. This is the case of a sinner if he repent not; if God pardon not, he is in the snare of Satan's temptation, he is in the snare of divine vengeance ; let him therefore cry aloud for hia deliverance, that he may have his feet in a large room. The "wicked lay snares for the righteous, but God either preventeth them that their souls ever escape them, or else he subventeth them : " The snares we broken, and we are delivered." No snares hold us so fast as those of our own sins; they keep down our heads, and stoop us that we cannot look up : avery little ease they are to him that hath not a seared conscience.\Samuel Page, 1646.

Verted.\" He shall rain snares." As in hunting with the lasso, the huntsman casts a snare from above upon his prey to entangle its head or feet, so shall the Lord from above with many twistings of the line of terror, surround, bind, and take captive the haters of his law.\C. H. 8.

Vere 0.\" He shall rain snares," etc. He shall rain upon them when they least think of it, even in the midst of their jollity, as rain falls on a fair day. Or, he shall rain down the vengeance when he sees good, for it rains not always. Though he defers it, yet it will rain.\ William Nicholson, Bithop of Gloucester, in " Davids Harp Strung and Tuned," 1662.

Verte 6.\" Upon the wicked he shall rain snares, fire and brimstone, and an horrible tempest." The strange dispensation of affairs in this world is an argument which doth convincingly prove that there shall be such a day wherein all the involucra and entanglements of providence shall be clearly unfolded. Then shall the riddle be dissolved, why God hath given this and that profane wretch so much wealth, and so much power to do mischief : is it not that they might be destroyed for ever t Then shall they be called to a strict account for all that plenty and prosperity for which they are now envied ; and the more they have abused, the more dreadful will their condemnation be. Then it will be seen that God gave them not as mercies, but as " snares.'1" It is said that God " will rain on the iricked snares, fire and brimstone, and an horrible tempest:1" when he scatters abroad the desirable things of this world, riches, honours, pleasures, etc., then he rains " snares" upon them ; and when he shall call them to an account for these things, then he will rain upon them "fire and brimstone, and an horrible tempest " of his wrath and fury. Dives, who caroused on earth, yet, iu hell could not obtain so much as one poor drop of water to cool his scorched and flaming tongue : had not his excess and intemperance been so great in his life, his fiery thirst had not been so tormenting after death ; and therefore, in that sad item that Abraham gives him (Luke xvi. 25), he bids him "remember, that thou, in thy lifetime, receivcdst thy good things, and likewise Lazarus evil things; but now he it comforted, and thou art tormented." I look upon this as a most bitter and a most deserved sarcasm ; upbraiding him for his gross folly, in making the trifles of this life his good things. Thou hast received thy good things, but now thou art tormented. Oh, never call Dives's purple and delicious fare good things, if they thus end in torments ! Was it good for him to be wrapped in purple who is now wrapped in flames ? Wus it good for him to fare deli- ciously who was only thereby fatted up against the day of slaughter ?\Ezekiel Hopkins.

Verse 6.\" Snares, fire and brimstone, storm and tempest: this shatt lie the portion of their cup." After the judgment follows the condemnation : prefigured as we have seen, by the overthrow of Sodom and Gomorrah. ' Snares:" because the allurements of Satan in this life will be their worst punishments in the next; the fire of anger, the brimstone of impurity, the tempest of pride, the lust of the flesh, the lust of the eyes, and the pride of life. " This shall be their portion ;" compare it with the psalmist's own saying, " The Lord himself is the portion of my inheritance and my cup." Psalm xvi. 5.\Cassiodorus, in J. M. Nettle's Commentary.

Verse 6.\" The portion of their cup." Heb., the allotment of their cun. The expression has reference to the custom of distributing to each guest his mess of meat. | William French and George Skinner, 1842.

Verse 7.\That God may jjive grace without glory is intelligible ; but to admit a man to communion with him in glory without grace, is not intelligible. It is not agreeable to God's holiness to make any inhabitant of heaven./ and converse freely with him in a way of intimate love, without such a qualification of grace: " The righteous Lord loveth righteousness; his countenance doth behold the upright;" he looks upon him with a smiling eye, and therefore he cannotfavourably look upon an unrighteous person ; so that this necessity is not founded ouly in the command of God that we should be renewed, but in the very nature of the thing, because God, in regard of his holiness, cannot converse with an impure creature. God must change his nature, or the sinner's nature must be changed. There can be no friendly communion between two of different natures without the change of one of them into the likeness of the other. Wolves and sheep, darkness and light, can never agree. God cannot love a sinner as a sinner, because he hates impurity by a necessity of nature as well as a choice of will. It is as impossible for him to love it as to cease to be holy.| Stephen, Charnoeic.

HLNTS TO THE VILLAGE PREACHER.

Verte 1.\Faith's bold avowal, and brave refusal.

Verne 1.\Teacheth us to trust in God, how great soever our dangers be ; also that we shall be many times assaulted to make us put far from us this trust, but yet that we must cleave unto it, as the anchor of our souls, sure and steadfast.\Thomas Wttcoclcs.

Yerie 1.\The advice of cowardice, and the jeer of insolence, both answered by faith. Lesson\Attempt no other answer.

Verm 2.\The craftiness of our spiritual enemies.

Yene 3.\This may furnish a double discourse. I. If QocFs oath and promite tevld remote, what could we do? Here the answer is easy. II. If all earthly tiiingi fail, and the very State fall to pieces, what can we do ? We can suffer joyfully, hope cheerfully, wait patiently, pray earnestly, believe confidently, and triumph finally.

Yene 3.\Necessity of holding and preaching foundation truths.

Yerte 4.\The elevation, mystery, supremacy, purity, everlastingness, invisibility, etc., of the throne of God.

Veneti, 5.\In these verses mark the fact that the children of men, as well M the righteous, are tried ; work out the contrast between the two trials in their design and result, etc.

Yene5.\" The Lord trieth the righteous." I. Who are tried? H What in them is tried 1\Faith, love, etc. in. In what manner ?\Trials of every sort. IV. How long ? V. For what purposes ?

Verne 5.\" His toul hateth." The thoroughness of God's hatred of sin. Illustrate by providential judgments, threatenings, sufferings of the Surety, and the terrors of hell.

Yene 5.\The trying of the gold, and the sweeping out of the refuse.

Verge 6.\" He shall rain." Gracious rain and destroying rain.

Yene 6.\The portion of the impenitent.

Yene 7.\The Lord possesses righteousness as a personal attribute, loves it m the abstract, and blesses those who practise it.

PSALM XII.

Title.\This Psalm is headed "To the Chief Musician upon Sheminith, a Psalm of David," which title is identical with that of the siacth Psalm, except thai Neginoth is here omitted. We have nothing new to add, and therefore refer the reader to our remarks on the dedication of Psalm VI. As Shfminith signifies the eighth, the Arabic version says it is concerning the end of the world, which shall be the eighth day, and refers it to the coming of the -We.sA'irt/i: without accepting so fanciful an Merpi'etation, we may read this song of complaining faith in the light of His comiruj who shall break in pieces the oppressor. The subject will be 'the better before the mind's eye if we entitle this Psalm: " Good Thoughts In Bad Times." /(is supposed to have been written while Haul was persecuting David, and i/tose who favoured his cause.

Division.\In the first and second verse,? David spreads Ms plaint before the Lord concerning the treacfiery of his age ; verses 3 and 4 denounce judgments jpon proud traitors ; in verse 5 Jehovah himself thunders out his wrath against oppressors; hearing this, the Chief Musician sings sweetly nf the faithfulness of God and his care of his people, in verses 6 and 7 ; but closes on the old key of lament in verse 8, as he observes the abounding wickedness of his limes. Those holy souls who dwell in Mesech, and sojourn in the tents of Kedar, may read and sing these sacred stanzas with hearts in full accord with their mingled melody of lowly mourning and lofty confidence.

EXPOSITION.

HELP, LORD ; for the godly man ceaseth ; for the faithful fail from among the children of men.

2 They speak vanity every one with his neighbour : with flattering lips and with a double heart do they speak.

"Help, Lord,'1" A short, but sweet, suggestive, seasonable, and serviceable prayer ; a kind of angel's sword, to be turned every way, and to be used on all occasions. Ainsworth says the word rendered "help," is largely used for all manner of saving, helping, delivering, preserving, etc. Thus it seems that the prayer is very full and instructive. The Psalmist sees the extreme danger of his position, for a man had better be among lions than among liars ; he feels his own inability to deal with such sons of Belial, for " he who shall touch them must be fenced with iron ;" he therefore turns himself to his all-sufficient Helper, the Lord, whose help is never denied to his servants, and whose aid is enough for all their needs. " Help, Lord," is a very useful ejaculation which we mny dart up to heaven on occasions of emergency, whether, in labour, learning, suffering, fighting, living, or dying. As small ships can sail into harbours which larger vessels, drawing more water, cannot enter, so our brief cries and short petitions may trade with heaven when our soul is wind-bound, and businnss-bound, as to longer exercises of devotion, and when the stream of grace seems at too low an ebb to float a more laborious supplication. " For thf godly man ceaseth;'1" the death, departure, or decline of godly men should be a trumpet-call for more prayer. They say that fish smell first at the head, and when godly men decay, the whole commonwealth will soon go rotten. We must not, however, be rash in our judgment on this point, for Elijah erred in counting himself the only servant of God alive, when there were thousands whom the Lord held in reserve. The present times always appear to be peculiarly dangerous, because they ar nearest to our anxious gaze, and whatever evils are rife are sure to be observed, while the faults of past ages are further off, and are more easily overlooked. Yet we expect that in the latter days, " because iniquity shall abound, (he love of many shall wax cold," and then we must the more thoroughly turn from man, and address ourselves to the Churches'Lord, by whose help the gates of hell shall be kept from prevailing against us. " T/te jaU/y'ul jail J'rom among the children of men;'1'1 when godliness goes' laithtuiae&s inevitably follows ; without fear of God, men have no jove of truth! Common honesty is no longer common, when cummon irreligion leads to universal godlessness. David had his eye on Doeg, and the men of Ziph and Keilau, and perhaps remembered the murdered priests of Nob, and the many banished outs whu consorted with him in the cave of Adullam, mid wondered where the state would drill without the anchors of its godly and faithful men. David, amid the general misrule, did not betake himself to seditious plotting but to solemn petitionings ; iior did ha join with the multitude to do evil, but took up the arms of prayer to withstand their attacks upon virtue.

" They speak vanity every one with his neigl&om.'1" They utter that which is ain to hear, because of its frivolous, foolii-h, want of worth ; vain to believe, because it was false and lying ; vain to tnist to, since it was deceitful and flattering ; vain to regard, for it lifted up the hearer, filling him with proud conceit of himself. It is a sad thing when it is the fashion to talk vanity. " Ca'me, and I'll ca'thee," is the old Scotch proverb ; give me a high-sounding chaiacter, and I will give you one. Compliments and fawning congratulations are hateful to honest men ; they know that if they take they must give them, and they scotn to do either. These accommodation-bills are most admired by those who are bankrupt in character. Bad are the times when every man thus cajoles and cozens his neighbour. " With f altering lips and Kith a double heart do they ipftii." He who puffs up another's heart, has nothing better than wind in his own. If a man extols me to my face, he only shows me one side of his heart, and the other is black with contempt for me, or foul with intent to cheat me. Flattery is the sign of the tavern where duplicity is the host. The Chinese consider a mau of two hearts to be a very base man, and we shall be safe in reckoning all flatterers to be such.

3 The Lord shall cut off all flattering lips, and the tongue that speaketh proud things :

4 Who have said, With our tongue will we prevail ; our lips are our own : who is lord over us ?

Total destruction shall overwhelm the lovers of flattery and pride, but meanwhile how they hector and fume 1 "Well did the apostle call them "raging waves of the sea, foaming out their own shame." Free-thinkers are generally very free-talkers, and they are never more at ease than when railing at God's dominion, and arrogating to themselves unbounded license. Strange is it that the easy yoke of the Lord should so gall the shoulders of the proud, while the iron bands of Satan they bind about themselves as chains of honour : they boastfully cry unto God, " Who is lord over us ?" and hear not the hollow voire of the evil ofle, who cries from the infernal lake, "I am your lord, and right faithfully do ye serve me." Alas, poor fools, their pride and glory shall be cut off like a fading flower ! Mny God grant that pur soul may not be gathered with them. It is worthy of observation that flattering lips, and tongues speaking proud things, arc classed together : the fitness of this is clear, for they aie fuilty of the same vice, the first flatters another, and the second flatters himself, m both cases a lie is in their right hands. One generally imagines that flatterers are such mean parasites, so cringing and fawning, that they cannot be proud ; pat the wise man will tell you that while all pride is truly meanness, there is in the very lowest meanness no small degree of pride. Csesar's horse is even more proud of carrying Cajsar, than Caesar is of riding him. The mat on which the emperor wiped his shoes, boasts vaingloriously, crying out, "I cleaned the imperial boots." None are so detestably domineering as the little creatures who creep into office by cringing to the great; those are bad times, indeed, in which these obnoxious beings are numerous and powerful. No wonder that the justice of God in cutting off such injurious persons is matter for a psalm, for bothearth and heaven are weary of such provoking offenders, whose presence is a very plague to the people afflicted thereby. Men cannot tame the tongues of such boastful flatterers ; but the Lord's remedy if sharp is sure, and is an. unanswerable answer to their swelling words of vanity.

5 For the oppression of the poor, for the sighing of the needy, now will I arise, saith the Lord ; I will set him in safety from him that puffeth at him.

In due season the Lord will hear his elect ones, who cry day and night unto him, and though he bear long with their oppressors, yet will he avenge them speedily. Observe that the mere oppression of saints, however silently they bear it, is in itself a cry to God : Moses was heard at the Red Sea, though he said nothing ; and Hagar's

*affliction was heard despite her silence. Jesus feels with his people, and their smarts
are mighty orators with him. By-and-by, however, .'."// begin to sigh and express their
misery, and then relief comes post-haste. Nothing moves a father like the cries of his
children ; he bestirs himself, wakes up his manhood, overthrows the enemy, and sets
his beloved in safety. A pvff is too much for the child to bear, and the foe is so haughty,
that he laughs the little one to scorn ; but the Father comes, and then it is the child's
turn to laugh, when he is set above the rage of his tormentor. What virtue is there in
a poor man's sighs, that they should move the Almighty God to arise from his throne.
The needy did not dare to speak, and could only sigh in secret, but the Lord heard,
and could rest no longer, but girded on his sword for the battle. It is a fair day when
our soul brings God into her quarrel, for when his bare arm is seen, Philistia shall
rue the day. The darkest hours of the Church's night are those which precede the
break of day. Man's extremity is God's opportunity. Jesus will come to deliver just
when his needy ones shall sigh, as if all hope had gone for ever. O Lord, set thy rune
near at hand, and rise up speedily to our help. Should the afflicted reader be able to
lay hold upon the promise of this verse, let him gratefully fetch a fulness of comfort
from it. Gurnal says, " As one may draw out the wine of a whole hogshead at one tap,
so may a poor soul derive the comfort of the whole covenant to himself through one
promise, if he be able to apply it." He who promises to set us in safety, means thereby
preservation on earth, and eternal salvation in heaven.*

*6 The words of the Lord are pure words : as silver tried in a furnace of earth,
purified seven times.*

*7 Thou shalt keep them, O Lord, thou shalt preserve them from this generation for
ever.*

*Verse 6. What a contrast between the vain words of man, and the pure words of
Jehovah. Man's words are yea and nay, but the Lord's promises are yea and amen. For
truth, certainty, holiness, faithfulness, the words of the Lord are pure as well-refined
silver. In the original there is an allusion to the most severely-purifying process known
to the ancients, through which silver was passed when the greatest possible purity
was desired ; the dross was all consumed, and only tho bright and precious metal
remained ; so clear and free from all alloy of error or unfaithfulness is the book of the
words of the Lord. The Bible has passed through the furnace of persecution, literary
criticism, philosophic doubt, and scientific discovery, and has lost nothing but those
human interpretations which clung to it as alloy to precious ore. The experience of
saints has tried it in every conceivable manner, but not a single doctrine or promise
has been consumed in the most excessive heat. What God's words are, the words
of his children should be. If we would be Godlike in conversation, we must watch
our language, and maintain the strictest purity of integrity and holiness in all our
communications.*

*7. To fall into the hands of nn evil generation, so as to be baited by their cruelty,
or polluted by their influence, is an evil to be dreaded beyond measure ; but it is an
evil foreseen and provided for in the text. In life many a saint has lived a hundred
years before his age, as though he had darted his soul into the brighter future, and
escaped the mists of the beclouded present : he has gone to bis grave unreverenced
and misunderstood, and lo ! as generations come and go, upon a sudden the hero is*

unearthed, and lives in the admiration and love of the excellent of the earth ; preserved for ever from the generation which stigmatised him as a sower of sedition, or burned him as a heretic. It should be our daily prayer that we may rjse above pur age as the mountain-tops above the clouds, and may stand out as heaven-pointing pinnacle high above the mists of ignorance and sin which roll around us. O Eternal Spirit, fulfil in us the faithful saying of this verse ! Our faith believes those two assuring words, and cries, " Thau itolt," "thm shalt."

8 The wicked walk on every side, when the vilest men are exalted.

8. Here we return to the fount of bitterness, which first made the psalmist ran to the wells of salvation, namely, the prevalence of wickedness. When those in power are vile, their underlings will be no better. As a warm un brings out noxious flies, so does a sinner in honour foster vice everywhere. Our turf would not so swarm with abominablcs if those who are styled honourable did not give their countenance to the craft. Would to God that the glory and triumph of our Lord Jesus would encourage us to walk and work on every side ; as like acts upon like, since an exalted sinner encourages tinners, our exalted Redeemer must surely excite, cheer, and stimulate his Mints. Nerved by a sight of his reigning power we shall meet the evils of the times in the spirit of holy resolution, and shall the more hopefully pray, " Help, Lord."

EXPLANATORY NOTES AND QUAINT SAYINGS.

Vent.\" Help, Lard." 'Twas high time to call to heaven for help, when Saul cried, " Go, kill me up the priests of Jehovah" (the occasion as it is thought of making this Psalm), and therein committed the sin against the Holy Ghost, as some grave divines are of opinion. 1 Sam. xxii. 17. David, fttr many sad thoughts about that slaughter, and the occasion of it, Doeg's malicious information, together with the paucity of his fast friend?, and the multitude of his sworn enemies at court, breaks forth abruptly into these words, " Utlp, Lwd," help at a dead lift. The Arabic version hath it, Deliver meby ᵀᴹ in forte, as with weapons of war, for " the Lord is a man of war." Ex. xv. 8. ton Trapp.

Vfrti. ifa faithful." "A faithful man," as a parent, a reprover, an MYiser, one "without guile," " who can find?" Prov. xx. 6. Look close. View thyself in the glass of the word. Does thy neighbour or thy friend, find thee faithful to him ? What does our daily intercourse witness 1 Is not the attempt to speak what is agreeable oft made at the expense of truth ? Are not professions of regard sometimes utterly inconsistent with our real feelings ? In common life, where gross violations are restrained, a thousand petty offences we allowed, that break down the wall between sin and duty, and, judged by the

mne standard, are indeed guilty steps upon forbidden ground.\Charlei

Verse 1.\ A "faithful" man must be, first of all, faithful to himself ; then, he must he faithful to God ; and then, he must be faithful to others, particularly the church of God. And this, as it regards ministers, is of peculiar importance. Joseph Irons, 1840.

Verse 1.\Even as a careful mother, seeing her child in the way when a company of unruly horses run through the streets in full career, presently whips up her child in her arms and taketh him home ; or as the hen, seeing the ravenous kite over her head, clucks and gathers her chickens under her wings ; even so when God hath a purpose to bring a heavy calamity upon a land, it hath been usual with him to call and cull out

to himself such as are his dearly beloved. He takes his choice servants from the evil
to come. Thus was Augustine removed a little before Hippo (wherein he dwelt) was
taken ; Parceus died before Heidelburg was sacked ; and Luther was taken off before
Germany was overrun with war and bloodshed.\Ed. Dunsterville in a Sermon at the
Funtral of Sir Sim. Harcourt, 1642.

Verse .\" Help, Lord ; for the godly man ceaseth,'1'1 etc. :\

Back, then, complainer, loathe thy life no more,
Nor deem thyself upon a desert shore,

Because the rocks the nearer prospect close.
Tct In fallen Israel arc there heurts und eyes,
That day by day in prayer like thine arise;

Thou knbwest them not, but their Creator known.
Go, to the world return, nor fear to cast
Thy bread upon the waters, sure at lost

In joy to Und it after many days.
John Keble, 1792\1860.

Verseil 1, 2, 4.\Consider our markets, our fairs, our private contracts and bargains,
our shops, our cellars, our weights, our measures, our promises, our protestations,
our politic tricks and villanous Machiavelism, our enhancing of the prices of all
commodities, and tell, whether the twelfth Psalm may not as fitly be applied to our
times as to the days of the man of God ; in which the feigning, and lying, and facing,
and guile, und subtlety of men provoked the psalmist to cry out, "Help, Lord ; for tlitre
is not a godly man left: for tft$ faithful are failed from among the children of men
: they speak deceitfully eaery one with his neighbour, Jtattering with their lips, and
speak with a double heart, which have said, With our tongue we will prevail; our lipa
are our own : who is Lord oter vs.'"\B. Wokombe, 1612.

Verse 2.\" The]/ speak ranity etery one with his neighbour: with Jlattering lips
and with a double heart do they speak." The feigned zeal is just like a waterman, that
looks one way and rows another way ; for this man pretends one thing and intends
another thing ; as Jehu pretended the zeal of God's glory, but his aim was at his
master's kingdom ; and his zeal to God's service was but to bring liim to the sceptre
of the kingdom. So Demetrius professed great love unto Diana, but his drift wns to
maintain the honour of his profession ; and so we have too many that make great show
of holiness, and yet their hearts aim at other ends ; but they may be sure, though they
can deceive the world and destroy themselves, yet not God, who knoweth the secrets
of all hearts.\ Or. Williams, 1636.

Verse 2.\" They speak vanity."\

Faithless is earth, and faithless are the skies!
Justice is fled, and truth Is now no more !

Virgil's Eneid, IV. 873.

Verse 2.\" With a double heart."\ Man is nothing but insincerity, falsehood, and hypocrisy, both in regard to himself and in regard to others. He does not wish that he should be told the truth, ho shuns saying it to others ; and all these moods, so inconsistent with justice and reason, have their roots in hie heart.\Blaine Pascal.

Z.\" With flattering lips and with a double heart do they tpeak." There is no such stuff to make a cloak of as religion ; nothing so fashionable, nothing Bo profitable : it is a livery wherein a wise man may serve two masters, God and the world, and make a gainful service by either. I serve both, and in lth myself, by prevaricating with both. Before man none serves his God with more severe devotion ; for which, among the best of men, I work my own ends, ind serve myself. In private, I serve the world ; not with so strict devotion, but with more delight; where fulfilling of her servants' lusts, I work my end and serve myself. The house of prayer who more frequents than I ? In all Christian duties who more forward than I ? I fast with those who fast, that I may eat with those that eat. I mourn with those that mourn. No hand more open to the cause than mine, and in their families none prays longer and witli louder zeal. Thus when the opinion of a holy life hath cried the goodness of my conscience up, my trade can lack no custom, my wares can want no price, my words can need no credit, my actions can lack no praise. If I am covetous, it is interpreted providence ; if miserable, it is counted temperance ; if melancholy, it is construed godly sorrow ; if merry, it is voted spiritual joy ; if I be rich, it is thought the blessing of a godly life ; if poor, supposed the fruit of conscionable dealing ; if I be well spoken of, it is the merit of holy conversation ; if ill, it is the malice of malignants. Thus I sail with every wind, and have my end in all conditions. This cloak in summer keeps me cool, in winter waim, and hides the nasty bag of all my secret lusts. Under this cloak I walk in public fairly with applause, and in private sin securely without offence, and officisite wisely without discovery. I compass sea and land to make a proselyte ; and no sooner made, but he makes me. At a fast I cry Geneva, and at a feast I cry Rome. If I be poor, I counterfeit abundance to save my credit ; if rich, I dissemble poverty to save charges. I most frequent prhii-matiral lectures, which I find most profitable ; from thence learning to divulge and maintain new doctrines ; they maintain me in suppers thrice a week. I use the help of a lie sometimes, as a new stratagem to uphold the gospel ; and I colour oppression with God's judgments executed upon the wicked. Charity I hold n eitraordinary duty, therefore not ordinarily to be performed. "What I openly reprove abroad, for my own profit, that I secretly act at home, for my own plrasure. But stay, I see a handwriting in my heart which damps my soul. It is chiiractered in these sad words, " Woe be to you, hypocrites." Matt, xxiii. 13. Frmeit Quarks' " Hypocrite'l Soliloquy."

Vene 2.\" With flattering lips," etc. The world indeed says that society ronld not exist if there were perfect truthfulness and candour between man and man ; and that the world's propriety would be as much disturbed if every man said what he pleased, as it was in those days of Israelitish history, when wry man did that which was right in his own eyes. The world is assuredly the best judge of its own condition and mode of government, and therefore I will not say what a libel does such a remark contain, but oh, what a picture does it present of the social edifice, that its walls can be cemented and kept together only by flattery and falsehood !\Barton Bovchier.

VeneZ.\"Flattering lips."1 The philosopher Bion being asked what animal he thought the most hurtful, replied, " That of wild creatures a tyrant, and of tome ones a flatterer." The flatterer is the most dangerous enemy we can have. Raleigh, himself a courtier, and therefore initiated into the whole art of flattery, ho discovered in his own career and fate its dangerous and deceptive power, tadeep artifice and deeper falsehood, says, " A flatterer is said to be a beast that wteth smiling. But it is hard to know them from friends\they are Bo obsequious and full of protestations : for as a wolf resembles a dog, so doth a flatterer a friend."\ The Book of Symlxih, 1844.

Verte 2.\" They apeak with it dovlle heart." The original is, " A heart and a wart:" one for the church, another for the change ; one for Sundays, another for working-days ; one for the king, another for the pope. A man without a heart is a wonder, but a man with two hearts is a monster. It is said of Judas"There were mnny hearts in one man ;" and we read of the saints, "There was one heart in many men." Acts iv. 32. Ddbo illis cor unum; a special blessing.\Thomas Adams.

Verse 2.\When men cease to be faithful to their God, he who expects to find them so to each other, will be much disappointed. The primitive sincerity will accompany the primitive piety in her flight from the earth ; and then interest will succeed conscience in the regulation of human conduct, till one man cannot trust another farther than he holds him by that tie. Hence, by the way, it is, that though many are infidels themselves, yet few choose to have their families and dependants such ; as judging, and rightly judging, that true Christians are the only persons to be depended on for the exact discharge of social duties. | Qeorge Home.

Verse 3.\" The Lord shaU cut off all flattering lips," etc. They who take pleasure in deceiving others, will at the last find themselves most of all deceived, when the Sun of truth, by the brightness of his rising, shall at once detect and consume hypocrisy. | George Home.

Verge 3.\" Out off" lips arid tongues.'1 " May there not be here an allusion to those terrible but suggestive punishments which Oriental monarchs were wont to execute on criminals ? Lips were cut off and tongues torn out when offenders were convicted of lying or treason. So terrible and infinitely more Bo are the punishments of sin.\C. II. 8.

Verses 3, 4.\It need not now seem strange to tell you that the Lord is the owner of our bodies, that he has so much propriety therein that they are more his than ours. The apostle tells us -as much. 1 Cor. vi. 20. " Glorify God in your bodies which are his." Our bodies, and every member thereof, are his ; for if the whole be so, no part is exempted. And therefore they spake proud things, and presumptuously usurped the propriety of God, who said, " Our lipt are our own ;" as though their lips had not been his who is Lord and Owner of all, but they had been lords thereof, and might have used them as they list. This provoked God to show what right he had to dispose of such lips and tongues, by cutting them off.\David Clarkson.

Verse 4.\" Who have said, With our tongues wiU v prevail; who is Lord oner va?" So it was: twelve poor and unlearned men on the one side, all the eloquence of Greece and Rome arrayed on the other. From the time of Ter- tullus to that of Julian the apostate, every species of oratory, learning, wit, was lavished against the church of God ; and the result, like the well-known story of that dispute between the Christian *peasant and the heathen philosopher, when the latter, having challenged the assembled fathers of a synod to silence him, was put to shame by the simple faith of the former "In the name of our Lord Jesus Christ, I command thee to be dumb." Wlw is Lord over us? "Who is the Lord, that I should obey his voice to let Israel go?" Ex. v. 2. "What is the Almighty, that we should serve him?" Jobxxi. 15. "Who is that God that shall deliver you?" Dan. iii. 15.\Michael Ayguan, in J. M. Neale's Commentary.*

Verse 4.\" Our lips are our own." If we have to do with God, we must quit claim to ourselves and look on God as our owner ; but this is fixed in the hearts of men, We will be our own ; we will not consent to the claim which God makes to us : "Our lips are our otcm." Wicked men might as well say the same thing of their whole selves ; our bodies, strength, time, parts, etc., are our own, and who is Lord over us I\John Howe.

Verse 4.\Prom the faults of the wicked we must learn three contrary lessons ; to wit : 1. That nothing which we have is our own. But, 2'. Whatsoever is given to us of God is for service to be done to him. 3. That whatsoever we do or say, we have a Lord over us to whom we must be answerable when he calleth us to account.\David Didcson.

Verse 5.\" For the oppression of the poor," etc. When oppressors and

persecutor? do snuff and puff at the people of God, when they defy them, and scorn them, and think that they can with a blast of their breath blow them away, then God will arise to judgment, as the Chaldee has it; at that very nick of time when all seems to be lost, and when the poor, oppressed, and afflicted people of God can do nothing but sigh and weep, and weep and sigh, then the Lord will arise and ease them of their oppressions, and make their day of extremity a glorious opportunity to work for his own glory and his people's good. Matt. xxii. 6, 7. " And the remnant took his servants, and entreated them spitefully, and slew them. But when the king heard thereof, he was wroth : and he sent forth his armies and destroyed those murderers, and burned up their city."\Thomas Brookt.

Verte 5.\Fear ye, whosoever ye be, that do wrong the poor ; you have power and wealth, and the favour of the judges, but they have the strongest weapons of all, sighings and groanings, which fetch help from heaven for them. These weapons dig down houses, throw up foundations, overthrow whole nations.\ Chryioitom.

Yene o.\" For the sighing of the needy, now will I arite, taith the Lord." God is pleased to take notice of etery grace, even the least and lowest, and every gracious inclination in any of his servants. To fear hit name is no great matter, yet these have a promise. To think on hi name less, yet set down in a "book of remembrance." God sets down how many good thoughts a poor soul hth had. As evil thoughts in wicked men are taken notice of\they are the first fruits of the evil heart (Matt. xv. 19)\so good thoughts are they which lie uppermost, and best discover a good heart. A desire is a small matter, especially of the poor man, yet God regards the desire of the poor, and calls a good desire the greatest kindness ; " The desire of a roan is his kindness." A fear makes no great noise, yet hath a voice, "God hath heard the voice of my weeping." It is no pleasant water, yet God bottles it up. A groan is a poor thing, yet is the best part of a prayer sometimes (Rom. viii. 26) ; a sigh is less, yet God it awakened and raited up by it. Psalm xii. 5. A look is less than all these, yet this is regarded (Jonah ii. 4) ; Ireathing is less, yet (Lam. iii 56), the church could speak of no more ; panting *is less than breathing, when one is spent for lack of breath, yet this is all the godly can sometimes boast of. Psalm ilii. 1. The description of a godly man is ofttimes made from his least quod tic. Blessed are thepoor, the meet,, they that mourn, and they who hunger and thirtt. Never did Hannah pray better than when she could get out never a word, but cried, " Hard, hard heart." Nor did the publican, than when he smote his breast and cried, "Lord, be merciful to me a sinner." Nor Mary Magdalene, than when she came behind Christ, sat down, wept, but kept silence. Hnw sweet is music upon the waters.' How fruitful are the lowest valleys ! Mourning hearts are most musical, lowest most fruitful. The good shepherd erer takes most care of his weak lambs and feeble sheep. The father makes moet of the least, and the mother looks most after the sick child. How comfortable is that of our Saviour, " It is not the will of your Father which is in heaven that one of these little ones should perish!" And that heaven is not to be entered but by such as are like the little child.\John Sheffield, 1654.*

Verte 5.\" The oppretsion of the poor.'" Insolent and cruel oppressing of the poor is a sin that brings desolating and destroying judgments upon a people. God sent ten wasting judgments one after another upon Pharaoh, his people, and land, to revenge the cruel oppression of his poor people. " Rob not the poor, because he is poor : neither oppress the afflicted in the gate : for the Lord will plead their cause." Prov. xxii. 22, 23. To rob and oppress the rich is a great sin : but to rob and oppress the poor is a greater ; but to rob and oppress the poor because he is poor, and wants money to buy justice, is the top of all inhumanity and impiety. To oppress any one is sin ; but to oppress the oppressed is the height of sin. Poverty, and want, and misery, should be motives to pity ; but oppressors make them the whetstones of their cruelty and severity, and therefore the Lord will plead the cause of his poor oppressed people against their oppressors withoutfee or fear ; yea, he will plead theircause with pestilence, blood, and fire. Gog was a great oppressor of the poor (Ezekiel xxxviii. 8\14), and God pleads against him with pestilence, blood, and tire (verse 22) ; " and I will plead against him, with pestilence and with blood ; and I will rain upon him, and upon his bands, and upon the many people that are with him, an overflowing rain, and great hailstones, fire, and brimstone."\Thomas Brooks.

Verse 0.\" The words of the Lord are pure words,'" etc. How beautifully is this verse introduced, by way of contrast to what was said before concerning ! Do sinners talk of vanity ? let saints then speak of Jesus and his gospel. Do they talk impure words ? then let the faithful use the pure words of God, which like silver, the more used the more melted in the fire, the more precious will they be. It is true, indeed, despisers will esteem both God and his word as trifling ; but oh, what an unknown treasure doth the word, the promises, the covenant relation of the divine things of Jesus contain ! They are more to be desired than gold, yea, than pure gold ; sweeter also than honey and the honeycomb.\Robert Hawker.

Verse 6.\" The word of the Lord are pure wrf," etc. They that purify silver to the purpose, use to put it in the fire again and again, that it may be thoroughly tried. So is the truth of God ; there is scarce any truth but hath been tried over and over again, and still if any dross happen to mingle with it, then God calls it in question again. If in former times there have been Scriptures alleged that have not been pertinent to prove it, that truth shall into the fire again, that what is dross may be burnt up ; the Holy

Ghost is so curious, so delicate, so exact, he cannot bear that falsehood should be mingled with the truths of the gospel. That is the reason, therefore, why that God doth still, age after age, call former things in question, because that there is still some dross one way or other mingled with them ; either in the stating the opinions themselves, or else in the Scriptures that are brought and alleged for them, that have passed for current, for he will never leave till he have purified them. The doctrine of God's free grace hath been tried over, and over, and over again. Pelagius begins, and he mingles his dross with it : he saith, grace is nothing but nature in man. Well, his doctrine was purified, and a great deal of dross purged out. Then come the semi-Pelagians, and they part stakes ; they say, nature cau do nothing without grace, but they make nature to concur with grace, and to have an influence as well as grace ; and the dross of that was burnt up. The Papists, they take up the same quarrel, but will neither be Pelagians nor semi-Pelagians, yet still mingle dross. The Arminians, they come, and they reflne popery in that point anew ; gtill they mingle dross. God will have this truth tried seven times in the fire, till he hath brought it forth as pure as pure may be. And I say it is because that truth is thus precious. T/iomtu Ooodwin.

Verse 6.|The Scripture is the sun ; the church is the clock. The sun we know to be sure, and regularly constant in his motions ; the clock, as it may fall out, may go too fast or too slow. As then, we should condemn him of folly that should profess to trust the clock rather than the sun, so we cannot but justly tax the credulity of those who wduld rather trust to the church than to the Scripture.|Bithop Hall.

Verse 0.|" The word of the Lord are pure words.'1" Men may inspect detached portions of the Book, and please themselves with some things, which, at first view, have the semblance of conniving at what is wrong. But let them read it, let them read the whole of it ; let them carry along in their minds the character of the persons to which the different portions of it were addressed ; the age of the world, and the circumstances under which the different parts of it were written, and the particular objects which even those portions of it have in view, which to an infidel mind appear the most exceptionable ; and they may be rationally convinced that, instead of originating in the bosom of ah impostor, it owes its origin to men who wrote " as they were moved by the Holy Ghost."Let them scrutinise it with as much severity as they please ; only let their scrutiny be well informed, wisely directed, and with a fair and ingenuous mind, and we have no fears for the issue. There are portions of it on which ignorance and folly have put constructions that are forced and unnatural, and which impure minds have viewed in shadows reflected from their own impurity. Montesquieu said of Voltaire, Lonque Voltaire lit un livre, il le fait, puis il ecrit ctmtre ce qu'il a fait: " When Voltaire reads a book, he makes it what he pleases, and then writes against what he has made." It is no difficult matter to besmear and blot its pages, and then impute the foul stains that men of corrupt minds have cast upon it. to its stainless Author. But if we honestly look at it as it is, we shall find that like its Author, it is without blemish and without spot.|Gardiner Spring, D.D.

Verte 6.|" The words of the Lord are pure words: as siker tried in a furnace tf earth, purified seven times." The expression may import two things: first, the infallible certainty of the word ; and, secondly, the exact purity. First, the infallible certainty of the word, as gold endureth in the fire when the dross is consumed. Vain conceits *comfort us not in a time of trouble : but the word of God, the more it is tried, the more you will find the excellency of it\the promise is tried, as well as we are tried, in deep afflictions ; but, when it is so, it will be found to be most pure. " The word of the Lord is tried ; he is a buckler to all those that trust in him" (Prov. xxx. 5) ; as pure gold suffers no loss by the fire, so the promises suffer no loss when they are tried, but stand to us incur greatest troubles. Secondly, it notes the exact perfection of the word : there is no dross in silver and gold that hath been often refined ; so there is no defect in the word of God.\Thomas Manton.*

Vent 6.\Fry thus translates this verse :
The words of Jehovah are pure words
Silver refined in the crucible
Gold, seven times washed from the earth.

pp?3 though sometimes applied to express the purity of silver, is more strictly aepithet of gold, from the peculiar method made use of in separating it from the soil by repeated washings and decantations.-\ John Fry, in lac.

Verte 0.\" Seven times." I cannot but admit that there may be a mystic meaning in the expression " seven times," in allusion to the seven periods of the (tech, or to that perfection, implied in the figure seven, to which it is to be brought at the revelation of Jesus Christ. This will be more readily allowed by those who admit of the prophetic interpretation of the seven epistles of the Book of Revelation. \ W. Wilson, D.D., in lot.

Verse 8.\" When the vilest men are exalted:" Heb., vilities, oir.Viai'ot, the abstract for the concrete, quisquttia, oi-i6avoi. Oft, empty vessels swim aloft, rotten posts are gilt with adulterate gold, the worst weeds spring up bravest. Chaff will get to the top of the fan, when good corn, as it lieth at the bottom of the heap, so it falls low at the feet of the fanner. The reason why wicked men "twft" on every side, are so brisk, so busy (and who but they ?) is given to be 'his, because losels and rioters were exalted. See Prov. xxviii. 12, 18, and Mil. 2. As rheums and catarrhs fall from the head to the lungs, iind cause a wnaimption of the whole body, so it is in the body politic. As a fish putrefies first in the head and then in all the parts, so here. Some render the text thus, " When they (that is, the wicked) are exalted," it is a " shame for the sons of men," that other men who better deserve preferment, are not only slighted, but vilely handled by such worthless ambitionists, who yet the higher they climb, as apes, the more they discover their defoimities."\John Trapp. rr8.\Good thus translates this verse :

Should the wicked advance on every Bide ;
Should the dregs of the earth be uppermost ?

The original is given literally. PlSt means " fceces, foeculences, dregs." 03 is here 111 adverb, and imports uppermost, rather than exalted.\J. Mason Good, in loc.

HINTS TO THE VILLAGE PREACHER.

Verte 1.\" Help, Lard.'1" L The Prayer itself, short, suggestive, seasonable, rightly directed, vehement. H. Occasions for its use. ILL Modes of its answer. IV. Reasons for expecting gracious reply.

Firtt two da'itet.\Text for funeral of an eminent believer.

Whole verte.\L The fact bewailed\describe godly and faithful, and show how they fail. H. The feeling excited. Mourning the loss, fears for church, personal need of *such companions, appeal to God. III. The fwebodingt a/rowed. Failure of the cause, judgments impending, etc. IV. The faith remaining: "Help, Lord."*

Verte 1.\Intimate connection between yielding honour to God and honesty to man, since they decline together.

Verse 2 (firtt claute).\A discourse upon the prevalence and pemiciousneea of vain talk.

The whole vene.\Connection between flattery and treachery.

"A double heart.1' Right and wrong kinds of hearts, and the disease of duplicity.

Verte 3.\God's hatred of those twin sins of the lips\Flattery and Pride (which is self flattery). Why he hates them. How he shows his hatred. In whom he hates them most. How to be cleansed from them.

Vertex 3, 4. \I. The revolt of the tongue. Its claim of power, self-possession, and liberty. Contrast between this and the believer's confession, " we are not our own." II. The method of its rebellion\"flattery, and speaking proud things." in. The end of its treason\"cutoff."

Verse 5.\The Lord aroused \How ! Why ! What to do ! When !

Latt dame.\Peculiar danger of believers from those who despise them and their special safety. Good practical topic.

Verte 6.\The purity, trial, and permanency of the words of the Lord.

Seven crucibles in which believers try the word. A little thought will suggest these.

Verte 7.\Preservation from one's generation in this life and for ever. A very suggestive theme.

Verte 8.\Sin in high placet specially infectious. Call to the rich and prominent to remember their responsibility. Thankfulness for honourable rulers. Discrimination to be used in choice of our representatives, or civic magistrates.

WORK UPON THE TWELFTH PSALM.

In " A Godly Meditation upon xx select Psalms By Sir Anthony Cope,

Knight, 1547," a thin, black letter 4to., is an Exposition, or rather Meditation, on this Psalm. Reprinted 1848.

PSALM XIII.

Occisioy.\The Psalm cannot be referred to any especial event or period in David" s history. AB attempts to find it a birthplace are but guesses. It was, doubtless, more titan once Um language of that much tried man of God. and is intended to express the feelings of the people of Hod in those ever-returning trials which beset them. If the reader has never yet found occasion to use the language of this brief ode, he witt do so ere long, if he be a man after the lord's own heart. We hai-e been won to call this the " How Long Psalm." We had almost said tke Howling Psalm, from the incessant repetition of the cry " how long ?"

Ditbioh.\This Psalm is very readily to be divided into three parts;\the question of ouwtj),!, 2 ; the cry of prayer, 3, 4 ; the song of faith, 5, 6.

EXPOSITION.

HOV long wilt thou forget me, O Lord ? for ever ? how long wilt thou hide thy face from me ?

2 How long shall I take counsel in my soul, having sorrow in my heart daily ? how long shall mine enemy be exalted over me ?

"Bme long?"\This question is repeated no less than four times. It betokens very intense desire for deliverance, and great anguish of heart. And "shit if there be some impatience mingled therewith ; is not this the more true a portrait of our own experience ? It is not easy to prevent desire from degenerating into impatience. O for grace that, while we wait on God, we may be kept from indulging a murmuring spirit! "How long?" Does not the oft- repeated cry become a very Howling ? And what if grief should find no other means of utterance ? Even then, God is not far from the voice of our roaring ; for he does not regard the music of our prayers, but his own Spirit's work in them in exciting desire and inflaming the affections.

"HmclongP'l Ah ! how long do our days appear when our soul is cast down within us!

" How wenrily the momeute seem to glide
O'er sadness! How the time
Delights to linger in iU flight! "

Time flies with full-fledged wing in our summer days, but in our winters he totters painfully. A week within prison-walls is longer than a month at liberty. Long sorrow seems to argue abounding corruption ; for the gold 'hichislong in the fire must have had much dross to be consumed, hence the question " how long ?" may suggest deep searching of heart. " How long will Urn forget m?" Ah, David ! how like a fool thou talkcst ! Can God forget f Can Omniscience fail in memory? Above all, can Jehovah's heart forget his own beloved child ? Ah ! brethren, let us drive away the thought, and hear the voice of our covenant God by the mouth of the prophet, " But Ziou said, The totd hath forsaken me, and my Lord hath forgotten me. Can a woman forget her sucking child, that she should not have compassion on the son of her womb ? jea, they may forget, yet will I not forget thee. Behold, I have graven thee upon the palms of my hands ; thy walls are continually before me." " For ever f" Oh, dark thought! it was surely bad enough to suspect a tern porary f orgctf ulness, butihall we ask the ungracious question, and imagine that the Lord will for ever wst aj-gy his people ? No, his anger may endure for a night, but his love shall abide eternally. " Horn long wilt thou hide thy face from me.'" This is afar more rational question, for God may hide his face, and yet he may remember still. A hidden face is no sign of a forgetful heart. It is in love that his face is tamed away ; yet to a real child of God, this hiding of his Father's face iaterrible, and he will never be at ease until, once more he hath his Father's smile. " Hate long shall I take counsel, in my- soul, having sorrow in my heart daily .'" There is in the original the idea of " laying up" counsels in his heart, as if his devices had become innumerable but unavailing. Herein we have often been like David, for we have considered and reconsidered day after day, but have not discovered the happy device by which to escape from our trouble. Such store is a sad sore. Ruminating upon trouble is bitter woik. Children fill their mouths with bitterness when they rebelliously chew the pill which tliey ought obediently to have taken at once. " How long shall mine enemy be exalted veer me ?" This is like wormwood in the gall, to see the wicked enemy exulting while our soul is bowed down within us. The laughter of a foe grates horribly upon the ears of grief. For the devil to make mirth of our misery is the last evince of our complaint, and quite breaks down our patience ; therefore let us make it one chief argument in our plea with mercy.

Thus the careful reader will remark that the question " how long?" is put in four shapes. The writer's grief is viewed, as it seems to be, ns it is, as it affects himself within, and his foes without. We are all prone to play most on the worst string. We set up monumental stones over the graves of our joys, but who thinks of erecting monuments of praise for mercies received ? We write four books of Lamentations and only one of Canticles, and are far more at home in wailing out a Miserere than in chanting a Te Deum.

3 Consider and hear me, O Lord my God : lighten mine eyes, lest I sleep the sleep of death ;

4 Lest mine enemy say, I have prevailed against him ; and those that trouble me rejoice when I am moved.

But now prayer lifteth up her voice, like the watchman who proclaims the daybreak. Now will the tide turn, and the weeper shall dry his eyes. The mercy-seat is the life of hope and the death of despair. The gloomy thought of God's having forsaken him is still upon the psalmist's soul, and lie therefore cries, " Consider and hear me." He remembers at once the root of his woe, and cries aloud that it may be removed. The final absence of God is Tophet's fire, and his temporary absence brings his people into the very suburbs of hell. God is here entreated to ee and hear, that so he may be doubly moved to pity. What should we do if wo had no God to turn to in the hour of wretchedness ?

Note the cry of faith, " 0 Lord My Gfod!" la it not a very glorious fact that our interest in our God is not destroyed by all our trials and sorrows ? We may lose our gourds, but not our God. The title-deed of heaven is not written in the sand, but in eternal brass.

" Lighten, mine eyes:" that is, let the eye of my faith be clear, that I may see my God in the dark ; let my eye of watchfulness be wide open, lest I be entrapped, and let the eye of my understanding be illuminated to see the right way. Perhaps, too, here is an allusion to that cheering of the spirits so frequently culled the enlightening of the eyes because it causes the face to brighten, and the eyes to sparkle. Well may we use the prayer, " Lighten our darkness, we beseech thee, O Lord !" for in many respects we need the Holy Spirit's illuminating rays. " Lest I sleep the sleep of death." Darkness engenders sleep, and despondency is not slow in making the eyes heavy. From this faintness and dimness of vision, caused by despair, there is but a step to the iron sleep of death. David feared that his trials would end his life, and lie rightly uses his fear as an argument with God in prayer ; for deep distress has in it a kind of claim upon compassion, not a claim of right, but a plea which has power with grace. Under the pressure of heart sorrow, the psalmist does not look forward to the sleep of death with hope and joy, as assured believers do, but he shrinks from it with dread, from which we gather that bondage from fear of death is novnew thing.

Another plea is urged in the fourth verse, and it is one which the tried believer may handle well when on his knees. We make use of our arch-enemy for once,and compel him, like Samson, to grind in our mill while we use his cruel arrogance as an argument in prayer. It is not the Lord's will that the great enemy of our souls should overcome his children. This would dishonour God. and cause the evil one to boast. It is well for us that our salvation and God's honour are so intimately connected, that they stand or fall together.

Our covenant God will complete the confusion of all our enemies, and if for awhile we become their scoff and jest, the day is coming when the shame will change sides, and the contempt shall be poured on those to whom it is due.

5 But I have trusted in thy mercy ; my heart shall rejoice in thy salvation.

6 I will sing unto the Lord, because he hath dealt bountifully with me.

What a change is here ! Lo, the rain is over and gone, and the time of the singing of birds is come. The mercy-seat has so refreshed the poor weeper, that he clears his throat for a song. If we have mourned with him, let us now dance with him. David's heart was more often out of tune than his harp. He begins many of his psalms sighing, and ends them singing ; and others he begins in joy and ends in sorrow; " so that one would think," says Peter Moulin, " that those Psalms had been composed by two men of a contrary humour." It is worthy to be observed that the joy is all the greater because of the previous sorrow, as calm is all the more delightful in recollection of the preceding tempest.

" Sorrows remembered sweeten present joy."

Here is hia avowal of his confidence : " But I have trusted in thy mercy." For many a year it had been his wont to make the Lord his castle and tower of defence, and he smiles from behind the same bulwark still. He is sure of his faith, and his faith makes him sure ; had he doubted the reality of his trust in God, he would have blocked up one of the windows through which the sun of heaven delights to shine. Faith is now in exercise, and consequently is readily discovered ; there is never a doubt in our heart about the existence of faith hile it is in action : when the hare or partridge is quiet we see it not, but let the same be in motion and wo soon perceive it. All the powers of his enemies had not driven the psalmist from his stronghold. As the shipwrecked mariner clings to the mast, so did David cling to his faith ; he neither could nor would give up his confidence in the Lord his God. O that we may profit by his example and hold by our faith as by our very life !

Now hearken to the music which faith makes in the soul. The bells of the mind are all ringing, " My heart shall rejoice in thy salvation." There is joy nd feasting within doors, for a glorious guest has come, and the fatted calf is killed. Sweet is the music which sounds from the strings of the heart. But this is not all ; the voice joins itself in the blessed work, and the tongue keeps tune with the soul, while the writer declares, " I will sing unto the Lord."

" I will praise thee every day,
Now thine anger's past away;
Comfortable thoughts arise
From the bleeding sacrifice."

The Psalm closes with a sentence which is a refutation of the charge of forgetfulness which David had uttered in the first verse, "He hath dealt bountifully vitkme." So shall it be with us if we wait awhile. The complaint which in our haste we utter *shall be joyfully retracted, and we shall witness that the Lord hath dealt bountifully with'us.*

EXPLANATORY NOTES AND QUAINT SAYINGS.

Verse 1.\" How long vrilt them forget, me, 0 Lordf" etc. The departures of God from true believers are never final ; they may be tedious, but they are temporary. As the evil spirit is said to depart frum Christ for a season (Luke ir. 13 ; though he quitted that temptation, he did not quit his design, so us to tempt no more), so the good Spirit withdraws from those that are Christ's, for a season only, 'tis with a purpose of coming again. When he hath must evidently forsaken, 'tis as unquestionable that sooner or later he will return ; and the happiness of his return will richly recompense for the sadness of his desertion ; Isa. liv. 7, " For a small moment have I forsaken thee ; but with great mercies will I gather thee ;" here is not only a gathering after a forsaking, but "great inercifs1' to make amends for " a small moment." He who hath engaged to be our God for ever, cannot depart for ever.\Timothy Cruso, 1696.

Verse 1.\" Haw long wilt than forget me, 0 Lord?" Whatever be the pressing need of Christ's followers in troubles, and their constant cleaving to duty for all that ; and whatever be Christ's purpose of love towards them, yet lie aeuth it fit ofttimes not to come to them at first, but will let the trial go on till it come to a height, and be a trial indeed, and put them seriously to it ; for before he came he lets them row " about five and twenty or thirty furlongs" (the last of which make near four miles, eight furlongs going to a mile) ; and (Mark vi. 48) he came not till the fourth watch of the night, which is the morning watch. We are indeed very sparing of ourselves in trouble, and do soon begin to think that we are low and tried enough, and therefore would be delivered; but our wise Lord seeth that we need more.\ George Hutefion 1657.

Verse 1.\" How long,'1'1 etc. Enquire into the causes of God's anger. He is never angry but when there is very great reason, when we force him to be so. What is that accursed thing in our hearts, or in our lives, for which God hides his face, and frowns upon us ? What particular disobedience to his commands is it for which he has taken up the rod ? Job x. 2 ; "I will say unto God, Do not condemn me ; shew me wherefore thou contendest with me ;" as if he

should say, Lord, my troubles and my sorrows are very well known We-

must not cease to be solicitous to know what are the particular sins that have made him to tear us up by the roots, to throw us down as with a whirlwind ; what is it that has made him so long angry with us, and so long to delay his help, that if any evil be undiscovered in our souls, we may lament it with a seasonable grief, and get a pardon for it. It is not the common course of God's providence to cover his servants with so thick a darkness as this is, which our troubled souls labour under in the day, or rather in the night of his displeasure ; and, therefore, we may with humility desire to know why he proceeds with us in a way that is so singular ; for it is some way delightful to the understanding to pierce into the reasons and causes of things.\Timothy Rogers.

Verse 1.\"Hue long wilt than forget me," etc. For God to forget David, not to mind him, or look after him, is much ! If his eye be never so little once off us, the spiritual adversary is ready presently to seize on us, as the kite on the chick if the hen look not carefully after it As a father will sometimes cross his son to try the child's disposition, to see how he will take it, whether he will mutter and grumble at it, and grow humorous *and wayward, neglect his duty to his father because his father seemeth to neglect him, or make offer to run away and withdraw himself from his father's obedience because he seemeth to carry himself harshly and roughly towards him, and to provoke him thereunto ; so doth God likewise ofttimes cross his childrenand seemeth to neglect them, so to try their disposition, what metal they are made of, how they stand affected towards him : whether they will neglect God because God seemeth to neglect them, forbear to serve him because he feemeth to forget them, cease to depend upon him because he seemeth not to look after them, to provide for them, or to protect them. Like Joram's pro- lhane pursuivant, " This evil," saith he, " is of the Lord ; what should I wait (or the Lord any longer ?" Or whether they will still constantly cleave to him, though he seem not to regard them, nor to have any care of them ; and say with Isaiah, " Yet will I wait upon God, though he have hid his face from us, and I will look for him though he look not on us ;" for, " They are blessed that wait on him ; and he will not fail in due time to show mercy unto all them that do so constantly wait on him." Isa. viii. 17 ; xxx. 18. As Samuel dealt with Saul; he kept away till the last hour, to see what Saul would do when Samuel seemed not to keep touch with him. So doth God with his saints, and with those that be in league with him ; he withdraweth himself oft, and keeps aloof off for a long time together to try what they will do, and what courses they will take when God seemeth to break with them and to leave them in the suds, as we say ; amidst many difficulties much perplexed, as it was with David at this time.| Tlunruu Gatoker, 1637.*

Verte I.\1. For desertions. I think them like lying fallow of lean and ak land for some years, while it gathers sap for a better crop. It is possible to gather gold, where it may be had, with moonlight. Oh, if I could but creep one fout, or half a foot, nearer in to Jesus, in such a dismal night as that when be is away, I should think it a happy absence ! 2. If I knew that the Beloved were only gone away for trial, and further humiliation, and not smoked out of the house with new provocations, I would forgive desertions and hold my peace at his absence. But Christ's bought absence (that I bought with my sin), is two running boils at once, one upon each side ; and what side then cau I lie on ? 3. I know that, as night and shadows are good for flowers, and moonlight and dews are better than a continual sun, so is Christ's absence of special use, and that it hath some nourishing virtue in it, and giveth sap to humility, and put- Uthanedge on hunger, and furnisheth a fair field to faith to put forth itself, and to exercise its fingers in gripping it seeth not what.\Samuel Rutherford, 1600- \ 1661.

Yerte 1, 2.\That which the French proverb hath of sickness is true of all evils, that they come on horseback and go away on foot ; we have often seen that a sudden fall, or one meal's surfeit, has stuck by many to their graves ; whereas pleasures come like oxen, slow and heavily, and go away like post- horses, upon the spur. Sorrows, because they are lingering guests, I will entertain but moderately, knowing that the more they are are made of the longer they will continue : and for pleasures, because they stay not, and do but call to drink at my dour, I will use them as passengers with slight respect. He is his own best (riend that makes the least of both of them.\Joseph Hall.

Venn I, 2.\" How Long wilt thou forget me? How Long wilt thou hide thy fate from, met How Lono shall I take counsel in my goulf" The intenseness of the affliction *renders it trying to our fortitude ; but it is by the continuance of it that patience is put to the test. It is not under the sharpest, but the longest trials, that we are most in danger of fainting. In the first case, the MmJ collects all its strength, and feels in earnest to call in help from above ; but, in the last, the mind relaxes, and sinks into despondency. When Job was accosted with evil tidings, in quick sucession, he bore it with becoming fortitude ; but when he could see no end to his troubles, he sunk under them.\ Jindrac Fuller.*

Vena 1\4.\Everything is strangely changed ; all its comeliness, and beauty, nd glory, vanishes when the life is gone : life is the pleasant thing ; 'tis sweet ud comfortable ; but death with its pale attendants, raises a horror and aver- ion to it everywhere. The saints of God dread the removal of his favour, and the aiding of his face ; and when it is hid, a faintness and a cold amazementand fear seizes upon every part, and they feel strange bitterness, and anguish, and tribulation, which makes their joints to tremble, and is to them as the very pan;) of death.\Timothy Jtogert.

Verges 1, 5. 6.\Prayer helps towards the increase and growth of grace, by drawing the habits of grace into exercise. Now, as exercise brings benefit to the body, so does prayer to the soul. Exercise doth help to digest or breathe forth those humours that clog the spirits. One that stirs little we see jjrow pursy, and is soon choked up with phlegm, which exercise clears the body of. Prayer is the saint's exercise-field, where his graces are breathed ; it is as tlic wind to the air, it brightens the soul ; as bellows to the fire, which clears the coal of those ashes that smother them. The Christian, while in this world, liven in an unwholesome climate ; one while, the delights of it deaden and dull his love to Christ; another while, the trouble he meets in it damps his faith on the promise. How now should the Christian get out of these distempers, had he not a throne of grace to resort to, where, if once his soul be in a melting frame, he (like one laid in a kindly sweat), soon breathes out the malignity of his disease, and comes into his right temper again ? How often do we find the holy prophet, when he first kneels down to pray, full of fears and doubts, who, before he and the duty part, grows into a sweet familiarity with God, nnd repose in his own spirit ! (Psalm xiii. 1), he begins his prayer as if he thought God would never give him a kind look more : " IIow long wilt thou foryet me., O Lord? for ererf' But by that time he had exercised himself a little in duty, his distemper wears off, the mists scatter, and his faith breaks out as the sun in its strength, verses 5, 6 : " Ihate trusted in thy mercy; my heart shall rejoiea in thy salvation. I will sing unto the Lord." Thus his faith lays the cloth, expecting a fcasl ere long to be set on : he that now questioned whether he should ever hear good news from heaven, is so strong in faith as to make himself merry with the hopes of that mercy which he is assured will come at last. Abraham began with fifty, but his faith got ground on God every step, till he brought down the price of their lives to ten. \ William Gurnall.

Verses 1, 6.\Whatever discouragements thou meetest with in thino attendance on God in ordinances, be like the English jet, fired by water, and not like our ordinary fires, quenched by it ; let them add to, not diminish, thy resolution and courage ; let not one repulse beat thee off ; be violent, give a second storm to the kingdom of heaven. Parents sometimes hide themselves to make their children continue seeking. He that would not at first open his mouth, nor vouchsafe the woman of Canaan a word, *doth, upon her continued and fervent petitions, at last open his hand and give her whatsoever she asks : " O woman, be it unto thee as thou wilt." Continued importunity is undeniable oratory. And truly, if after all thy pains thou findest Jesus Christ, will it not make amends for thy long patience ? Men that venture often at a lottery, though they take blanks twenty times, if afterwards they get a golden bason and ewer, it will make them abundant satisfaction. Suppose thou shouldst continue knocking twenty, nay, forty years, yet if at last, though but one hour before thou diest thy heart be opened to Christ, and he be received into thy soul, and when thou diest heaven be opened to thee, and thy soul received into it, will it not infinitely requite thee for all thy labour ? Oh, think of it, and resolve never to be dumb while God is deaf, never to leave off prayer till God return a gracious answer. And for thy comfort, know that he who began his Psalm with, " How long wilt thou forget me, 0 Lordt for evert how long wilt thou hide thy face from me.'" comes to conclude it with, " I will sing unto the Lord, because he hath dealt bountifully with me."|George Swinnock.*

Verse 2.|" How long?" There are many situations of the believer in this life in which the words of this Psalm may be a consolation, and help to revive sinking faith. A certain man lay at the pool of Bethesda, who had an infirmity thirty and eight years. John v. 5. A woman had a spirit of infirmity eighteen years, before she was "loosed." Luke xiii. 11. Lazarus all his life longlaboured under disease and poverty, till he was released by death and transferred to Abraham's bosom. Luke xvi. 20|22. Let every one, then, who may be tempted to use the complaints of this Psalm, assure his heart that Ood does not forget his people, help will come at last, and, in the meantime, all things shall work together for good to them that love him.| W. Wilson, D.D.

Vere 2.|" Sow long shall I take counsel in my soul, having sorrow in my heart daily f" There is such a thing as to pore on our guilt and wretchedness, to the overlooking of our highest mercies. Though it be proper to know our own hearts, for the purposes of conviction, yet, if we expect consolation from this quarter, we shall find ourselves sadly disappointed. Such, for a time, appears to have been the case of David. He seems to have been in great distress ; and, as is common in such cases, his thoughts turned inward, casting in his mind what he should do, and what would be the end of things. While thus exercised, he had torrow in his heart daily: but, betaking himself to God for relief, he succeeded, trusting in his mercy, his heart rejoiced in his tahaiion. There are many persons, who, when in trouble, imitate David in the former part of this experience : I wish we may imitate him in the latter.|Andrew Fuller.

Verfei 2,4.|" How long shall mine enemy be exalted-orer me?" 'Tis a great relief to the miserable and afflicted, to be pitied by others. It is some relief when others, though they cannot help us, yet seem to be truly concerned for the sadness of our case ; when by the kindness of their words and of their actirms they do a little smooth the wounds they cannot heal ; but 'tis an unspeakable addition to the cross, when a man is brought low under the sense of God's displeasure, to have men to mock at his calamity, or to revile him, or to speak roughly ; this does inflame and exasperate the wound that was big enough before ; and it is a hard thing when one has a dreadful sound in his ears to have every friend to become a son of thunder. It is a small matter for people that are at ease, to deal severely with such as are afflicted, but they little know how their severe speeches and their angry words pierce them to the very soul. "Tis east to blame others for complaining, but if such had felt but for a little while what it is to be under the fear of God's anger, they would find that they could not but complain. It cannot but make any person restless and uneasy when he apprehends that God is his enemy. It is no wonder if he makes every one that he sees, and every place that he is in, a witness of his grief ; but now it is a comfort in our temptations and in our fears, that we have so compassionate a friend as Christ is to whom we may repair, " For we have not an high priest which cannot be touched with the feeling of our infirmities ; but was in all points tempted like as we are, yet without sin." Heb. iv. 15.|Timothy Sogert.

Vme 8.|"Lighten mine eyes, lest I sleep the sleep of death." In time of sickness and grief, the " eyes" are dull and heavy ; and they grow more and more so as death approaches, which closes them in darkness. On the other hand, health and joy render the organs of vision bright and sparkling, seeming, as it were, to impart " light" to them from within. The words, therefore, may b fitly applied to a recovery of the body natural, and thence, of the body politic, from their respective maladies. Nor do they less significantly describe the restoration of the soul to a state of spiritual health and holy joy, whiph will manifest themselves in like manner, by " the eyes of the understanding being enlightened ;" and in this case, the soul is saved from the sleep of sin, as the bod? is in the other, from the sleep of death.|George Home.

Verie 3.|Why dost than hide thy face f happily thou wilt say, None can see thy face and live. Ah, Lord, let me die, that I may see thee ; let me see thee, that I may die : I would not live, but die ; that I may see Christ, I desire death ; that I may live with Christ, I despise life.|Augustine.

Yerte 3.|" How long wilt thou hide thy face from me?" Oh, excellent hiding, which is become my perfection 1 My God, thou hidcst thy treasure, to kindle my desire ! Thou hidest thy pearl, to inflame the seeker ; thou delayestto give, that thou mayest teach me to importune ; seeinest not to hear, to make me persevere.|John Anaelm, 1034|-1109.

Verse 4.|

Ah ! can you bcnr contempt; the venom'd tongue
Of those whom ruin plciises. the keen sneer,
The lewd reproaches of the niscitl herd ;
Who for the selfsame actions, if successful,
Would be as grossly lavish in your praise ?
To sum up all in one|can you support
The scornful glances, the malignant joy,
Or more deteatrd pity of a rival|
Of a triumphant rival ?

James Thomson, 1700|1748.
Verse 4.|" And those that trouble me rejoice when I am mo-ted"|compose comedies out of my tragedies.|John Trapp.

Verge 5.|" 1 hate trusted in thy mercy ; my heart shall rejoice in thy salvation." Faith rejoiceth in tribulations, and triumpheth before the victory. The patient is glad when he feels his physic to work, though it make him. sick for the time ; because he hopes it will procure health. We rejoice in afflictions, not that they are joyous for the present, but because they shall work for our good. As faith rejoiceth, so it friumpheth in assurance of good success ; for it seeth not according to outward appearance, but when all means fail, it keepeth God in sight, and beholdeth him present for our succour.\John Ball.

Verse 5.\" I hate trusted in thy mercy; my heart Khali rejoice in thy salvation." Though passion possess our bodies, let " patience possess our souls.71 The law of our profession binds us to a warfare ; patiendo vincimus, our troubles shall end, our victory is eternal. Here David's triumph (Psalm xviii. 38\40), " I have wounded them, that they were not able to rise ; they are fallen under my feet. Thou hast subdued under me those that rose up against uie. Thou hast also given me the neck of mine enemies," etc. They have wounds for their wounds ; and the treaders down of the poor are trodden down by the poor. The Lord will subdue those to us that would have subdued us to themselves ; and though for a short time they rode over our heads, yet now at last we shall everlastingly tread upon their necks. Lo, then, the reward of humble patience and confident hope. Speramus et superamw. Deut. xxxii. 31. " Our God is not as their God. even our enemies being judges." Psalm xx. 7. " Some put their trust in chariots, and some in horses." But no chariot hath strength to oppose, nor horse swiftness to escape, when God pursues. Verse 8. " They are brought down and fallen ; wo are risen and stand upright." Their trust hath deceived them ; down they fall, and never to rise. Our God hath helped us ; we are risun, not for a breathing space, but to stand upright for ever.\ Thomas Adams.

Verse 5.\None live so easily, so pleasantly, as those that live by faith.\ Matthew Henry.

Verse 5.\Wherefore I say again, " Live by faith ;" again I say, always live by it, rejoice through faith in the Lord. I dare boldly say it is thy fault and neglect of its exercise if thou suffer either thy own melancholy humour or Satan to interrupt thy mirth and spiritual alacrity, and to detain thee in dumps and pensiveness at any time. What if thou beest of a sad constitution ? of a durk complexion ? Is not faith able to rectify nature ? Is it not stronger than any hellebore ? Doth not an experienced divine and physician worthily prefer one dram of it before all the drugs in the apothecary's shop for this effect ? Hath it not sovereign virtue in it, to excerebrate all cares, expectorate all fears and griefs, evacuate the mind of all ill thoughts and passions, to exhilarate the whole man ? But what good doth it to any to have a cordial by him if he use it not ? To wear a sword, soldier-like, by his side, and not to draw it forth in an assault ? When a dump overtakes thee, if thou wouldst say to thy soul ina word or two, " Soul, why art thou disquieted ? know and consider in whom thou believest,1' would it not presently teturn to its rest again ? Would not the Master rebuke the winds and storms, and calm thy troubled mind presently I Hath not every man something or other he useth to put away dumps, to drive away the evil spirit, as David with his harp? Some with merry company, some with a cup of sack, most with a pipe of tobacco, without which they cannot ride or go. If they miss it a day together they are troubled with rheums, dnluess of spirits. They that live in fens and ill airs dare not stir out without. a morning draught of some strong liquor. Poor, silly, smoky helps, in comparison with the least taste (but for dishonouring faith I would say whiff) or draught of faith.\Samuel Ward, 1577- -1653.

Venn 6.\"/ win ring unto the Lord, because Tie hath dealt "bountifully with me." Faith keeps the soul from sinking under heavy trials, by bringing in former experiences of the power, mercy, and faithfulness of God to the afflicted soul. Hereby was the psalmist supported in distress. Oh, saith faith, rtmember what God hath done both for thy outward and inward man : he hath not only delivered thy body when in trouble, but he hath done great things for thy soul ; he hath brought thce out of a state of black nature, entered into a covenant relation with thee, made his goodness pass before thee ; he hath helped thee to pray, and many times hath heard thy prayers and thy tears. Hath he not formerly brought thee out of the horrible pit, and out of the miry clay, and put a new song in thy mouth, and made thee to resolve never to give way to such unbelieving thoughts and fears again ? and how unbecoming is it for thee now to sink in trouble ?\John Willison, 1680\1750.

Verse 6.\" / will ring unto the Lord." '1 Mr. John Philpot having lain for some time in the bishop of London's coal-house, the bishop sent for him, and amongst other questions, asked him why they were so merry in prison ? singing (as the prophet speaks) Extdtantes in relrus pesiimit, rejoicing in your naughtiness, whereas you should rather lament and be sorry. Mr. Philpot answered, " My lord, the mirth which we make is but in singing certain Psalms, as we are commanded by Paul, to rejoice in the Lord, singing together hymns and Psalms, for we are in a dark, comfortless place, and therefore, we thus solace ourselves. I trust, therefore, your lordship will not be angry, seeing the apostle saith, ' If any be of an upright heart, let him sing Psalms ;' and we, to declare that we are of an upright mind to God, though we are in misery, yet refresh ourselves with such singing." After some other discourse, saith he, " I was carried back to my lord's coal-house, where I, with my six fellow prisoners, do rouze together in the straw, as cheerfully (I thank God) as others do in their beds of down." And in a letter to a friend, he thus writes : " Commend me to Mr. Elsing and his wife, and thank them for providing me some ease in my prison ; and tell them that though my loid's roal-house be very black, yet it is more to be desired of the faithful than'thc Queen's palace. The world wonders lw we can be so merry under such extreme miseries; but our God is omnipotent, who turns misery into felicity. Believe me, there is no such joy in the world, as the people of God have under the cross of Christ: I speak by experience, and therefore believe me, and fear nothing that the world can do into you, for when they imprison our bodies,, they set our souls at liberty to converse with God -, when they cast us clown, they lift us up ; when they kill "'i then do they send us to everlasting life. What greater glory can there be tian to be made conformable to our Head, Christ 8 And this is done by affliction. O good God. what am I, upon whom thou shouldst bestow so great "mercy? This is the day which the Lord hath made; let us rejoice and be sM in" it. This is the way, though it be narrow, which is full of the peace of d, and leadeth to eternal bliss. Oh, how my heart leapeth for joy that I am w near the apprehension thereof ! God forgive me my unthankfulness, and "nworthiness of so (Treat glory. I have so much joy, that though I be in a Place ol darkness and mourning, yet I cannot lament; but both night and dayam so full of joy as I never was so merry before ; the Lord's name be praiaed for ever. Our enemies do fret, fume, and gnash their teeth at it. O pray instantly that this joy may never be taken from us ; for it passe th all the delights in this world. This is the peace of Qod *that passeth all understanding. This peace, the more his chosen be afflicted, the more they feel it, und therefore cannot faint neither for fire nor water."\Samuel Clarke's " Afirrour," 1671.*

Verse 6.\" / wM sing unto the Lord.' 1 " *How far different is the end of this Psalm from the beginning !\John Trapp.*

Versed.\" I will ting unto the Lord," etc. *I never knew what it was for God to stand by me at all turns, and at every offer of Satan to afflict me, etc., as I have found him since I came in hither ; for look how fears have presented themselves, so have supports and encouragements ; yea, when I have started, even as it were at nothing else but my shadow, yet God, as being very tender of me, hath not suffered me to be molested, but would with one Scripture or another, strengthen me against all ; insomuch that I have often said, Were it lawful, I could pray for greater trouble, for tlui greater comfort's sake. Eccles. vii. 14 ; 3 Cor. i. 5.\John Bunyan, 1628\1688.*

HINTS TO THE VILLAGE PREACHER.

Verse 1.\The apparent length of sorrow, only apparent. Contrast with days of joy, with eternal misery and eternal joy. Impatience, and other evil passions, cause the seeming length. Means of shortening, by refusing to forestall, or to repine afterwards.

Verse 1 (second clause). \Hiding of the divine face. Why at all ? Why from me? Why so long?

Verse 2.\Advice to the dejected, or the soul directed to lock out of itself for consolation.\A. Fuller.

Verse 2 (first clause).\Self-torture, its cause, curse, crime, and cure.

Verge 2.\"Having sorrow in my heart daily." I. The cause of daily sorrow. Great enemy, unbelief, sin, trial, loss of Jesus' presence, sympathy with others, mourning for human ruin. II. The necessity of daily sorrow. Purge corruptions, excite graces, raise desires heavenward. III. The cure of daily sorrow. Good food from God's table, old wine of promises, walks with Jesus, exercise in good works, avoidance of everything unhealthy.\B. Sanies.

Verse 2 (second clause).\Time anticipated when defeat shall be turned into victory.

Verse 3.\By accommodating the text to the believer. I. True character of Satan, "enemy." II. Remarkable fact that this enemy is exalted over us. HI. Pressing enquiry, "How long?"\I). Davits.

Verse 3.\" Lighten, mine eyes.' 11 A prayer fit for (1) Every benighted sinner. (2) Every seeker of salvation. (3) Every learner in Christ's school. (4) Every tried believer. (5) Every dying saint.\S. Danes.

Verse 4.\Noteth the nature of the wicked two ways ; namely, the more they prevail the more insolent they are ; they wonderfully exult over those that are afflicted.\T. Wdcockt.

Verse 5.\Experience and perseverance. " I have," " my heart shall."

Verse 6.\The bountiful giver and the hearty singer.

The whole Psalm would make a good subject, showing the stages from mourning to rejoicing, dwelling especially upon the turning point, prayer. There are two verses for each, mourning, praying, rejoicing.\A. 0, Brown.

PSALM XIV.

*Titli.\ This admirable ode is simply headed, "To the Chief Musician, by David."
The dedication to the Chief Musician stands at the head of fifty-three of the Psalms,
and deoriy indicates that such psalms were intended, not merely for the private use
of believers, fctd to be sung in the great assemblies by the appointed choir at whose
head was the overseer, or superintendent, called in our version, "the Chief Musician,"
and by Ainsworth, "tlie Master of the Music." Several of these psalms have little or
no praise in them, and were not adiirtssed directly to the Host High, and yet were to
be sung in public worship; which is a efcor indication that the theory cf Augustine
lately revived by certain hymn-book makers, that anftiiyj but praise should be sung,
is far more plausible than scriptural. Not only did the mrini Church chant hallowed
doctrine and offer prayer amid her spiritual songs, but even iht uxiUing notes of
complaint were put into her mouth by the sweet singer of Israel who was inspired j
God. Some persons grasp at any nicely which has a gloss of apparent correct- nrjs
upon it, and are pleased with being more fancifully precise than others; nevertheless
it irffi cur be the way of plain men, not only to magnify the Lord in sacred canticles,
but also. awordinj to PauT s precept, to leach ana admonish one another in psalms
and hymns and ifariiual songs, singing with grace in their hearts unto the Lord.*

*As no distinguishing title is given to thli Psalm, we would suggest as on assistance
to the memory, the heading\ Conctebning Pbactical Atheism. The many conjectures as
to the occasion upon which it was written are so completely without foundation, that
it would be a vast; nftime. to mention them at length. The apostle Paul, in Romans in.,
has s/ioicn in- ribntally thai the drift of the inspired writer is to show that both Jews
and Gentiles are all twfersi'n; there was, therefore, no reason for facing upon any
particular historical occasion, trAn iff history reeks with terrible evidence of human
corruption. Wth instructive alterations, Dorid has given us in Psalm liii. a second
edition of this umuiating psalm, being moved of 0 Holy Ghost thus doubly to declare
a truth which is ever distasteful to carnal minds.*

*Dmsios.\The world's foolish creed (verse 1); itspractical influence in corrupting
morals, 1,4,3. The persecuting tendencies of sinners, 4 ; their alarms, 6 ; their ridicule
of the godly, 6; and a prayer for the manifestation of the Lord to his people's joy.*

EXPOSITION.

*'T'HE fool hath said in his heart. There is no God. They are 1 corrupt, they have
done abominable works, there is none that doeth good.*

*"The fool." The Atheist is the fool pre-eminently, and a fool universally. He iroulil
not deny God if he were not a fool by nature, and having denied God it is no marvel
that he becomes a fool in practice. Sin is always folly, and as it i the height of sin to
attack the very existence of the Most High, so is it also the greatest imaginable folly.
To say there is no God is to belie the plainest evidence, -which is obstinacy ; to oppose
the common consent of mankind, which is stupidity; to stifle consciousness, which is
madness. If the sinner could by his atheism destroy the God whom he hates there were
some sense, although much-wickedness, in his infidelity ; but as denying the existence
of fire does not prevent its burning a man who is in it, so doubting the existence of
God will nut stop the .Judge of all the earth from destroying the rebel who breaks his
laws ; nay, this atheism is a crime which much provokes heaven, and will bring down
terrible vengeance on the fool who indulges it. The proverb says, "A fool's tongue*

cuts his own throat," and in this instance it kills both soul and body for ever : would to God the mischief stopped even there, but alas ! one fool makes hundreds, and a noisy blasphemer spreads his horrible doctrines as lepew spread the plague. Ainsworth, in his "Annotations," tells us that the 'ord here nsed is Nabal, which has the signification of fading, dying, or falling awy, as a withered leaf or flower ; it is a title given to the foolish man as having lost the juice and sap of wisdom, reason, honesty, and godliness. Trapp hits the mark when he calls him " that sapless fellow, that carcase of a man, that walking sepulchre of himself, in whom all religion and right reason is withered and wasted, dried up and decayed." Some translate it the apostate, and others the wretch. With what earnestness should we shun the appearance of doubt as to the presence, activity, power and love of God, for all such mistrust is of the nature of folly, and who among us would wish to be ranked with the fool in the text ? Yet let us never forget that all unregenerate men are more or less such fools.

The fool " hath said in kin heart."" .May a man with his mouth profess to believe, and yet in heart say the reverse ? Had he hardly become audacious enough to utter his folly with his tongue ? Did the Lord look upon his thoughts as being in the nature of words to Him though not to man ? Is this where man first becomes an unbeliever ?\in his heart, not in his head ? And when he talks atheistically, is it a foolish heart speaking, and endeavouring to clamour down the voice of conscience? We think so. If the affections were set upon trulh and righteousness, the understanding would have no difficulty in settling the question of a present personal Deity, but as the heart dislikes the good and the right, it is no wonder that it desires to be rid of that Elohim, who is the great moral Governor, the Patron of rectitude and the Punisher of iniquity. While men's hearts remain what they are, we must not be surprised at the prevalence of scepticism ; a corrupt tree will bring forth corrupt fruit. " Every man," says Dickson, " so long as he lieth unrenewed and unreconciled to God is nothing in effect but a madman." What wonder then if he raves ? Such fools as those we are now dealing with are common to all time, and all countries ; they grow without watering, and are found all the world over. The spread of mere intellectual enlightenment will not diminish their number, for since it is an affair of the heart, this folly and great learning will often dwell together. To answer sceptical cavillings will be labour lost until grace enters to make the mind willing to believe ; fools can raise more objections in an hour than wise men can unswcr in seven years, indeed it is their mirth to set stools for wise men to stumble over. Let the preacher aim at the heart, and preach the all-conquering love of Jesus, and he will by God's grace win more doubters to the faith of the gospel than any hundred of the best reasoners who only direct their arguments to the head.

" The fool hathsnid in his /leart, There in no God," or " no God." So monstrous is the assertion, that the man hardly dared to put it as a positive statement, but went very near to doing so. Calvin seems to regard this saying " no God," as hardly amounting to a syllogism, scarcely reaching to a positive, dogmatical declaration ; but Dr. Alexander clearly shows that it does. It is not merely the wish of the sinner's corrupt nature, and the hope of his rebellious heart, but he manages after a fashion to bring himself to assert it, and at certain seasons he thinks that he believes it. It is a solemn reflection that some who worship God with their lips may in their hearts be saying, " no God." It is worthy of observation that he does not say there is no Jehovah, *but there is no Elohim ; Deity in the abstract is not so much the object of attack, as the covenant, personal, ruling and governing presence of God in the world. God as ruler, lawgiver, worker, Saviour, is the butt at which the arrows of human wrath are shot. How impotent the malice ! How mad the rage which raves and foams against Him in whom we live and move and have our being ! How horrible the insanity which leads a man who owes his all to God to cry out, " No God" ! How terrible the depravity which makes the whole race adopt this as their hearts' desire, " no God !"*

11They are corrupt." This refers to all men. and we have the warrant of the Holy Ghostfor so saying ; see the third chapter of the Epistle to the Romans. Where there is enmity to God, there is deep, inward depravity of mind. The words are rendered by eminent critics in an active sense, " tliey have done corruptly :" this may serve to remind us that sin is not only in our nature passively as" the source of evil, but we ourselves actively fan the flame and corrupt ovfrselves, making that blacker still which was black as darkness itself already. Wo rivet our own chains by habit and continuance.

" They hate done abominable works." When men begin with renr-.mcing the Most High God, who shall tell where they will end ? When the Master's t'jcs are put out, what will not the servants do ? Observe the state of the world bef01 e the flood, as pourtrayed in Genesis vi. 12, and remember that human nature is unchanged. He who would see a terrible photograph of the world without God must read that most painful of all inspired Scriptures, the first chapter of the epistle to the Romans. Learned Hindoos have confessed that the description is literally correct in Hindostun at the present moment ; und were it not for the restraining grace of God, it would be so in England. Alas ! it is even here but too correct a picture of things which are done of men in secret. Things loath- come to God and man are sweet to some palates.

" There u none that doeth good." Sins of omission must abound where transgressions are rife. Those who do the things which they ought not to have done, are sure to leave undone those things which they ought to have done. What a picture of our race is this 1 Save only where grace reigns, there is none that doeth good ; humanity, fallen and debased, is a desert without an oasis, a night without a star, a dunghill without a jewel, a hell without a bottom.

2 The LORD looked down from heaven upon the children of men, to see if there were any that did understand, and seek God.

3 They are all gone aside, they are all together become filthy : there is none that doeth good, no, not one.

" The Lord looked down from heaven vjion the children of men.'1'1 As from a iratchtower, or other elevated place of observation, the Lord is represented as gazing intently upon men. He will not punifh blindly, nor like a tyrant command an indis- criminate massacre because a rumour of rebellion has come up to his ears. What condescending interest and impartial justice are here imaged ! The case of Sodom, visited before it was overthrown, illustrntcs the careful manner in which Divine Justice beholds the sin before it avenpes it, and searches out the righteous that they perish not with the guilty. Behold then the tyes of Omniscience ransacking the globe, and prying among every people and nation, " to set if there were any that did understand and seek God." He who is looking down knows the good, is quick to discern it, would

be delighted to find it; but as be views all the unregenerate children of men his search is fruitless, for of all the race of Adam, no unrenewed soul is other than an enemy to God and goodness. The objects of the Lord's search are not wealthy men, great men, fir learned men ; these, with all they can offer, cannot meet the demands of the great Governor : at the same time, he is not looking for superlative eminence in virtue, he seeks for any that understand themselves, their state, their duty, their destiny, their happiness ; he looks for any that seek God, who, if there be a God, are willing and anxious to find him out. Surely this is not too great a matter to expect; for if men have not yet known God, if they have nny right understanding, they will seek him. Alas ! even this low degree of good is not to be found even by him who sees all things : but men love the hideous negation of "NoGod," and with their backs to their Creator, who is the sun of their life, they journey into the dreary region of unbelief and alienation, which is a land of darkness as darkness itself, and of the shadow of death without any order and "here the light is as darkness.

" They are all gone aside." Without exception, all men have apostatized from the Lord their Maker, from his laws, and from the eternal principles of right. Like stubborn heifers they have sturdily refused to receive the yoke, like errnnt sAeep they have found a gap and left the right field. The original speaks of the race as a whole, as a totality ; and humanity as a whole has become depraved in heart anddefiled in life. " They have altogether become filthy ;" as a whole they are spoiled and soured like corrupt leaven, or, as some put it, they have become putrid and even stinking. The only reason why we do not more clearly see this foulness is because we are accustomed to it, just as those who work daily among offensive odours at last cease to smell them. The miller does not observe thenoise of his own mill, and we are slow to discover our own ruin and depravity. But are there no special cases, are all men sinful ? " Yes," says the Psalmist, in u manner not to be mistaken, " they are." He has put it positively, he repeats it negatively, " There is none that doeth good, no, not one."" The Hebrew pUrase is an utter denial concerning any meie man that he of himself doelh good. What can be more sweeping ? This is the verdict of the all-seeing Jehovah, who cannot exaggerate or mistake. As if no hope of finding a solitary specimen of a good iii n: among the unrenewed human family might be harboured for an instant. The Holy Spirit is not content with saying all and altogether, but adds the crushing threefold negative, " none, no, not one." What say the opponents to the doctrine of natural depravity to this ? Rather what do we feel concerning it ? Do we not confess that we by nature are corrupt, and do we Dot bless the sovereign grace which has renewed us in the spirit of our minds, that sin may no more have dominion over us, but that grace may rule and reign ?

4 Have all the workers of iniquity no knowledge ? who eat up my people as they eat bread, and call not upon the LORD.

Hatred of God and corruptness of life are the motive forces which produce persecution. Men who having no saving knowledge of divine things, enslave themselves to become workers of iniquity, have no heart to cry to the Lord for deliverance, but seek to amuse themselves 'with devouring the poor and despised people of God. It is hard bondage to be a " worker of iniquity ;" a worker at the galleys, or in the mines of Siberia, is not more truly degraded and wretchtd ; the toil is hard and the *reward dreadful ; those who have no knowledge choose such slavery, but those who are taught of God cry to be rescued from it. The same ignorance which keeps men bondsmen to evil, makes them hate the free- born sons of Gud ; hence they seek to eat them up " as they eat bread,' "\daily, ravenously, as though it were an ordinary, usual, every-day matter to oppress the saints of God. As pikes in a pond eat up little fish, as eagles prey on smaller birds, as wolves rend the sheep of the pasture, so sinners naturally and as a matter of course, persecute, malign, and mock the followers of the Lord Jesus. While thus preying, they forswear all praying, and in this act consistently, for how could they hope to be heard while their hands are' full of blood ?*

5 There were they in great fear : for God is in the generation of the righteous.

Oppressors have it not all their own way, they have their fits of trembling and their appointed seasons of overthrow. There\where they denied God and hectored against his people ; there\where they thought of peace and safety, they were made to quail. " There, were they"\these very loud-mouthed, iron-handed, proud-hearted Nimrods and Herods, these heady, high-minded sinners\" there were they in great fear." A panic terror seized them : " they feared a fear," as the Hebrew puts it ; an undefinable, horrible, mysterious dread crept over them. The most hardened of men have their periods when conscience casts them into a cold sweat of alarm. As cowards are cruel, so all cruel men are at heart cowards. The ghost of past sin is a terrible spectre to haunt any man, and though unbelievers may boast as loudly as they will, a sound is in their ears which makes them ill at ease.

" For Ood is in the generation of the righteous." This makes the company of godly men so irksome to the wicked because they perceive that God is with them. 8hut their eyes as they may, they cannot but perceive the image of God in the character of his truly gracious people, nor can they fail to see that he works for their deliverance. Like Haman, they instinctively feel a trembling when they see God's Mordecais. Even though the saint may be in a mean position, mourning at the gate where the persecutor rejoices in state, the sinner feels the influence of the believer's true nobility and quails before it, for God is there. Let scoffers beware, for they persecute the Lord Jesus when they molest his people ; the union is very close between God and his people, it amounts to a mysterious indwelling, for God is in the generation of the righteous.

Lightning Source UK Ltd.
Milton Keynes UK
26 October 2009

145440UK00001B/79/P